Praise

"Begin reading at any p _____ _eachers in the Forest and you will discover a calm curiosity towards the natural world. Babcock's voice inspires with rich lessons on the history, culture, plants and animals of our wild places. The teachings in this collection are like the wolf; timeless and alive." —Maureen Hackett, MD, Founder and President of Howling For Wolves

"The teachings contained within this book belong to the author's decades afield as both hunter and self-provider, and are also strongly influenced by his close ties to the Ojibwe people and their connection to the land and its animals." —Traditional Bowhunter Magazine

"Babcock is a curious, persistent, conscientious man who cares deeply about the land." —Katie Carter, KAXE Radio

"This book is a deeply poetic account of one man's quest to live off the land and his battle-cry to protect it." —Julia Huffman, Director of Medicine of the Wolf and Wolf Spirit

"This book will heighten the way you interpret and value our remaining wild places." —Daniel J. Rice, author of The Unpeopled Season

"This book is a powerful tool for anyone yearning to forge a stronger spiritual and physical relationship with wild nature, no matter where you live." —David Petersen, author of On the Wild Edge: In Search of A Natural Life

"Babcock has written a powerful book in defense of the natural world ... he echoes Aldo Leopold's conservation values with the spiritual values of the Ojibwe culture. This book belongs in your library if you understand the need for wild places." —Steve Voiles, wildlife photographer

"Babcock uses his extraordinary ability for recall to blend his own vast knowledge of living off-the-grid and the teachings of Henry David Thoreau, Aldo Leopold, and Chi-Ma'iingan." —Michael Meuers, author of Road to Ponemah: The Teachings of Larry Stillday

This book is dedicated to Chi Ma'iingan (Big Wolf - Larry Stillday), and my friends of Ponemah, the Red Lake Nation, and of Obaashiing University.

Teachers in the Forest

Barry Babcock

Riverfeet Press

Livingston, MT

www.riverfeetpress.com

TEACHERS IN THE FOREST

Barry Babcock

Copyright 2022 © by the author

Non-fiction: Nature/Environment

Edited by Daniel J. Rice and Elise Atchison (www.eliseatchison.com)

All rights reserved.

ISBN-13: 978-1-7360894-3-9

LCCN: 2021952430

This book is available at a special discount to booksellers, librarians, and educational institutions. Contact the publisher for orders: riverfeetpress@gmail.com

Typesetting by Daniel J. Rice
Cover design by Eubank Creative
Title page art of wolf tracks © shutterstock_ALMAGAMI
Cover art of leaf © shutterstock_Svetlana Zhukova
Cover art of watercolor trees © shutterstock_ Anastasiya Bleskina
Cover art of wolf face © shutterstock_mountain beetle
Cover art of watercolor sky © shutterstock_Anelina
Chapter header art of tree branch © shutterstock_ sibiranna

Contents

<u>Author's note:</u>

I was fortunate enough to share the company and friendship with a great Red Lake Nation spiritual healer named Chi Ma'iingan (Big Wolf - Larry Stillday). Much of our conversations in this book are taken as his exact language from his teachings and our conversations together, and some are represented to the best of my memory with the intention of honoring his words and his message. I have also included quotes and excerpts from numerous authors who I believe have contributed greatly to environmental literature. I have taken great care in ensuring their words are accurately represented here, and are used for the purpose of sharing their educational message and in hopes that the reader may discover a new piece of work or revisit an old favorite.

Teachers in the Forest

Barry Babcock

My Dream

I have had a dream that has reoccurred to me in recent years. It is exactly the same every time.

It is early winter and I am walking alone in the woods. This forest is made of northern hardwoods. The canopy oaks are around one hundred years old, and the understory is open which provides a good view unobstructed by underbrush. There is no wind and it's snowing heavily. The silence is only broken by the uninterrupted swishing sound of the snow as it sifts through the few dried remaining leaves still clinging to the small ironwood trees. The snow is accumulating fast and there is at least four inches on the ground. The visibility is no more than thirty or forty yards and lessening as the snow increases. It is a peaceful scene: quiet, serene, yet melancholy.

As I walk, I must squint my eyes in order to see through the falling snow, but I observe a gray object moving toward me. Several more begin to approach. It isn't until the first object is within twenty yards that I recognize it as a wolf. Then I make them all out as a wolf pack. There are perhaps six or seven of them, spread out from left to right and staggered, some behind and to the sides of the forward wolves. As they get nearer, I see their heads are couched somewhat lower than their shoulders, and their eyes are locked in on me like lasers. They appear in a stalking position. As they get closer, the outer most wolves begin to circle around me, and the front most animals slow to almost a halt.

I should be fearful due to their stance and posture, but for some reason I am fascinated by this unusual encounter. As their flanks circle behind me, they close in and the center animals that had slowed turn and all begin to move at the same speed and direction I have been moving. As I walk in the snow, surrounded by wolves, it is as though they are escorting me somewhere. They make no vocal sounds, no hackles up, no curled lips, no body language. Only stoicism on their part. They walk with me as though I belong.

I have what can only be described as an out-of-body experience. My conscious self remains behind motionless, standing there alone, watching the image of myself, surrounded by the wolves, moving deeper into the forest and heavy snow, fading and fading, getting fainter in the snow until the wolves and I disappear completely.

Then I awake.

Henry Thoreau, Aldo Leopold, and Chi Ma'iingan

All men are brothers, we like to say, half-wishing sometimes in secret it were not true. But perhaps it is true. ... We are obliged, therefore, to spread the news, painful and bitter though it may be for some to hear, that all living things on earth are kindred.

— Edward Abbey

I was born in 1948 on the great plains of South Dakota when the land was still dominated by family farms. My grandparents and extended family were small farmers or connected to farming. My earliest memories are of the land. I recall the meadowlarks and bobolinks singing in the heat of the summer sun, being a small boy shagging pheasants and jackrabbits for my father in the red sunsets of autumn, the deep snowdrifts in winter and great flocks of geese and mallards returning in the spring. My dad ran a small country grain elevator and my mom was a housewife. We had electricity but no running water. My mother had to heat water on a stove in which to bathe my sister and me. There was no store-baked bread in those days in rural America, so Friday nights were bread-baking nights, to be followed by donuts in the deep fat fryer. Our large garden was not a pastime but subsistence. Our lives were shaped by the land on which we lived.

When my dad got a job with the federal government, we moved to the big city of Minneapolis, and my life was greatly altered. I was now immersed in an unknown anonymity among the masses of urban life. I felt no inspiration as the culture of our institutions was like being caught up in a strong current and being swept along. Life was focused on working, getting and spending. I was resigned to a lifestyle similar to domestic cattle, and I didn't question what society expected of me. As a small boy, I longed to move back to the great open places of Dakota and hear the meadowlarks again.

It was during an autumn in the mid-1960s that I accompanied a friend to his parent's lake cabin in northern Minnesota. The objective of the trip was to hunt ducks. The memory of this first experience in the Northwoods is as vivid to me now as if it happened yesterday. We woke up early and drove to a neighboring lake where we put in my friend's twelve-foot boat. While crossing the lake, the northern lights flickered and the mauve color of first daylight showed in the east. Across the lake was the Mississippi River, and when we got into the mouth of the river we shut off the motor and oared. In the silence of the pre-dawn, I heard the tenor hoots of a great horned owl in the deep, dark and mysterious forest. When we selected a place to hunt, we made crude blinds, and at first light a low-flying flock of mallards came directly at us, just above the cane grass. The anticipation and excitement swelled within me as they approached. Then came the firing of our 12-gauge shotguns with the flame exploding from the barrels. We missed our targets, but the entire morning was a seminal moment in my life.

From that experience on the Mississippi River my interests became focused on things natural, wild and free. These avocations were first manifested in hunting, but the time spent in the woods furthered my interests in birds, trees, wild flowers and anything else that I found related to my relationship with the Northwoods. As my thinking progressed, I discovered the genre of nature writing. Most of the nature writings I encountered focused on people who lived in the woods and wrote intimately of their experiences with wildlife. I then enlarged my interests to field manuals like bird, animal and plant identification guides. I had a lot of loose ideas bouncing around in my head but was yet unable to put them together into some fundamental idea or value of where they were taking me.

My life was about to change, and it came about in a most inconspicuous fashion.

I owe a great deal to three men who profoundly changed my life and gave it meaning. First, Aldo Leopold and the deep philosophical nature of his book, *A Sand County Almanac*, which shook me to my core. Even today, his words have as much importance, if not more, than when I first read them. Secondly, Henry Thoreau made me look at the way we live and that our lives need questioning along with our institutions, and that there is a greater purpose to our lives than debt and mortgages. And lastly, it was a Native American spiritual leader from the Red Lake Band of Ojibwe in Minnesota who, in flesh and blood, impacted me in ways I have never been affected before. His name was Chi Ma'iingan—Big Wolf—also known as Larry Stillday.

Aldo Leopold

It was sometime in 1968 while perusing the nature section of a local bookstore when I came across a paperback with a black and white sketching of three geese on the cover. It was entitled *A Sand County Almanac and Sketches Here and There*. When thumbing through the pages it was the artwork by Charles Schwartz that interested me most. I had never heard of the book or Leopold up to that time in my life, but it looked to be right up my alley so I bought it, read it repeatedly, carried it with me, and my life has not been the same since. It gave beautiful meaning to all I searched for in my life and is one of the great philosophic writings in American literature.

As a senior in high school, I had an English teacher, Miss Telander, who encouraged my appetite for literature and told me that a person may read hundreds of books in a lifetime, but perhaps only two or three impact you enough to transform the way you live and think. *A Sand County Almanac* was one of those books for me.

Leopold was the master wordsmith, working and reworking his writings. He was economical with words yet his prose was poetic, still bringing a tear to my eye with his beautiful and sensitive anecdotes and portrayals of individual life forms in the natural world and their role in the stability of the greater whole.

There has been a historical record of environmentalism in our country, but there hasn't been a good track record of our history towards the environment. We continue to see the land as an economic commodity. Leopold, more than anyone else in our history, articulated a different way – an ethical way – to see the land. He realized that human evolution must develop a land ethic and that if we did not start thinking and treating the land as we do one another, we would be in deep trouble. He stated that a "land ethic changes the role of *Homo sapiens* from conqueror of the land-community to plain member and citizen of it. It implies respect for his fellow members, and also respect for the community as such." He saw man as part of a biotic community, not apart or removed from the biotic community, and that community included all life, from the bacteria in the soil to the birds in the sky. Aldo Leopold's legacy to us is not only that he articulated a land ethic, but that he did it so eloquently. He gave us a road map with directions with which to navigate our way out of the mess we have gotten ourselves into. His land ethic isn't just for nature lovers, but meant for all people to embrace. He notes the development of ethics in the development of civilization, starting with man's relationship to one another on an individual scale, and then man's relationship to society. He tells us that we now need an ethic to deal with our relationship to the land, and that land is a community to be loved and is the source of our culture.

On April 14, 1948, Aldo Leopold and his family drove to his beloved woodland farm near Baraboo, Wisconsin, to plant a few pine trees. That afternoon he noticed smoke coming from a neighbor's farm. They gathered some firefighting gear and hurried to help. The family split up with Leopold and one daughter monitoring a marsh in order to prevent sparks from jumping a road. Aldo sent his daughter to phone the authorities. It was then that Leopold, alone, felt the chest pain and lay down and died. The fire swept over his body, and later one of his daughters would remark that her dad would probably want it that way as he was an advocate of fire as a management tool. He was sixty-one years old.

It has been over sixty-five years since Leopold's masterpiece was published posthumously. The book stands as a great edifice today and marks a bearing on which we can set our compasses. It will go down as one of the great philosophical works to come out of our nation.

Henry David Thoreau

Thoreau's *Walden* was mandatory reading in high school, but I failed at it then and several tries later. I was never able to get beyond his first chapter, "Economy." It was not until sometime in my mid-thirties that I again picked up the book. This time it was like a light turned on in my head, and in fact that first chapter became the most important chapter to me.

Thoreau wrote that "the mass of men lead lives of quiet desperation" and equated their condition to those of the twelve labors of Hercules. He saw his townsmen as carrying the debt and burden of farms around from the cradle to the grave, unable to see the beauty and true meaning in life. Whereas Hercules only had twelve labors, there was at least an end to his tasks.

Thoreau's experiment of living in the woods only lasted a little over two years. He did not advocate that everyone should do so or live like him, but he did argue that we need to enlarge our lives beyond the "quiet desperation" he saw in us. He felt that in order to achieve this he had to simplify life, to drive it into a corner and reduce it to its lowest denominator. He wrote, "My purpose in going to Walden Pond was not to live cheaply nor to live dearly there, but to transact some private business with the fewest obstacles; to be hindered from accomplishing which for want of a little common sense, a little enterprise and business talent, appeared not so sad as foolish."

Walden can be read in many ways and seen through many perspectives. There is humor, sarcasm, and philosophy, but to me, most importantly, Thoreau was looking at achieving happiness outside the normal life of being detached from nature. He said, "I was a self-appointed inspector of snow-storms and rain-storms, and did my duty faithfully; surveyor, if not of highways, then of forest paths and all across-lot routes, keeping them open, and ravines bridged and passable at all seasons, where the public heel had testified to their utility."

Thoreau is often thought of as a recluse or hermit and as being rejected by society. This is not true. In fact, there was hardly a day during his experiment at Walden that he didn't walk into his hometown of Concord. He was a lover of wilderness and on three different occasions took canoe trips into the wilds of Maine, but he had no desire to live in wilderness. Walden Pond was only a mile from Concord. His attraction to the wild was spiritual, mental, emotional, and physical. In his essay "Walking" he wrote, "I am alarmed when it happens that I have walked a mile into the woods bodily, without getting there in spirit ... What business have I in the woods, if I am thinking of something out of the woods?"

Thoreau moved environmental thinking ahead to new places. As for wilderness, he said, "From the forest and the wilderness come the tonics and barks which brace mankind."

Through reading Thoreau I gained an understanding about living life a better way, and this was accomplished by simplifying it and reducing my material needs. I also gained a better perspective on wild lands, their cultural significance, and that they can renew us as a tonic can.

For the last two weeks of Thoreau's life, he was working on his *Maine Woods* papers which were of the three trips he had taken into the wilderness. While Thoreau lay on his deathbed on the last day of his life, May 6, 1862, coming in and out of consciousness, the last two words he uttered before he died were "Moose" and "Indian."

Chi Ma'iingan, aka Larry Stillday

Aldo Leopold and Henry David Thoreau were powerful

voices for bringing us back into alignment with nature, shedding all the superfluous and material encumbrances of life, and understanding the interconnectedness of all living things on earth. I thought that their voices along with other contemporary environmentalists were the only voices seeing man as part of nature rather than separate from it, but I was in error. There are other civilizations who view man as a co-tenant with all other life on earth.

Living in northern Minnesota, in Indian Country, I eventually came into friendships with Ojibwe people. As an advocate for the environment, it was inevitable that I would develop relationships with Native American people as battles over clean water and other resources would bring us together.

In 2008 I volunteered my services for a healing run. The run went from Cass Lake on the Leech Lake Indian Reservation to Red Lake on the Red Lake Indian Reservation, and was in memoriam to the tragic school shooting at Red Lake a few years prior, and also the death of Grandma Duck, a much beloved Elder from Leech Lake. The distance of the run was forty miles, and my help was needed to pull two porta-potties behind my truck for the participants. A ceremony was held in Cass Lake prior to the run, offering tobacco, and then sage was burned and used to smudge participants. The run went smoothly with no hitches and we were expecting more participants to meet us at the Red Lake Reservation north of Bemidji. A contingent of elite long-distance runners from Red Lake was going to join the healing run.

When we approached the boundary of Red Lake, and as the expected Red Lakers were there waiting, we stopped with youths and Elders for water, food, and alternate runners. While everyone was milling around, I noticed a tall Anishinaabe man approach the group. He was attired in a manner that would not indicate anything out of the ordinary other than his height. He wore a pair of slacks, a plain pull-over shirt, and a pair of loafers. His hair was cut rather short and parted. He had a neat moustache and his overall appearance was well-groomed and not what I would expect an Indian healer and spiritual leader should look like. He was very tall, perhaps six foot four or more, and as he approached, he carried a large oyster-like shell with sage and an eagle feather. Everyone present had solemn faces and moved forward without any oral instruction to do so. It appeared that everyone knew instinctively what they should do, and they encircled him as he commenced to smudge everyone with the sage burning in the shell, and then he used the eagle feather to direct the fragrant smoke at each individual, including my little springer spaniel that I brought along. He said a prayer in Ojibwemowin, turned and went his way, and disappeared from the entourage. His demeanor and the demeanor of everyone toward him greatly impressed me and left me with the feeling that this man was of some great importance to the people present.

When the runners and caravan reached the shores of Red Lake, another ceremony was held at the pow wow grounds. The tall Indian healer was present, and I also saw his wife for the first time who was a white woman, and I learned his name, Larry Stillday, whose spirit name is Chi Ma'iingan (meaning Big Wolf). He was introduced to all the runners and gave the invocation at the ceremony. The name Stillday was familiar to me as it's a Red Lake name used by other highly respected healers.

Later that summer an Irish-American friend of mine, Michael Meuers, who worked for the Red Lake Band, invited me to accompany him to a teaching and sweat lodge put on by Larry at Ponemah. Ponemah is often called Obaashiing by its residents, and it is located near the end of the long peninsula that extends out and separates Lower Red Lake from Upper Red Lake. Larry referred to Ponemah-Obaashiing as the heart of the Rez, and the peninsula it is on as the aorta, and Lower and Upper Red Lakes as the lungs. Ponemah is considered one of the most traditional Anishinaabeg communities in the nation, and it has the highest percentage of first language speakers anywhere among the Ojibwe. Ponemah is also the birthplace of Larry, and he came into this world on May 14, 1944.

This was the second teaching lodge that Larry had administered, and it was my first. There was not a large crowd, maybe twenty people at most. Perhaps a half dozen whites were present, mostly women. Larry's wife, Violet, assisted Larry, and the two made a welcoming and entertaining pair. Violet was from Louisiana and had a distinct southern drawl. I later learned that Larry met her while in Louisiana. Larry often poked fun at her accent, and Violet was almost always with him and assisting Larry at his teaching lectures.

Early in life Larry left the reservation, served in Vietnam, and lived, worked and had a family in the Twin Cities area. When the family grew up, Larry returned to Red Lake in order to serve his people.

Most of the late morning and afternoon of the teaching lodge was spent instructing the attendees about the Teachings of the Seven Grandfathers, which was of most interest to me. But what made the greatest impression at this first lodge I attended wasn't the classroom business that day, it was the sweat lodge held that evening. Larry's son, Larry Jr., heated the rocks in the fire while Larry Sr. explained to us the prescribed manner in which the whole sweat ceremony was to be done. Once inside the lodges, with the entrance cover open, we were instructed to only enter and leave in a clockwise manner. Larry prepared us for what was to commence, and that he would be speaking only in Ojibwemowin, as the spirits and ancestors only understood this language. He made certain that we understood the sweat would be in rounds or sessions, and anyone feeling overcome by the heat should not be ashamed to ask to exit.

As Larry said, "It's not a test of endurance and has nothing to do with manliness or stamina." I do not remember any more details about the sweat ceremony or proceedings other than to say that during the third session, we were to offer a prayer in which I made some wishes for the environment while most of the white women in the lodge talked at length about their marital problems, the troubled lives of their children, and what I perceived to be personal problems. The lodge was pitch black, the sun had set, and it was so dark inside I could not see my hand in front of my face. While the ladies were going on about their lives, my emotional reaction was to be really turned off by it, and I wished it would end. I was feeling very uncomfortable during what I considered a whining session.

As soon as this session was finished and we were all outside the sweat lodge, Larry called me to him and sat me down. He was direct, yet tactful, when he told me that I needed to work on my female side. I always felt that I had a good handle on that side of myself, so I was taken aback by his criticism. He went on to tell me that he could feel the negativity oozing out of me in the sweat lodge. I was stunned by what he was telling me, but he was exactly right. Besides being flabbergasted at his correct perception, I was dumbfounded at how he could have known this. He was not exhibiting any anger or rudeness but was simply matter-of-fact about what I thought were my well-hidden emotions.

Driving home late that evening with Michael, my consternation continued by what Larry told me. Not so much because he was right, but because I couldn't understand how he knew what I was feeling. It was so dark in the lodge, he could not see me, I couldn't see a thing, and it was as if I was blind. I made no verbal tones, no grunts or groans of discontent at what I was listening to. Later that night, lying in bed, I tried to rationalize his ability to perceive my emotions, and I even theorized that he had night-vision goggles in which he could see my facial features. I ultimately reconciled myself to the belief that he had some power of perception I couldn't understand.

At the next teaching lodge, Larry focused on the Teachings of the Seven Grandfathers. Leopold had articulated the need for society to develop a land ethic, and I began to realize that Larry was articulating the same thing in a different way. He described the Teachings of the Seven Grandfathers as the foundation of all Ojibwe beliefs. It was the way to be not only good stewards of Mother Earth, but also good people. He repeatedly taught that everything we need to understand in being good people and living in harmony with nature was learnable by observing the animals around us in the natural world. For white people immersed in a culture that was driven by the marketplace of getting and spending, this would be a difficult concept to wrap our brains around. Larry knew this, and so gave us his teachings piecemeal. This way we could grasp its meaning, though it may be slow in coming.

Later in our conversations and email exchanges, Larry often used the word "equality," and he used it not to discuss equality among men, but between all living things. This new use of the term equality was key in understanding the interconnectedness of all life that was foremost in the teachings. As he put it in citing Ojibwe creation stories: Man was not created until after all the other animals and plants. He was the weakest and most pitiful, and though no other life form needed man, man needed all the others to survive. In response to a message I sent Larry about my own personal day-to-day relationships with the animal communities where I live, Larry emailed: "What we believe is who we are, it doesn't matter what the world says, our relatives in nature know who we are and that's what matters. All those you mentioned are life, nothing more, nothing less, and that's equality. It can't get any more real than that."

16

Many times Larry talked about coming to an understanding of the interconnectedness of all life as helping us being physically, emotionally, mentally and spiritually in balance within ourselves. Understanding how Mother Earth works isn't just about being good environmentalists, it also enables us to be better people by being balanced. "It goes right in line with the teachings I've been using, it's all about connectedness and relatedness and of course interdependence. Another way of putting this is being in alignment with all that is of nature."

Aldo Leopold, in his "Land Ethic," was essentially saying the same thing as Larry Stillday, but Leopold was educating through a scientific perspective whereas Larry's message was spiritual.

Larry notes that our disconnection with nature is the source of so many ills in society as well as the natural world. He often would say that the Elders told us, "a man's heart hardens when he is removed from nature." In an email message he once wrote, "Yes we can attribute the mess and/or misery that so many are experiencing in life today to the disconnection from our Earth Mother, many miss the nourishment as well as the nurturing our Earth Mother has for us. It is when man decided to place himself at the center, which is the place of our Creator, that man therefore shifted the flow of the spirit. Man strikes out because of the pain he caused himself, in this way man has reduced everything in life down to a weed, therefore has no conscience of the harm he creates, it has become brother killing brother. Now he doesn't know where to stop or how to stop."

Both Stillday and Leopold were talking about ethics, but through the lens of different cultures. Stillday saw health through balance within, and within each of us is the spiritual, emotional, mental, and physical. When Stillday got out his sage and smudged, he burned sage in a shell by lighting it with fire and creating smoke. Smudging is said to be a purifying ceremony, but he explained that beyond purifying, the shell and the sage represented water and earth, and the burning and fragrant smoke represented fire and air. The smudging ceremony itself was renewing the covenant with life and the four basic elements: earth, fire, water, and air. These four basic elements are necessary for life and this was the Ojibwe ceremonial way of honoring them. Leopold said the same when he wrote that a land ethic includes a larger community of all living things.

These are the Teachings as taught to me by Chi Ma'iingan:

- The origin of the Teachings of the Seven Grandfathers came in ancient times when the Grandfathers asked a messenger to survey the human condition and found the condition was not good. The teachings were delivered to the people as seven principles in order to follow a path that would enable them to be good human beings. They became the spiritual foundation of the Anishinaabeg, and each teaching or law was represented by an animal.

- The Great Spirit placed all the lessons we need to learn in the natural world. If we look deep into nature, we have a better understanding of everything. The Elders tell us that connecting with animal guides helps us to be better and healthier people physically, mentally, emotionally, and spiritually. We can learn a lot by watching animals, both in the physical and spiritual forms. We will see the world and all things in it with clarity and understanding.

- We learn to live with nature, be comfortable within it, and trust our instincts. Our animal guides can bring us messages of guidance and offer protection to shield us from negative energies. But we must be open to the animal spirits and the messages they bring.

• Every animal is different just like we are, each having their own attributes that give them advantages in their daily lives. Every experience we have with them has something to teach us. We may have a connection or attraction with a certain animal.

• We are given the Teachings of the Seven Grandfathers to act as our spiritual foundation. These laws offer direction to those who wish for a balanced life. Each law is represented by an animal. These teachings of the animal world offer us the help we need to live close to the natural laws.

The Teachings of the Seven Grandfathers, as taught to me by Chi Ma'iingan, are: Courage, Truth, Respect, Wisdom, Love, Humility, Honesty. What follows are his descriptions:

Courage/Bravery as represented by *Makwa,* the Black Bear. In its home, the bear shows us the spirit of courage. The bear is a gentle creature but threaten its cub and it becomes fearless in its defense. The virtues taught us by *Makwa* are power, industriousness, instinctive healing, gentle strength, introspection, and dreams. The bear is closely connected to the Grand Medicine Society as a teacher. Midewiwin members are said to "follow the bear path." Because of his claws which are good for digging, the bear pays attention to healing herbs that many other animals pass up.

Truth is represented by *Mikinaak,* the Snapping Turtle. When the Great Spirit gave the Anishinaabe these laws, the turtle was present to ensure that the laws would never be forgotten or lost. There are thirteen markings on the back of the turtle to denote the thirteen moons which represent the truth of one cycle of earth's rotation around the sun. There are also twenty-eight markings on the back of *Mikinaak* to denote one cycle of the moon around earth. These signs are evidence of the truth which the turtle represents. The turtle represents self-containment, Mother Earth (*Gidakiiminaan*), and knowledge.

Respect is represented by *Mashkode-Bizhiki*, the Buffalo. Every part of the buffalo provided Native Peoples with some valuable tools for life: shelter, clothing, food, utensils, and even fuel for fire—its dung. Through giving its life and sharing every part of its being, the buffalo shows the deep respect it has for people. *Bizhiki* teaches us we must respect all life and the interconnectedness between us all.

Wisdom is represented by *Amik*, the Beaver. To know and understand wisdom is to know that the Great Spirit gave everyone special gifts to be used to build a peaceful and healthy community. *Amik* uses his sharp teeth for cutting trees and branches, a special gift he received from the Great Spirit.

Love is represented by *Migizi,* the Bald Eagle. The eagle in Anishinaabeg creation stories was a savior for man by showing his love for them before the Great Spirit. *Migizi* is the one animal who can reach the highest in bringing vision to the seeker. *Migizi* values are divine spirit, clear vision, great healing powers, courage, sacrifice, and connection to the Creator.

Humility is represented by *Ma'iingan*, the Wolf. The wolf represents loyalty, perseverance, courage, stability, teacher and intuition. Practicing humbleness means we always consider our fellow humans before ourselves. In the natural world, the wolf expresses this humbleness in great clarity. The wolf bows his head not out of fear but out of humbleness, he humbles himself in our presence. A wolf that has hunted food will take the food back to the den to eat with the pack before he takes the first bite or he regurgitates all he has for the pups. *Ma'iingan* is an animal guide for true teaching.

Honesty is represented by *Masaba,* the Wilderness Man or Bigfoot. *Masaba* is honesty and innocence. The Elders say, "Never try to be someone else. Live true to your spirit, be honest to yourself, and accept who you are and the way the Great Spirit made you.

After every lodge Larry would tell us: "*Gidinawemidimin* (we are all related) and "*Gigaagiigidotamaagoom, maada'ooyok gaa-miinigooyeg*" (you are speakers for us now, share what you have learned). Larry's life ended in his sleep on May 20, 2014. His death was a shock for not only Anishinaabeg, but for many white people also. His kindness was equally extended to non-Anishinaabe as well as Anishinaabe people. His wisdom and teachings were widely respected and he was sought out as a speaker by the Mayo Clinic, state government, schools and churches. His humility was shown to everyone who attended his talks. A friend who was in attendance at a church in Bemidji told me about an audience member who, after a lecture on the medicine wheel, asked where Jesus fit into these teachings. Larry responded that just like Jesus, we spend our time with the poor, the downtrodden and the needy. Larry's teachings transcended education and kindness as he was a bridge between Anishinaabe and white communities. His death left a gaping hole in many of us. There isn't a day that goes by that I do not think of him, but what I must never forget is that he now resides in my heart and his words made me a better person, and those words will continue to resonate within and continue to show me the right path to take in life.

Gijigijigaaneshiinh:
The Little Bird That Says *Gijigiji*

Look deep, deep into nature, then you'll understand everything better.

— Albert Einstein

Now is the time of year when lakes begin to freeze over. It is the end of autumn and the start of the long cold winter up north. The sunny skies of October with the brilliant colors of autumn are now of the past, and the forests of November are naked and stark. The wind rattles the dried leaves of the oaks; the skies are blue-gray with low hanging clouds from horizon to horizon. The cold November wind is sharp, and something in the air says "Old Man

Biboon" is at the door and another year is at an end. It both signals and is a symbol for death in much of the forest community.

The warblers and other insectivorous birds are long gone. The seasonal finches and seed eaters such as purple finches, goldfinches and rose-breasted grosbeaks have flown away. The geese, ducks and shorebirds have traveled south. Only a few trumpeter swans remain where there is some open water. Even many hawk species have left. The many varieties of sparrows such as juncos, fox sparrows, white-throated, and tree sparrows, just to name a few, that found temporary haven here on migration, have also departed with the first snows covering the ground. All that remain are my resident, sedentary birds who make this land their year-round home.

I made the decision to feed birds as they are a great source of inspiration and enjoyment to me. The year-round residents who frequent my bird-feeder are blue jays, an occasional gray jay, white-breasted and red-breasted nuthatches, downy woodpeckers, hairy woodpeckers, pileated woodpeckers, red-bellied woodpeckers and northern shrikes. Often, as winter proceeds, large flocks of the nomadic, showy and colorful evening grosbeaks and pine grosbeaks appear along with red polls and pine siskins, but the real star of my winter bird world is my year-round neighbor the black-capped chickadee.

This little bundle of energy and industriousness—the chickadee—has been a model and a teacher for me. He is always here, all year, and has never abandoned me.

Early one morning I was filling my bird feeder when a chickadee landed on my shoulder and spoke into my ear, "jig-ah-ji-ji-ji-ji-ji," and with each note, his voice rose in volume. It's curious how my animal neighbors around here get to know me and also understand my intentions. I have always admired the little black-capped chickadee. I marvel at how this tiny bundle of feathers can survive and flourish in the harsh winters of northern Minnesota when much larger and more powerful creatures cannot. They do not migrate, but instead are year-rounders, sharing every day of the calendar — good and bad — with me. With him, I am never alone. My friend Larry Stillday teaches that we can learn from watching the animals of the land. I believe the chickadee has something of importance to teach us.

The great Crow Chief, Plenty Coups, had a dream during his vision quest, and among other things in his dream, he saw a great forest knocked down by a powerful wind. Only one tree remained standing. The following are Plenty Coups' words: "Only one tree, tall and straight, was left standing where the great forest had stood. 'Listen Plenty Coups,' said a voice. 'In that tree is the lodge of the chickadee. He is least in strength but strongest in mind among his kind. The chickadee-person is a good listener. Whenever others are talking together of their successes or failures, there you will find the Chickadee-person listening to their words. He gains success and avoids failure by learning how others succeeded or failed, and without great trouble to himself. There is scarcely a lodge he does not visit, hardly a person he does not know, and yet everybody likes him, because he minds his own business. The lodges of countless bird-people were in that forest when the Four Winds changed it. Only one is left unharmed, the lodge of the chickadee-person.'" (*Plenty-Coups: Chief of the Crows*, Frank Linderman.)

There is an old adage that says, "It's not how big the dog is in the fight, it's how big the fight is in the dog." If there was an honor reserved for the toughest, most determined and indefatigable life form in the Northwoods, it would be the little chickadee.

Just the other day, while sitting in my tree stand waiting for a whitetail buck to come my way, I observed a small band of chickadees moving from tree to tree and bush to bush, scouring them for insect larvae or ant eggs, and then one landed on the barrel of my gun. Although I have pondered the short lives of the chickadee sorrowfully, I also recognize how fast everything moves in their lives. It is fast-forward every minute of their existence. I wonder if their lives are really shorter than ours, or does it just move by at a much faster pace, as if they are in another dimension of time.

As this chickadee rested on my rifle barrel, she cocked her head from side to side and gave me some "wheezy zee-zee-zees." I tried my best to respond to her through my tightly puckered lips. The bird then proceeded to flutter around my head, landing on many small twigs around me with as much, or more, curiosity than I had of her.

Deer hunting is made up of countless hours doing nothing but sitting silently in the woods waiting for that one dramatic moment when everything in the world seems to stop. It is in between these widely spaced events that one can observe what most of the non-human world is doing. For one who keeps their eyes and ears open, sits motionlessly, and keeps their mouth shut, it is in these extended periods of observation that the world can reveal a great deal of truth.

In one instance while deer hunting in a stand of mature jack pines, I watched several chickadees landing on the trunks of these trees, each carrying a single sunflower seed in its beak. Upon landing on the jack pines, they stuffed the sunflower seeds in crevices in the bark of the trees and then flew off. I watched them for the duration of the evening and discovered that they flew to and came from the same direction—my cabin—which is about a quarter mile away. These little chickadees were carrying sunflower seeds to their haunts and building up a storehouse against the long, cold winter.

And then there is the world-famous chickadee, 65290, made famous by Aldo Leopold in *A Sand County Almanac*. In Leopold's chapter titled "65290" he writes of banding chickadees and the joy of catching banded birds in order to witness their longevity. He writes that to "band a bird is to hold a ticket in a great lottery." In 1937, Leopold trapped and banded seven chickadees, 65290 being one of the seven, but at that time the little bird "showed no visible evidence of genius." By the second winter, the class of 1937 had shrunk to three, and by the third winter to two. By the fifth winter, 65290 was the only survivor, and "signs of genius were still lacking, but of his extraordinary capacity for living, there was now historical proof." Maybe this was the first time that a human paid ode to the lowly little chickadee. Leopold's closing paragraph written eleven years later reaffirms his love of life: "65290 has long since gone to his reward. I hope that in his new woods, great oaks full of ants' eggs keep falling all day, never with a wind to ruffle his composure or take the edge off his appetite."

Waawaashkeshi:
The Spiked Buck

Nothing exists for itself alone, but only in relation to other forms of life.

— Charles Darwin

While drinking coffee and listening to the radio news this mid-November morning, I heard a gunshot nearby. I put on my blaze orange and went down my driveway and found a hunter looking in the ditch. He and his partner, a bearded man who never got out of the truck, said they shot a doe standing in the ditch alongside the township road and it ran into my woods. I asked him if they had a doe permit and he replied yes, and said he just paid a considerable amount of money for a new scope for his rifle which allowed him to see it was a doe and made him feel certain that he had made a good shot.

They, like many hunters today, drive the roads looking for deer. I told them they could look around on my land, as I did not want to see a wounded animal suffering. They spent ten minutes or less looking for a blood trail but couldn't find any and got back in their truck and off they went. I am sure no lingering regrets or sorrow ever haunted them about this deer. For them, it was off to the next road-hunting episode in the heated cab of their truck and the next unlucky deer.

The last thing I wanted this morning was to track someone else's wounded deer, but I continued to look around and found blood. I went back to my cabin and got my rifle and picked up the blood trail. After a short distance of tracking, I found the deer, and it was not a doe as the road hunters said, but a one-and-a-half-year-old spiked buck. He jumped up from his bed and hobbled off for twenty yards and stopped. They had hit him in the shoulder and his front leg was hanging uselessly, and my shot put him out of the suffering that would have caused him a slow and lingering death.

I sat by the dead animal and meditated for a while—in my way—feeling sorrow for him and expressing my regret at the way things ended for this young buck. Pondering his lifeless body, I admired his sleekness and beauty. He was an abnormally large yearling buck who likely had a good future ahead of him had he lived. I suspect that if he had survived another year, he might be well on his way to becoming one of the dominant bucks in these woods. I thought about how many times I may have seen him and that he was likely one of many young bucks I have observed at my salt lick in mid-summer, or that he would have been one of the many fawns I'd seen the previous summer when their mothers felt they were big enough to safely bring out of hiding and secrecy. I thought of the encounters he had with the local wolf pack and how he had hidden in the grasses as a scentless newborn while the black bears were scouring the woods for fawns. By now, he had learned where the locations of the best oak woods yielding acorns were, and the best cedar swamps as wintering areas, and he was surely acquainted with my neighbor's lush hay field. This was his home range that he knew so well, but the increased testosterone in his body had caused him to be in the wrong place at the wrong time. Now he lay here before me and I did my best to let his spirit know he existed and I admired him, and I was sorrowful his powerful will to survive was no more.

Killing a deer is only the first step in a process before the gift of the deer becomes food. Within two hours the spiked buck was skinned, quartered, and the rib cage was on a tree as suet for the birds. The hide was on a platform for the ravens to pick on and the bones were in the woods for the coyotes and foxes—nothing goes to waste. While paying my sorrow to the deer, I thought of a quote by William Faulkner: "I slew you; my bearing must not shame your quitting life. My conduct forever onward must become your death." I complain about deer being overpopulated and their having a detrimental impact on forest ecology, but know in my heart that the deer are not the problem; they are only symptomatic of a problem of our own creation. I admire them—they are the soul of caution. They, like all the other plant and animals that I live with, have important lessons to teach me. I call whitetails the "soul of caution." These words were carefully chosen. I have watched many an adult deer, and the wary whitetail do not often make a mistake. Their senses are beyond amazing. They possess radar ears, a super nose and eyes that can acutely detect movement along with what seems to be an intuitive sense of perception that is beyond our understanding as humans. The sensitive, moccasin-like pads between the hard shells of their hoofs can detect slight vibrations on the ground. So many times while hunting, a deer, usually a doe with a fawn, will come along while I am ten feet or more up in a tree, hidden behind a limb, downwind, and completely still and silent, yet the deer, for a reason inexplicable to me, will stop and sense something wrong. You can see it in their ears, tail, and overall body language that they know something is not right, and when this happens, they are gone and nothing can get them to come back. The two guiding principles for deer are caution and vigilance.

I have killed many deer in my life with both a traditional bow and a rifle, but the killing gets more difficult every year for me. The day is coming when I will no longer hunt deer. Whether it becomes a decision made on judgment, the manner in which hunting has been transformed today, or my old body giving out, one way or another, deer hunting will likely become a thing of my past. But for now, I am a hunter, and when possible, I prefer to obtain meat myself and not from the grocery store, but I have had to think hard about this thing called hunting. I was born in rural America and hunting, to my parents, was more about food than being a sport. Wild game was often on the table. Death for both farm animals and wild game was an everyday experience for rural folks. Some of my earliest memories as a small boy being raised on the plains of South Dakota are of my dad bringing home pheasants and jackrabbits. In my mother's baby book, she wrote of carrying me along with her as an infant, wrapped in a blanket, as she accompanied my dad pheasant hunting (which probably helps account for my loss of hearing), so my experiences as a hunter go back a long way.

My first experience with killing an animal was when I was eight years old. It was with my dad on a relative's farm shooting gophers. The "gophers" were thirteen-lined ground squirrels, commonly called "striped gophers." Everybody shot gophers for the reason that they dug holes in pastures or grain fields. On this particular day, the first day I ever shot at a living thing with a .22 rifle, I drew bead on a little gopher sitting attentively erect at the entrance to his den. I pulled the trigger and the gopher dropped dead where it sat. When I ran up to the burrow, there was this small, limp and lifeless body in my hand. I would not have been capable of articulating my feelings at that early time in my life other than having a feeling of senselessness. For my dad and everyone else, the gopher was just a varmint that was causing destruction to the farm. They would never consider killing a gopher or any other varmint wrong.

Trying to explain to a non-hunter why I hunt is indeed a difficult task if even fully possible. There are too many instincts buried deep within us to articulate, but I can tell you that when I am within wild or semi-wild places, hunting in a manner that is considered fair chase, I feel most connected to the earth and am able to touch that primitive place inside me that says, *You are a part of this.*

Never do I feel as close to nature as when I am on a hunt. Our existence as hunter-gatherers consumed a much greater part of our existence on earth as compared to our lives as civilized beings. Joseph Campbell perhaps said it best when he wrote, "Neither in body nor in mind do we inhabit the world of those hunting races of the Paleolithic era, to whose lives and ways we nevertheless owe the very forms of our bodies and structures of our minds. Memories of their animal envoys still must sleep somehow within us; for they wake a little and stir when we venture into wilderness."

For Native Americans, hunting was not a sport—it was sustenance. Fair chase was not part of their hunting culture, it was more about putting up meat for survival. Yet they had respect for the hunted and believed that a deer, or whatever it was they hunted, gave itself to them. The respect component should be an essential part of all hunters, though it often is not. Nothing on earth is as precious as life, and everything we do as hunters should be in regard to this sacred truth.

As I sat by the dead spiked buck, with the aspen branches

rattling in the November wind, it was as though the scene itself was an act in the play of creation. This entire act had great meaning to my life, and I understood that if I was going to take a life, then I had a debt to pay. I respect the deer and I respect the wolf, and if my life could be as good and true as the deer and the wolf, my life would be a success.

Trash Trees

The greater part of the phenomena of Nature are...concealed from us all our lives. There is just as much beauty visible to us in the landscapes as we are prepared to appreciate, not a grain more ... A man sees only what concerns him.

— Thoreau

In July of 1995, two violent storms with seventy to eighty miles per hour straight-line winds wreaked havoc in the region where I live in northern Minnesota. The first storm came out of the southwest and the second storm came out of the northwest. At the time, my wife and I owned and operated a small business in nearby Hackensack, Minnesota. The wooded property where I now live is a half-hour drive from the town.

Much of the entire region was without power, and roads

and driveways were closed due to the massive blowdown. My anxiety about what the storm did to my land could not be suppressed, so I made the half-hour drive and was shocked and saddened by what I found. In a wide swath from west to east, hundreds of mature jack pines and aspens were piled up in places five to six feet high in a mix resembling giant pickup sticks. Included in this devastation were a few of my beloved one-hundred-year-old red pines. It was bad, but perhaps sixty of my eighty acres had been spared, and within the damaged area the majority of trees in the understory survived.

Days later after the shock wore off I called several loggers to inquire if they could clean up the mess in my woods. I was told that since it was salvage work on damaged trees I would not get anywhere close to market prices for stumpage. I also had numerous lone trees standing out in the open that survived the winds, making them extremely vulnerable to blowdown in the next strong wind storm. The logger agreed to do the work for me, but since he wouldn't be able to start until he finished his current job, the delay gave me an opportunity to ask several forester friends to walk through my land and allow me to pick their brains for ideas and suggestions as how to best go about this logging process which would have a major impact on my beloved land. This also gave me the opportunity to experience the difference between foresters, which enlightened me to the wide range in forestry's school of thought. Several advised me to cut many or all of various non-marketable species of trees because of their lack of economic value, another stressed the impact on the forest ecology, and another suggested a compromise between economics and ecology.

In northern Minnesota in 1995, the only principal market for timber was aspen and pine. The aspen was principally used for pressed board and pine for dimensional lumber. Of the two, aspen was the most valuable, bringing about seventy dollars a cord in 1995, of which I got close to half, and the logger received the remainder for his work and investment in expensive equipment.

One forester of the economic persuasion had referred to "trash trees" and used that reference to recommend clear-cutting land where there was a network of aspen roots in the soil, thereby giving aspens the greatest chance for maximum regeneration. His point was that removing the "trash trees" would allow more sunlight and heat to reach the ground, thus enabling aspens to regenerate at a much greater concentration. Young aspen shoots are called suckers and are actually clones, all genetically identical, and will regenerate up to 50,000 suckers an acre under ideal conditions. The forester who advised me to propagate the greatest aspen regeneration in harvesting methods was doing so for two reasons: one being economic and the other being for deer and grouse habitat. To him, species like ironwood, cherry, even birch and burr oak were "trash trees" for the simple reason they impeded aspen regeneration and had, as he saw it, little or no economic value or desirable habitat for game species. Other foresters with more forest ecology in mind saw value in these other tree species but all emphasized that in the final analysis, it was up to me.

I spend most of my leisure time tromping around in the woods. In doing so, I see much of our state forest lands as tree farms for big timber companies. This land is logged for maximum aspen regeneration which makes vast amounts of state forest land look like monocultured tree farms, primarily devoid of diversity. I did not want this on my land, and had drilled into my head Leopold's thinking that diversity was stability. I spent many hours wrapping bright lime green tape around these "trash trees" so the logger would recognize these marked trees and take care not to damage them with the massive equipment he used. This was nearly twenty years ago, and the resulting impacts of my decision to save these "trash trees" is paying off dividends, though not in an economic sense but in an ecological sense.

An example of ecological benefit, rather than economic gain, was made evident one cold morning in early December after the rifle hunting season for deer had come and gone. I was in a tree stand in a white spruce in a woodland hollow. On the north rim of high ground around this depression was a small stand of *Ostrya virginiana*, also known as hop hornbeam, but more commonly known around here as ironwood. This far north, many hardwoods are at the limits of their northern range. Ironwoods seldom reach fifteen or twenty feet in height in this region. It is a sub-canopy tree, residing well below other larger hardwoods like oaks and maples. Ironwoods are members of the birch family but the only manner in which this is recognized is by the catkins at the end of branches like birches. Their trunks are usually in clumps and as the trees age, the bark gets a shaggy appearance like shagbark hickory (of which none grow around these parts). The flowers develop into overlapping papery clusters with a single seed attached and resemble hops, hence the other name used for this tree: hop hornbeam. The hornbeam comes from when pioneers used the extremely hard wood of this tree as yokes for oxen. The trees have a rugged and sculpted appearance in the manner in which they lean and bend outward from the base. The shaggy bark adds to the rugged appearance.

As I stood on my tree stand in the spruce, I heard something up on the rim and took note. It was eleven ruffed grouse who made their appearance in the ironwoods. I pulled out my small binoculars and watched them. They all were in the ironwood tops, moving about and eating the catkins whole and extracting the seeds from the hops. They spent over an hour there before moving on. To these birds, these "trash trees" had ecological value. The seeds in the hops and the high-energy catkins provided much-needed energy on this cold December morning for these hungry birds. Ironwoods, like most members of the plant communities, have good years, average years and bad years in seed production—that's where diversity comes in. If one species is having a poor year, you can be assured another species will be having a good year.

Pioneers used the hard wood of this little tree for tool handles and Ojibwe people used the one-inch trunks of young ironwoods as framing for their wigwams due to its resiliency and strength. The wood is also excellent for making bows. Perhaps this little "trash tree" may have no value to modern day man as a lumber or paper product, but it provides nourishment for wildlife, makes good tool handles, is used as framework for native dwellings, and can make a weapon to provide meat. Native Americans found medicine in this tree. The heartwood was ground up so a tea could be made from it that was reputed to be a cure for colds and lung ailments.

The ruffed grouse may be king of game birds, but they are also the living embodiment of all the trees in the forests including ironwoods, which some call a "trash tree."

The lesson I learned this December morning, as I watched ruffed grouse feeding in my ironwood trees, was the importance these inconspicuous trees play in the greater scheme of this forest.

Our Relatives

When we try to pick out anything by itself, we find it hitched to everything else in the universe.

— John Muir

It is the weekend before the deer firearms season opens in the Northwoods. Every weekend for the next two or three weeks hunters will be traveling from their homes south of here to come and investigate the condition of their hunting grounds in the north. It is an annual tradition—a cyclical pilgrimage for people who hunt deer—and I imagine they look forward to it all year.

It was early on a Sunday morning when my dog and I decided to head out with a shotgun and see if we could flush up a ruffed grouse or two. We were making our way back when a group of these pre-season deer hunters from central Minnesota, on four ATVs, encountered us, and one of them stopped to chat. He told me the last several years were bad for deer hunting. Last year their group of eight hunters only killed one small deer. He told me that when they arrived to their base camp, there was a wolf waiting for them as though he was giving them a message: "We got your deer." He then continued on his rant about too few deer and too many wolves. I sensed that he wanted to say more, but was aware that I valued the wolf, and so he tried not to insult me.

I find it a bit presumptuous that someone who doesn't live here would be telling me, one who lives here year-round close to the heartbeat of the land, what the problem is with deer and wolves. The comings, goings and status of the plant and animal communities are not an avocation for me, they are my vocation. From a wild aster to an apex predator, they are all relatives to me. As a hunter, I find plant dynamics to be of great relevance to everything else. What is happening in plant communities is an open book in which we can make judgments and predictions of the future. They set the agenda for the season to come.

The land where I live and hunt is dependent on native plant communities. The individual members of this community are variable from year to year. Here in north-central and northwestern Minnesota, we are at the extreme northern limits of many tree species. Red oaks are not found much farther north of here and nearly all the sugar maples have frost cracks in them caused by being north of the forty-below-zero range. This isn't great hardwood forest country like the eastern states. If you want to find the great hardwood forests, you have to go south and east.

White-tailed deer are survivors and opportunists. They have their own mysterious way of drawing infallible conclusions about where to get the necessary fat for the next six months or more of winter. The acorn crop is not always dependable. Some years there is a bumper mast crop in one species of oak, other years both species yield abundant acorns, and some years there is not enough in either oak species to support gray squirrels. When the oak limbs are laden with acorns, starting in late August for burr oaks and into September for red oaks, the acorns begin to drop, especially in the morning hours. When I walk through these woods dominated by mature oaks, it sounds like thousands of golf balls falling from the treetops, with the knock-knock of the hardened and seasoned nuts falling and bouncing off branches on their way to the ground. The loud knocking of these acorns can be heard far and wide and are the dinner bell for the white-tailed deer. These wary whitetails can hear this for up to a mile away and readily make their way to the feast of falling nuts. There have been years when walking through my stand of one-hundred-year-old red oaks in the autumn is like walking on ground covered with marbles. It is such years as these that white-tailed deer will hunker down in these woods as they know better than us that these fat- and protein-laden nuts will put on the necessary body fat to get them through the winter. But it's not just deer that benefit from bumper acorn production. Black bears will turn their noses from bear-hunter baits of prime rib and candied apples for the fat-filled acorns; gray squirrels will industriously bury them for the future cold; blue jays, flying squirrels, chipmunks, deer mice and many more creatures will harvest and store these nuts. Wildlife know what and where the best nutritional sources are.

With all this having been said, the many wolf-hating deer hunters around me fail to notice if there is even one acorn on the ground. They think of themselves as good deer hunters, but many can't tell me what the difference is between a red oak and burr oak, let alone telling me what wild plant food is prospering and is responsible for providing sustenance to deer and other wildlife. If these deer hunters would spend less time on their ATVs, or building starter castle tree stands, or cutting shooting lanes and scouring the halls of the nearest department-size outdoor store, and spend more time learning the ways of the white-tailed deer, which really means learning what is going on in the plant communities, they may be more successful and have a higher-quality experience in the outdoors. The current American hunter is more attuned to a commercial experience than an experience with the living forest.

Reading what is happening in the plant community is important, but there are other population fluctuations and interactions within wildlife communities that tell me about what, where and when deer can be found. This year, the oaks yielded a well below normal acorn crop. In fact, other natural foods were down, and when this happens, the local deer herd will stay close to two small cattle farms. Each of these farms have large hay fields of succulent red clover, something deer will capitalize on as this is their last chance to take in a lush green food before the long hard winter. When this happens, deer hunting can be diminished as most of the deer that frequent my woods are a mile or two away grazing on these last seasonal greens. This is when other wildlife can be an advantage to me.

The year 2014 was a good example, as few acorns and other natural foods forced the deer to vacate my woods and move to the clover hay fields of nearby farms. There was almost no deer sign around my woods, and then one night after midnight I stepped out and heard the deep chesty howl of a wolf coming from the location of my farmer-neighbor's hay field. The next morning the deer were back on and around my land. The wolves had scattered the deer, and when they scatter them, it's not just moving them a hundred yards or so — they run many of them off the farm. The wolves, unbeknownst to them, did me a favor, which reminds me of something I read about wolves and man hunting together. As among most Native people, the Koyukons of Alaska have stories about the hunting relationship between wolves and humans: "In the Distant Time, a wolf-person lived among people and hunted with them. When they parted ways, they agreed that wolves would sometimes make kills for people or drive game to them, as a repayment for favors given when wolves were still human." (*Make Prayers to the Raven*, Richard K. Nelson.) This lesson was taught to me in a meaningful way last year. On the second morning of the season, my son-in-law heard something coming through the brush and witnessed a large doe trotting out into an opening in front of him. She stopped and looked behind her, then continued off at a fast gait. Shortly after, the sound of more brush-busting came, and within seconds behind the doe a large solitary wolf appeared. The wolf too stopped in front of us, but it looked up at my son-in-law in his tree stand with what seemed a contemptuous glance, and then continued on after the doe. If my son-in-law had a doe permit, he could say that a wolf drove the deer to him.

The lesson the forest has to offer us is the interconnection of all life. What happens to one particular species will impact every species. If springtime oak flowers are damaged due to hard frosts or some other natural calamity, this can have far-reaching impacts. I cite a single example of an oak tree, but the plant communities that form the living foundation for all life, even the air we breathe, are numerous and range from microorganisms and fungi in the soil, ground layering herbs and forbs, shrubs, sub-canopy and all the way up to the top canopy. My Anishinaabeg friends call all life, including plant communities, their "relatives." This notion seemed rather quaint to me at first, but the more I pondered this relationship, the more truth I recognized in it. A single molecule of chlorophyll, the food-manufacturing source of plants which forms the bottom layer of the food chain in which all life is dependent and even the air we breathe, is made up of 136 atoms of carbon, hydrogen, oxygen and nitrogen arranged in a specific molecular structure. A molecule of red blood is made up of the same 136 atoms arranged in the same molecular structure. The only difference is that an atom of magnesium is attached to the molecule of chlorophyll while an atom of iron is attached to the molecule of red blood. Switch the magnesium and iron atoms and green chlorophyll becomes red blood and vice versa. Plants are our relatives from some warm prehistoric sea containing amino acids or algae or some other early plant life which first saw life—from there we can trace our origins. Yes, plants are our relatives and we have a direct and meaningful connection to them. They deserve all the attention we can give them.

Living with Wolves

Those unable to decipher the hidden meaning know nonetheless that it is there, for it is felt in all wolf country, and distinguishes that country from all other land.

— Aldo Leopold

It was a warm dewy morning in early October 2008 when my little field springer spaniel, Babsy, and I opted to make our first foray into the autumn woods after our favorite quarry, the woodland rocket, commonly known as the ruffed grouse. The old logging trail we walked started near my cabin and meandered two miles through county and state lands of mostly mixed hardwoods and conifers. It was a weekday and the opening of grouse hunting was several weeks ago so I knew we wouldn't be bumping into anyone else.

We chose an old trail that was commonly called by locals the "Twin Pines Trail" due to two large old-growth white pines growing along its path which are located on top of a hill overlooking a tamarack wetland that seeps northeastward to a small undeveloped wilderness lake. The lake is flanked on the south and west by a cedar swamp, and on the north by high ground with old-growth white and red pines. On the slope of these old-growth pines were several wolf dens that had been active during the denning season in April. In late spring or early summer, the pups were removed from the den to a rendezvous site a short distance away. For years, my wife and I have listened to the howling and yipping of adult wolves and their pups.

Along the Twin Pines Trail, the forest cover alternates between aspen of different age categories, scattered balsam firs, burr oaks, red maples and understory hazel with scattered sentinel white pines. The immediate region in a one-mile radius is excellent habitat with mast-bearing oak trees, thick dog-hair stands of aspen for cover and lowland conifers for deer yarding habitat during the harsh winters.

As we began our hunt, we noticed the ground was covered by heavy dew. Our footsteps were silent in the wet forbs and grasses on the old trail, but even with our hushed footsteps, something seemed different about this morning. I had a strange feeling that we had company, though I neither heard nor saw anything. It was just that strange sensation one has when he or she feels they are being watched.

At the end of the trail there was a small clearing of ten yards in diameter that was formed by ATVs turning around. At this point I seated myself on a large aspen blowdown so my dog and I could take a rest. I unloaded my side-by-side twenty-gauge shotgun, as more hunters are shot by rambunctious dogs than by themselves, like my hyper little dog who jumps around and could knock the loaded gun over. I ate an apple from my game bag, and then I took out my pipe and filled it with tobacco and lit it. As I started puffing away, Babsy stepped forward several yards and started to growl with the hackles up on her back. She scented something upwind in the trees and brush. I assumed it was a deer moving towards us not realizing our presence. In seconds, I began to make out something moving in the thick hazel brush, and to my surprise an adult wolf stepped into the small clearing. The wolf was a mottled black, gray and brown. I stood up in my blaze orange game vest with Babsy standing between me and the wolf. The wolf looked me in the eye and then focused its attention on my dog, I called Babs and she immediately responded by returning, not to my side, but behind me. The wolf, without any vocalization or outward sign of aggression, or any other gesture other than the curiosity of one dog encountering another dog, began to approach us. Wolves are mysterious and I'll never know what was on its mind.

This all happened in a matter of seconds, so I had no time to think about it, only to react. I was standing erect with no loaded gun, and my dog was directly behind me. The wolf stood in front of me, within arm's reach and showed no intention of stopping, and was keenly focused on Babsy. My immediate gut reaction was that I had to do something, so I removed my cap and hit the wolf on the head, which caused it to back off, somewhat surprised, and it began to pace back and forth. I walked toward it swinging my cap, and it backed off, staying out of reach. Within seconds it turned and left by the same way it came, disappearing into the forest. This whole episode happened so quickly, perhaps only thirty seconds and it was over. Or so I thought. I decided it best to load my gun, sit down, finish smoking my pipe, regain some composure, and let the wolf put some distance between us before heading back. So that's what I did, and when I finished smoking, I knocked the ash out of my pipe and started back, but this time, on the return, I kept Babsy right out in front of me within ten yards or less, and she too seemed to understand that circumstances were different now.

By now the ground was drying out from the heavy dew and the sound of footsteps could be more easily heard. It wasn't far after we started back that I heard something paralleling us and that feeling I had earlier, of being watched, returned. Was my mind playing tricks on me now after the wolf encounter? But as I began questioning myself, about a hundred yards down the trail I got a fleeting glimpse of a wolf just off the trail as it bounded off into the dense forest cover. Things started to get real weird as I continued to hear something moving in the woods a short distance off the trail on my flank. Then for a second time, about another hundred yards or so down the trail, I got another quick look at a wolf. Whether this was the same wolf I hit on the head or several different wolves, I cannot say with any certainty. It wasn't until I was within a half mile of my cabin that I felt the wolf or wolves had disappeared. I have heard wolves called "gray ghosts" but after that morning the name took on new meaning to me.

What happened that day with the wolf has taken me several years to fully wrap my brain around. In fact, I am still pondering the full meaning of the experience. I do not intend to make this out to be something it's not. Perhaps it was no more than a chance encounter and I should not interpret a moral lesson in it. But the uniqueness of this special incident is irrefutable. A great and powerful spirit of the forest met me that day face to face, and everything in life has some meaning whether it is of lesser or greater consequence, and to me this was of great significance. It taught me something about this mysterious entity. This lesson was not an academic teaching; it was a real-life experience that brought the definition of a wolf out of the pages of a book and into as intimate of an experience as one can have with such a being that has had more of a polarizing effect on us than any living creature. The wolf, the bear, the raven and the eagle are all powerful spirits in these wild places. The time we spend in wild places adds great meaning to our lives, and my life certainly has been broadened because of it.

I looked into its eyes, it looked into mine and then it became more interested in my dog, this distant relative of his. I touched him as we met one another in his world as though it happens every day. It was a chance meeting but I recognized there was something behind his eyes, something deeper and more perceptive than any other forest creature whose eyes I have looked into with the exception of *Makwa*, the bear.

Minnesota has always had ideal habitat for wolves and we have always had wolves. Our wolves are of the same genetic stock of the wolves that have lived here for thousands of years. They are not transplants; they are natives. Three biomes come together here: the northern temperate forests, the prairie biomes, and an abundance of surface water (lakes, streams, and wetlands). It would be difficult to find country with more diversity.

When Joseph Nicollet traveled to the headwaters of the Mississippi River 180 years ago, at a campsite in the Kabekona River valley, not more than five or six miles from the exact spot where I hit a wolf on the head with my cap, he wrote in his journal on August 25, 1836: "This morning for the first time in my life I attended a terrifying concert performed at dawn by wolves whose bands are wont to haunt these totally deserted and virgin forests. It was like a choir of chilling howls that could be heard in the distance on both sides of the river, spreading far and wide across the echoing solitudes. Had I not recalled that these forest animals, well provided for by the abundant game they devour, are more inclined to flee than to attack a solitary traveler, I would have shuddered with fear."

When wolves had been extirpated in most of the lower forty-eight, including the Rocky Mountain States who wiped out their wolves in the 1920s, Minnesota still had wolves roaming the northland, even though the state and federal wildlife agencies targeted them by gun, trap, and poison like the rest of the country. But the fact that by 1974, 750 wolves were able to cling to existence in Minnesota had nothing to do directly with us. Minnesota, like the rest of the nation, was hell-bent on killing wolves. The reason they survived here was due to the large contiguous wilderness that existed where wolves could find refuge. For Minnesota's wolves, their salvation was the wild. By the time of the establishment of the Endangered Species Act of 1973, those 750 wolves were principally found in the northern extremities of the five northeastern-most counties of Cook, Lake, St. Louis, Koochiching, and Lake of the Woods, and the major factor in this was the 1.25 million acre wilderness of the Boundary Waters Canoe Area (BWCA) in Superior National Forest located along the United States and Canadian border in Cook, Lake and St. Louis Counties. Even in this wilderness, wolves were still hunted, trapped, and poisoned. Even the wilderness icon Sigurd Olson was among those who trapped and poisoned wolves in the BWCA in the 1930s because he and most natural resource managers thought fewer wolves meant more deer. Olson called wolves "gray marauders." Aldo Leopold did likewise as he wrote, "we never heard of passing up a chance to kill a wolf." But both Leopold and Olson, through their experiences in nature, realized the errors of their ways and became powerful advocates for the wolf. The reason this vast wilderness in Minnesota was the salvation for wolves was due to its difficult and demanding means of access. It was a roadless area and access for humans was only by canoe or foot.

Up until twenty-five to thirty years ago wolves in the part of northern Minnesota where I live were rarely seen. In the early 1970s while living in Bemidji, if a coyote trapper would get a wolf, it was news enough to make the Bemidji newspaper. Aside from these unusual occurrences there was no viable population of wolves in this region of northern Minnesota.

As a young man in my twenties I would make trips to the Boundary Waters Canoe Area Wilderness during all four seasons to be in wolf country, never imagining at that time someday I would be living with wolves. On many occasions I would go to Ely on the edge of the BWCA and either winter camp or stay at the old Shagawa Hotel in town and drive up the Echo Trail and strap on either my army surplus skis or rawhide laced snowshoes and travel down one of the rivers such as the Little Indian Sioux, Moose, or Stuart Rivers and find tracks of wolves and follow them with the hope of seeing or hearing them. When on my eighty acres near Bemidji, the best I could see was coyotes. Listening to several coyote groups yipping away in the evening was fun to hear but coyotes are not wolves and with wolves, believe me, the character of the land is uniquely different than having coyotes around. When the Endangered Species Act of 1973 was passed by Congress, and signed by President Nixon, wolves became, for first time in America, innocent until proven guilty.

One winter day in the late 1980s, while I was tromping in the woods around my home on snowshoes, I came across the first wolf sign I had seen in this part of northern Minnesota. I found the tracks of two large canids and I followed them as they wandered throughout the woods in a random fashion. The tracks were larger than any dog track I have seen and they were where I would never expect to find a dog roaming. Soon thereafter I unmistakably heard wolves howling, and then I started seeing more tracks, then scats and then wolf kills. The big gray ghosts were back and a walk in the woods would never be the same again. The whole character of the Northwoods had changed and no longer would coyotes rule the day. A more powerful spirit was present and every living thing in the woods knew this. I remember the first time I came upon a fresh wolf kill. It was a mid-winter day of beauty. I was on snowshoes as the snow was twenty inches deep, and it was bitter cold, perhaps fifteen below zero, and the shadows were long. My dog and I first noticed a large number of ravens becoming airborne a short distance ahead of us, more than I had ever seen at one time, and my curiosity made me investigate. As I approached, I saw that the snow was covered with bright red blood. Every square inch had raven tracks and raven droppings over an area ten yards or more in diameter. The tracks, the blood, everything was recent, maybe no more than twelve hours ago. As my dog and I took in all this I started to sense the presence of something much greater than myself. I stood and scanned the woods around me. My mind pondered the scene with some concern: Were they close? Were they watching me? I sensed that I was no longer at the top of the food chain. No animal could change the character of the land as the presence of the wolf had that day.

With the return of the wolf, I wondered how this would impact deer hunting. My deer hunting goes back to the 1960s before any local deer knew what a wolf was. The chief predator of deer in those days was Old Man Biboon (winter). Winter was the chief limiting factor of deer with coyotes and black bear being somewhere in second or third place. From the time I started hunting in the Bemidji and Cass Lake areas in and around Chippewa National Forest in the mid-sixties, to when I bought the land that has become my home in the same area, deer hunting was tough. Deer populations were much fewer in those years. Deer were so few and far between that if you wanted venison, you shot the first one you saw, if you were one of the lucky ones or good enough of a hunter to see a deer. It wasn't until the late 1990s that the deer herd exploded in northern Minnesota.

From 2000 to 2015, Minnesota had the largest white-tailed

deer population in our history. This has been the golden age of deer hunting in Minnesota. According the Minnesota Department of Natural Resources (MN DNR), the deer herd has varied between one million to 1.25 million during this same period. These years of record deer numbers have also coincided with the largest wolf population in our state's history, approximately 3,200 wolves. I am not implying that three thousand wolves are responsible for over a million deer. The reason for these high deer numbers is our land practices. For three to four decades, Minnesota's public lands were tree farms that had human applications, such as pulp wood. These extractive wood industries created ideal habitat for deer.

Wildlife managers have repeatedly made the claims that the wolf density in northern Minnesota was the highest in North America, and I would not argue this, but this has nothing to do with wolves being overpopulated. Wolves are living in balance with their prey base. What it does say is that our deer herd is enormous. If one wants to lower the wolf population, lower the deer population. Any predator population will be correlated to its prey base.

As for the outcry from the agriculture sector concerning livestock losses, this is in some cases a legitimate issue that needs to be dealt with quickly and with measures that focus on the "problem" wolves and not non-offending wolves, but the livestock depredation problem is grossly overstated. It certainly happens, but some of the culpability rests with the farmers who refuse to adapt, alter their husbandry practices, or adamantly refuse to enlist measures to safeguard their livestock such as the use of guard dogs.

Parts of northern, western, and north-central Minnesota are cattle country. Cass County in the heart of northern Minnesota produces more calves annually than any other county in the state. When I see the numbers of livestock losses or percentages of losses, I am surprised they are so low.

The last year that depredation numbers were made available from the Fish and Wildlife Service (FWS) was 2011. In that year, only slightly over two hundred complaints or 1.7% of farms in Minnesota had confirmed claims of livestock depredation by wolves, which included cows, calves, geese, llamas, and dogs.

The MN Department of Agriculture statistics at the end of 2014 show Minnesota with a cattle herd of 2.3 million. The article indicates sixty-six calves and seventeen cows were killed by wolves. That is a total of eighty-three killed by wolves out of 2.3 million head. That means in 2014 the wolf depredation was .000037% of the total cattle herd, or less than one cattle killed for every 25,000. For comparison, a study conducted by the Humane Society of the United States concluded that nine times as many cattle die each year from the weather.

Also, at the end of 2014, the MN Department of Agriculture stated: "Minnesota had a sheep herd of about 130,000. Twelve sheep were killed by wolves." That means .0092% of the sheep herd were killed by wolves.

Concerning deer hunters, much hunter hatred for the wolf is, in my opinion, rather ironic and misguided. We love the chase when it comes to deer hunting because of the elusiveness of the wary whitetail. Their keen senses and extreme wariness make them sought after by all big-game hunters. The great archer and bow hunter, Fred Bear, said that of all the big game animals he had hunted in North America, the white-tailed deer was the most difficult to bag. The whitetail is a product of the wolf. It was over thousands of years of being chased and stalked by the wolf that the deer, through natural selection, evolved into the fleet-footed and keen-sensed creature hunters admire today. The deer would not be what it is if not for the wolf and other large predators. The wolf and the deer are in a sense related through their interaction in this event called life on earth. They are intrinsically linked and will be forever.

Wolves have always had great spiritual significance to people. To the Anishinaabeg, they are one of the Seven Grandfathers and the teacher of humility, and they are depicted as a brother who has a clan named in his honor. To white people he is hated and is rooted in myths and fairy tales as a treacherous killer and evil. But there are contradictions among white people in their attitude toward wolves. White people love dogs, but what is a dog other than a wolf in our living rooms? For white people, four or five thousand years ago in Europe, before the advent of agriculture and cultigens, we had an earth-based religion. We, like our Indian brothers and sisters, were co-tenants on earth with all other life. We did not see ourselves as having dominion over other life—we too were related to everything else. The cave walls of Lascaux, France, with their beautiful depictions of wild animals, are evidence of our past and our connection to the land.

To feel and understand this interconnectedness to all other life has to come from the heart first, and many people have not arrived there yet. The urge to kill wolves is politically and economically driven by Big Ag, extraction industries, sportsmen and politicians. Prior to the first wolf hunt in Minnesota after delisting in 2012, the MN DNR had an online survey in which 79% of respondents opposed hunting wolves. A year later a poll was taken and 80% of Minnesotans wanted wolves protected. The Creator did not create anything to be evil, and if he did, we only need to look in the mirror to find it.

In 2012 the wolf was delisted under the Endangered Species Act after many back-and-forths in court between environmentalists, legislators and anti-wolf folks. In Minnesota the wolf was reclassified by state government as a small game animal thus making penalties for illegal killings a mere pittance. As of writing this, Minnesota has had three wolf hunts. The first year there were over 400 wolves killed, the second year over 220, and the third year over 250 were shot or trapped, and more wolves were being killed in other ways. There were more "problem" wolves being killed for livestock depredation and poaching of wolves was believed to have greatly increased. Many of the legislators and citizens who had despised the wolf during forty years of protection were now in the driver's seat in managing the wolf. The marketplace is directing the management of the wolf, and even the Commissioner of the Minnesota Department of Natural Resources has noted that a wolf hide brings big dollars in China and that people will come to Minnesota to kill a wolf. During the first wolf hunt in 2012, the DNR hoped that wolf hunting would bring in $400,000. The Minnesota Deer Hunters Association, the Minnesota Trappers Association, Cattlemen's Associations, the Minnesota Legislature, our Governor and our two Senators in Washington D.C. support the hunt. All of us watching the events unfolding in front of us see that delisting wolves has brought out the worst elements of society toward the wolf, yet all surveys and polls show that most Minnesota citizens do not want a hunt.

To us in Minnesota, the wolf is special. This is the last bastion of the wolf, as it was the only state in the lower forty-eight where gray wolves survived. He has special meaning to us. I love to hunt but feel it is wrong to kill a wolf, and there are others like me. For many of those on the other side, I hear them say, "Kill them all." There is zero tolerance for the wolf and this intolerance is in power, sitting in the driver's seat. I cannot help but think of Aldo Leopold's words in *A Sand County Almanac* when he spoke of the government trapper who killed the last grizzly in Arizona which appropriately applies to the wolf: "He did not know he had toppled the spire off an edifice a-building since the morning stars sang together."

After several years of pondering my unique face-to-face

encounter with a wolf, I have realized its subjective meaning to me.

Several winters later while again out on snowshoes with Babsy on the Twin Pines Trail, I came across an old deer kill from earlier that winter. All that was left were the rib bones in the middle of the trail bleached white by the winter sun. Babsy was out ahead of me and stopped to sniff the bones with more than her usual interest. As I approached, I noticed two sets of fresh wolf tracks in the snow and some bright yellow urine on the rib bones that was still wet and unfrozen which meant it happened recently. As I knelt to get a closer look, I noticed Babsy's attention was focused elsewhere. I stood and looked off to the south side of the trail, and on a small rise in some old tamaracks I saw two wolves beautifully yet mysteriously silhouetted against the low sun. They were standing one directly behind the other, appearing to be relaxed and attentively watching us. There was no fear, no hatred, only four living organisms meeting one another, and then they casually turned and disappeared. My only emotion was of contentment that they were here. Nothing has more symbolic meaning for me than the wolf. For thousands of years we have waged a campaign of eradication against the wolf in the worst possible manner.

I often recall something that happened about twenty years ago and had a great impact on me. At that time, my wife and I owned and operated a small motel in northern Minnesota, and one winter day we were cleaning rooms together and had the TVs on, as we normally did while we made beds and cleaned rooms. The Discovery Channel or some similar channel was on and airing a program about wolves. A segment of the film had what appeared to be an old 8 MM movie camera clip filming a tractor and wagon pulling up to a poisoned deer or elk carcass. Around the carcass were many dead wolves with a few foxes and bobcats. Several men were lifting the lifeless bodies of wolves on their shoulders and throwing them on the wagon as though they were cordwood. As one large male wolf was hoisted up around the neck of a human, I could see he was still conscious, though paralyzed and dying, and he lifted his head with open eyes. This gruesome scene shook me to the core. An epiphany took place at that time in my life. What we have done to wolves on earth for thousands of years is not simply an unjust deed — it is a great ethical and moral injustice that we must bear forever.

For years I have had difficulty responding to the arguments given by some ethical hunters who want to maintain a population of wolves as a game species so they can continue to hunt them. These are not the hate-filled anti-wolf hunters, but people who I have much in common with. After mulling this over in my head the answer I would give to those hunters who have some feeling of respect for the wolf is that for thousands of years the wolf has been the most persecuted animal on earth. Think of our history with the wolf this way: We humans have created a huge moral and ethical debt in the cosmos. It is now our obligation to pay off that debt and all the interest that debt has incurred. We do that by getting our ethics right. Getting our ethics right applies to human beings as well as the environment.

I recall reading an account about an old wolf trapper in northern Minnesota. The old trapper, who had lost his reason for living without wolves in his life, told of a time when he was checking his trap line and found a large, beautiful, black male wolf with his leg in a foothold trap. The wolf looked at him and lifted his foot as if to ask the trapper, "Help me," and the trapper thought of how he wanted to let him live but then thought, "I need the bounty money," and he shot him. It is time for humankind to stop seeing the wolf through the lenses of politics and economics, and start seeing him as a cog in the greater wheel of things. More and more I come to believe that man's efforts to rid from the earth big predators in some of the cruelest and heinous fashions are reflected back on the way we behave ethically toward one another and society. In order to live the good way toward ourselves, we have to live that good way toward the wolf and the greater land organism. If we are to take life, it has to be done for a good reason, not for hatred or ego.

At the time of my writing, the wolf was relisted under the Endangered Species Act (ESA) by Federal Court. There are efforts in Congress by Big Ag, sportsmen groups, and others to permanently remove the Great Lakes Wolves from protection under the ESA, but there are also thousands of people throughout America that are mobilized and urging their elected officials to not remove the wolf from the Endangered Species list. These people are giving their time and resources to ensure that wolves will be protected. To see so much of America fighting for the wolf gives me hope that we can live in peace with the greater community on earth. The wolf symbolizes the great trial before us humans. If we cannot come to terms with the wolf, we may not be able to come to terms with anything, including ourselves.

Grosbeak Woods

Every farm woodland, in addition to yielding lumber, fuel, and posts, should provide its owner a liberal education. This crop of wisdom never fails, but it is not always harvested.

— Aldo Leopold

It's early December and winter has overtaken the land. All the migratory and seasonal birds are long gone. The remaining birds at my feeder are year-round neighbors: the chickadees, nuthatches, blue jays and a host of woodpeckers. The countryside is under a blanket of snow, the lakes are frozen and the short days and long nights combined with the long shadows of winter give the country a melancholy mood.

This is the time of year that I long for evening grosbeaks to appear at my bird feeder. Such an event is a joyous occasion.

It is uplifting to see these brilliantly colored birds. When one appears, it is certain that there will be more because this bird moves in flocks of large numbers. Their colorful markings of golden-yellow, plus black and white, brighten up any gloomy winter day and the sparrow-like chirping of three dozen birds or more, all perched in the boughs of my pines, is a thing to behold. They give me hope in a season of cold, darkness and death—the long winter of the northland.

Unfortunately they do not always appear. Their nomadic movements and irruptive appearances are unpredictable. Some years they are not to be seen, while in other years they appear in great numbers and bring delight to those of us who appreciate them. I did not see them the previous two years, but did the previous four or five consecutive years. I await them with great anticipation and anxiety and if my woods will be without them this year, it will be a sad thing because, for me, seeing my bird feeder covered with them busily and voraciously opening sunflower seeds in their powerful bills is a scene demonstrating a lust for life, and they can pass on this lust to a melancholy man.

The name itself, "grosbeak," means a large bill, and this bill can open or crush seeds and pits that require 125 pounds of force to fracture or open in testing devices. I like to think of these beautiful birds along with their relatives, pine grosbeaks and rose-breasted grosbeaks, as the "parrots of the north." But they are not strict vegetarians. On a canoe trip many years ago into northwestern Ontario's Woodland Caribou Provincial Park, we camped one evening on a lake with black spruce and balsam fir dominating the shoreline. The spruce and fir needles had turned red due to an infestation of spruce budworms, a larval form of a moth that aggressively attacks these conifers. The infected trees were full of evening grosbeaks who were busily feasting on the budworms. During the maple season, while working in my sugar bush, I have noticed evening grosbeaks drinking sap that was dripping from a wounded or broken twig. On another occasion, I filled a mixing bowl with water to soak after emptying its contents of pancake batter and placed it outside my door. Several minutes later I turned and noticed a half dozen evening grosbeaks perched on its rim and savoring the water which was tainted with pancake batter.

I remembered then that the Ojibwe called evening grosbeaks *paushkun-damo* which means "berry-breaker." I was fully familiar with these birds breaking open seeds of various trees, but I never made the connection with the Ojibwe name "berry-breaker" until one winter day while I was snowshoeing through a black ash lowland with many highbush cranberries in the understory. Highbush cranberry has many clusters of bright red cranberry-like berries all winter. When wandering through these frozen wooded wetlands I cannot pass up grabbing a handful of these fruits for a flavorful pick-me-up. Often I would notice the empty pinkish skins or hulls lying on the snow under the bushes. It wasn't until one cold winter afternoon when visiting these ash swamps that I observed a flock of grosbeaks extracting the pulp and seeds from the highbush cranberries while discarding the skins.

It is wonderful when evening grosbeaks appear, but what can make the winter even more special is the arrival of the less common pine grosbeaks. These "parrots of the north" are a bit larger than the evening grosbeaks and are more erect in posture. They are an unmistakable wine red with black wings. They move in smaller flocks than the evening grosbeaks and are often seen along northern roads presumably to pick at the salt and gravel on the shoulders. They have a soft, plaintive whistle that I will never forget. Of all the grosbeaks, the pine grosbeak is a rather tame bird, allowing close approach. They too are berry-breakers, and in fact the grosbeaks that I witnessed extracting the contents of highbush cranberries were these handsome and noble birds.

If you should have a winter bird feeder covered with the gold, black and white evening grosbeaks and a dozen or so pine grosbeaks underneath on the ground, consider yourself fortunate as you have been smiled upon by the woodland spirits, for this is nature in its finest.

But the real essence and spirit of my woods is the grosbeak of summer, the rose-breasted grosbeak. Between the fourth and sixth of May, like clockwork every year, arrives the rose-breasted grosbeaks in my woods and surrounding area.

When the early arriving males first appear, they are rather silent until the females arrive a week or so later. With the arrival of the females comes the rich bubbling warble and whistle of the rose-breasted grosbeak, making them one of the most melodic bird songs in the forest.

The woods in which I live are blessed with an uncommonly large number of these handsome and melodic birds. When walking in my woods in mid-May and through the month of June, the air is filled with their music. As I age, I find myself sitting up against a tree deep in the forest with my dogs and closing my eyes while savoring the beautiful song of this bird, and forgetting the worries of the outside world. There is contentment to be found in the natural world that is difficult to capture elsewhere, and hearing dozens of grosbeaks singing in close proximity is one of the sources.

When these birds arrive there is a flurry of activity at the feeder, but it drops off abruptly by mid-June and the singing slows to sporadic musings. The reason for their sudden absence at the bird feeder and less vigorous singing is the nesting activity of which the male birds share in the nest construction, incubating and feeding. During this period, it is not difficult to find them and their nests. The nests are usually within arm's reach from the ground, and typically in some thickets like hazel. The nests are the most shabbily built nests of any bird I am familiar with. They are built with as few twigs as possible, and often, standing directly underneath, I can see through the nest well enough to count the eggs. It is rather humorous to see these plump birds overlapping this hastily built assemblage of twigs, but they seem to make do as there is always an abundance of youngsters. By August they reappear with numbers many times greater than when they arrived in May. I have counted as many as two dozen birds on my twenty-four-inch bird-feeding platform at once with countless more in the trees around the feeder awaiting room for their turn. By mid-September they are gone until another spring comes with the renewal of life.

On a winter's day when a person's spirits may be low, to behold thirty to one hundred evening grosbeaks busily gorging themselves on birdseed while perched in a stand of pines with all of them creating a cacophony of sparrow-like chirps — this is real therapy for me. It is an act of contagious optimism. It is at such times I realize that a bird can do more for me than a shrink. The same can be said for the pine grosbeaks and the rose-breasted grosbeaks. What I witness and learn from all these "parrots" is camaraderie and a social togetherness that is perhaps unmatched in the bird world. They rarely squabble or fight and get along marvelously. If I were to put a lesson to be taken from these "parrots of the north," it is optimism and cohesive unity. Never are they downcast and there is an affectionate unity among them.

I am truly fortunate to live with a great many creatures of the forest: wolves, bears, deer, eagles, grouse, swans and much more, but if I had to choose one animal that is outstanding in presence and spirit, and whose presence represents the woods in which I live, it is grosbeaks. This is "Grosbeak Woods."

Old Man *Biboon*

Winter is not a season, it's an occupation.

—Sinclair Lewis

Winter in northern Minnesota can be brutal. Forty below zero or colder is not that uncommon and it can get colder. The state records from Tower and Embarrass are sixty and sixty-one below zero on February 2, 1996, and I am not talking wind chill: this is air temperature. Where I live, it got down to fifty-six degrees below zero on that same February day in 1996. That same winter, my records show over twenty mornings that the low temperature was forty below zero or colder. I used to scoff at people and say anything colder than fifteen below zero is indistinguishable until I walked to the mail box one frigid morning. When I inhaled, my nostrils closed and didn't want to reopen. That same year, we had slightly over ninety inches of snow, and the following winter we had ninety-eight inches. This isn't that much snow for places like U.P. Michigan, but the cold temperatures combined with the deep snow was devastating for much of northern Minnesota's wildlife. Deer took a major hit, and many winter bird species suffered terribly. Small owls like the saw-whet were almost wiped out. That winter made my woods almost squirrel-less. It took at least two years for the squirrel species — reds, grays and flying squirrels — to recover. Winter, or *biboon*, as the Ojibwe call it, is the great limiting factor in the northland.

We live in a sixteen-by-twenty-four-foot cabin. Our only heat source is a cast iron Norwegian wood stove. We have no running water which means we have an outhouse, and the trips there on frigid days are less than an enjoyable experience. There is something to be said about going outside late at night to relieve one's self. The things I've heard in the night air or what I've seen in the skies — northern lights, shooting stars or birds high in the night skies on migration — all make the discomfort of going into the chilly night air well worth it. One autumn night while I was outside, I heard a blood-curdling scream coupled with vicious snarling, growling and scuffling. I thought to myself, what in the world is this? The cries of the banshee? The next morning I checked it out and found it to be a porcupine dispatched by a fisher — I knew this by the manner in which the fisher had done the deed: the bloodied and mauled head of the porcupine, and the fact that it was eaten from the unprotected underside, which fishers do to avoid the quills.

I am a chronic early riser, often being up by 4:00 A.M., but my wife likes to sleep much later. My first task upon rising is to rekindle the fire. On these cold nights we stoke up the stove before we go to bed so hot coals remain in the morning which enables me to simply throw a few small pieces of wood in, and they quickly ignite, bringing the heat again. If the coals are dead, I have paper and kindling always at hand to start a new fire. On frigid mornings of subzero outside temps, the temperature inside will be in the fifties, but within an hour my little stove has it in the sixties and rising. I know my dogs think I am a worker of miracles, creating this warm and comfortable source of heat as they try to squeeze between me and the stove. The cat too believes I am a miracle worker but waits until the dogs have moved away before she gets closer. Every winter morning of bitter cold I think of Aldo Leopold and his masterpiece, *A Sand County Almanac* and his essay in February entitled "Good Oak." I too have developed a deep appreciation for firewood and especially oaks. It is at this time I realize the life-giving properties this wood has for me. Being a wood burner, I can walk by a stove, downwind, and tell you what type of wood is burning by smelling the smoke. They all have their own distinctive smell but pine and birch are my favorite. Pine smoke is the incense of the north and birch has a spicy odor that I wish I could bottle.

Living the way I do has allowed me a deeper appreciation for many things in life that would be easy to take for granted within other lifestyles. Wood gathering—culling the dead trees from my northern hardwoods, bucking them up to stove size, hauling them back to my yard, and splitting, stacking and covering them—is not just a chore, it is an annual ritual. When my wood is split, stacked and covered, I draw satisfaction and great contentment to gaze upon it for I know what these woodpiles mean to me. I sleep deeply knowing that I have an adequate supply of dry oak put up for winter. This wood enables me to survive another winter—it permits life and I am indebted to the trees from which it grew. I think of these things a lot here. My oaks are more than just nice trees. I rely on them, and I need them. They do not need me. They cause me to consider what else in my woods does need me. The answer is nothing. I also consider how much I depend on all the life around me. I am thankful for oaks because without the plant and animal communities on earth how would we survive? They are far more than fuel, they are lumber for shelter, food, medicine, homes for birds and animals, plus so much more.

There have been nights in mid-winter when I have stepped outside and the extreme cold is so intense that I feel as though it is crushing. It reminds me what I've heard of deep-sea diving and the intense crushing pressure at great depths in the ocean. That is how twenty, thirty or forty below can feel when you are not properly dressed. Old Man Biboon can crush you and show you how small and vulnerable you are.

Normally when it's that cold the wind is calm and the skies are clearer than at any other season. Such nights can have a mystical or magical effect. On such a night, my wife and I strapped on our snowshoes and made the short trip to the small wilderness lake on one end of our property. It was in early January and the moon was almost full, the wind was calm and the smoke of our chimney was rising so straight that you could plumb a line with it. The winter sky was extraordinarily clear. There is no light pollution here and the brightness of the moon that evening only slightly lessened the brilliance of the stars. The night air had the most complete silence one could find on earth. It was so quiet that it was deafening. The only noise was the squeak of snow under our snowshoes when we moved. As we stopped on the middle of the lake and gazed into the cold night air we saw millions of twinkling lights, not just skyward but all around us—within inches of our faces, and we were surrounded by a surreal light show. We both thought that we were hallucinating in some kind of ethereal kaleidoscopic. It was the cold night air freezing the minute water particles which were suspended, and those frozen particles caught the moon light and twinkled as they drifted aimlessly in the sub-zero air. It is at such times when the forbidding cold of the north can be a thing of great beauty and mystery. Winter can be pitiless but it can cast a spell and aura that transcends the ordinary.

My mother told me that as I aged, I would come to dislike winter. The reverse is true—the older I get, the more I appreciate winter. It can be a most peaceful season. The woods are silent, the tourists, hunters and cabin people are gone. There are nights when I can hear the drone of snowmobiles in the distance, but for the most part they don't come back here. By the onset of winter, my chores are done and I am ready for the long cold season. It is a time to rest, sleep longer, read, reflect, write, watch the bird feeder, snowshoe and read the tracks and animal sign that can be an endless manuscript.

I ponder the frozen countryside and I think it odd that with so many lakes and rivers now iced-over in the frozen grip of winter, and the land covered with snow, this water-rich land is a virtual frozen desert, waterless and white. But our perception of a frozen and dead landscape is deceiving. For life still goes about, just out of sight. Bears give birth in their winter dens, mice and shrews have networks of tunnels below the surface of the snow, snowshoe hares live it up in the darkness of winter, owls become the tigers of the night and then there are wolves.

The full moon of January is the Ojibwe moon of the wolf. This is the preferred time of year for the wolves. They are not hampered by the cold with their thick, insulated coats of dense fur, there are no ticks to plague them, and in the snow and cold, they are the supreme hunters of the land. *Ma'iingan* thrives in the winter—this is their time.

Bird watching is our winter form of television. We enjoy all that frequent our bird feeder. Besides our year-round resident birds, our winter visitors are evening and pine grosbeaks, occasional pine siskins, and redpolls. They are all welcome for they each bring their unique traits and characters. About every ten years we get huge irruptions of redpolls, and when that happens we are on alert for the hoary redpoll to be seen among the scores of common redpolls. The little redpoll comes down from where the taiga meets the tundra. When our feeder is covered with these little bundles of life, we watch for one that appears to have some albinism in it, for this is the hoary. The hoary redpoll breeds in the arctic which accounts for his much whiter shade. All redpolls have a bright red cap and forehead with a black chin and what accounts for this is told in a Cree story: A great bear stole the fire from the people during a severe winter which caused great suffering and death among the people. Many a great hunter tried to enter the cave of the great bear to retrieve the fire, only to be killed. It was the little redpoll who took pity on the people and flew into the cave and snatched a hot coal from the bear's fire in his little beak and flew back with it to the people and enabled them to kindle a fire and save themselves. As a result, the brave little redpoll burned his face which is signified today by his red cap and black chin. You don't think our animal neighbors can save a human? It happens every day where I live.

Beaver Lake

For was it not in the stagnant muddy waters, in the heavy humidity of saturated lands, under the heat of the sun, that the first germ of life moved, vibrated and opened itself to the light?

—Guy de Maupassant

Water, along with the earth, air, and fire, is one of the four elements essential for life. We would not exist without fresh water. The Anishinaabe word for water is *nibi*. Water is sacred to Native people and the places where clean water is found are shrinking. Where I live, there is lots of water, most of it still good, but we are not being good stewards of this precious resource, and with a lack of an ethic toward the land, water is seen as a commodity.

Some of our most important and treasured lakes are being

used as giant water recreation areas with no regard for the health of the lake. People live on and use these lakes with no regard for the plant and animal communities that maintain their health. Many people could not care less about water quality. I visited a relation on one of the more popular lakes, and he complained endlessly about the weeds in the lake. I could see what he called weeds were a native species of pond weed that have been part of submerged plant communities in many healthy lakes. They provide habitat for pike, pan fish, amphibians and food for waterfowl. He told me that he had complained to the Department of Natural Resources and demanded that they remove it or he would poison it.

The day is coming and not far off when water will be more valuable than oil, yet judging by the conduct of our political leaders and Big Oil towards the lakes, wetlands, and rivers that Minnesota is known for, one would assume they could not care less. Oil pipelines are crossing northern Minnesota and more are planned, some to carry the volatile Bakken oil from North Dakota and the corrosive and environmentally damaging oil from the tar sand deposits in Alberta.

Leopold's essays, Thoreau's ideas of simplifying our lives, Larry Stillday's teachings, and my connections to the land have given me an appreciation and respect for water.

There is a range of hills that lay south of me that were created by the retreat of the last glacier and they have hundreds of small yet deep lakes. This entire area is within a state forest and there is no development here. The lakes are at the top of a watershed and are so clear and unpolluted that on a clear calm day one can see the bottom at twenty feet. I would not hesitate to dip my cup in one of these lakes for a drink. This is one reason why I live here.

I live within the Leech Lake Watershed in north-central Minnesota. The watershed itself is 854,659 acres in size and within it are 277 miles of rivers and over 750 lakes. Within and overlapping the watershed is the Leech Lake Indian Reservation, Chippewa National Forest and several Minnesota State Forests. Leech Lake is the third largest lake in Minnesota with a water surface area of 103,000 acres and 195 miles of shoreline. Leech Lake and its watershed have some of the most prolific wild rice (*manoomin*) beds in the state. Leech Lake is so large and dominating, the forests within a certain distance are influenced by its microclimate.

The eighty acres I bought over forty years ago had all the requirements I desired. I knew virtually nothing about geology and was at the low end of a learning curve about the flora of the region, but I had some sound logic in what I wanted: I wanted a small lake or stream, I wanted diversity of forest types, and I wanted it off the beaten path. All those requirements were found on this eighty—it was a mile and a half from the nearest county road, it had pines, hardwoods, and a birch-aspen component, and it had a small remote lake.

Upon my first look at this lake, I knew I wanted to live here. The first object that caught my eye was a large beaver lodge; the second thing was a group of wood ducks. It was August and a hot, muggy day. I was impressed enough with the hardwoods and the lake and gave the realtor two hundred dollars down and signed a contract for deed that required three thousand dollars to be made in fifty-dollar payments at a small interest rate I cannot remember. I now had a wild place on earth that I could call home. I paid it off in two years.

I later learned from neighbors that the lake was nameless thus I would call it Beaver Lake but changed that in time to *Amik* which is the Ojibwe name for beaver.

In time I became educated about the regional glacial geology, and I learned that Amik Lake is a Type 5 wetland which has open water and shallow fresh water ponds and lakes. It is at the top of a small tunnel valley where seepage creates some wetlands that connect it to several small lakes by small creeks. This small creek flows into a primary river that enters Leech Lake. The further you go downstream on this micro-watershed the more abundant become the wetlands. The variety is astounding: cedar swamps, peat bogs, muskegs, vernal pools, seasonal grassy wetlands, cattail stands, and shallow ponds.

My appreciation for the abundance of lakes and rivers in the region came early in life but it took longer for me to understand the crucial role that wetlands play.

About ten years ago I was asked to guide a Massachusetts film crew on the Mississippi for a film they were doing for the Mississippi River Museum. None had been in northern Minnesota before and near the end of the time I spent with them, I asked what in our state impressed them most, thinking it would be our lakes or forests. All stated it was the prolific wetlands we have.

This was a surprise as I believed most Minnesotans overlooked these unique features to our landscape and some even viewed them with a degree of contempt. Some people saw them as an obstacle to development or simply as morasses or sloughs. Most people did not realize the vital roles they played for the health of all our water systems. Wetlands not only provided buffering and filtration systems, but also critical habitat for plant and animal communities.

Minnesota's wetlands are young according to the geologic clock. Their development dates back only 8,000 to 10,000 years ago to the retreat of the last glacier. Some are as recent as the pond created by a beaver dam.

Northern Minnesota is a bonanza of wetlands. For instance, Beltrami Island State Forest, a state forest of over 700,000 acres, is 93% wetlands according to the National Wetlands

Inventory. Unfortunately, we have eliminated over half of our wetlands on a national scale. Most of northwestern Minnesota was wetlands but was ditched and drained for agriculture. Chippewa National Forest of which my home is adjacent to has 100% of its pre-settlement wetlands intact.

I recently read an article that defended ATV riding in wetlands as the ruts would open this "stagnant monoculture" to diversity and compared a wetland to a sterile red pine tree farm. *Minnesota Wetlands: A primer on their nature and function,* a publication put together by a group of hydrologists and biologists for the Audubon Society, states: "Wetlands produce as much plant and animal life as do similarly sized areas of rain forest."

There are eight types of classifications for wetlands in Minnesota: Seasonally Flooded, Wet Meadow, Shallow Marsh, Deep Marsh, Shallow Open Water, Shrub Swamp, Wooded Swamps, and Bogs. These wetlands can range from vernal pools in upland forests that may be wet for no more than several weeks, to shallow ponds with up to as much as ten feet of water.

Wetlands have been referred as nature's kidneys — absorbing nutrients and pollutants like phosphorus and nitrogen. Much of these nutrients and pollutants are stored in the vegetation and some are trapped in the wetland itself. These are held in the wetland through the summer and generally flushed out the following spring in high water.

Wetlands, besides being nature's kidneys, are also known as nature's pumps, taking in water as rain, snow, runoff, streams, and groundwater, and then pumping this moisture back into the ecosystem through evaporation, transpiration, streams, and seepage into our groundwater. While the wetland is doing its pumping process, it is also purifying the water by absorbing pollutants, acting as a holding basin by slowing down the flow of water through ecosystems, buffering rivers and lakes from eroding wave action, and reducing flooding in the spring. There is no other substitute for these beneficial actions done by our wetlands. And the frosting on the cake is that wetlands are home to a tremendous variety of habitats and life ranging from microscopic organisms, rare orchids like *Arethusa*, and carnivorous plants like the pitcher plant, breeding places for frogs and amphibians, habitat for reptiles, bog lemmings, water fowl, furbearers, game animals, and much more. They can be something as familiar as a cattail marsh or as foreboding and unfrequented as the muskeg.

In 1991, the people of Minnesota deemed that our wetlands were important enough to protect and passed the Wetlands Conservation Act. It was seen then as one of the most sweeping wetland protective measures in the country. Representative Willard Munger was a driving force in this legislation. The basic premise of this law was, "no net loss of wetlands." But even today, mining and various forms of development are still creating ways of circumventing these protective measures.

When I ponder all the important functions of wetlands to the health of the land, I cannot help but think about millions of years ago when some amino acid in some warm and soupy sea mutated into the first life on earth. When pondering such life on earth, I am dwarfed by the importance of wetlands.

From the air or map, Amik Lake is shaped like a powder horn, running southwest to northeast. Both the north and south ends are peat bogs. The center is the lake which is perhaps four or five acres of open water, and at the center of the open water it has a depth of eighteen feet where the water is a cold forty-five degrees in July due to an active spring. The shoreline around the lake is a mixed forest with pine, hardwoods and stands of aspen. All around the marshy portion of the lake the beavers have constructed canals they can use to access the aspen and alders, of which they cut and eat the nutritious bark.

The water is rather clear with a slight tea-like tint from the adjacent peat. Aside from the deeper open water, it's full of lily pads: white water lily, yellow water lily, water shield, pond weeds and many more unique water species. In shallows near the shore there are cattails, wild iris, marsh cinquefoil, sedges, and related plants.

The bogs on both ends of Amik Lake are habitat for entirely different plant groups. Here sphagnum moss dominates, with scattered leatherleaf, cranberries, wild rosemary, dwarf birch, cotton grass with stunted black spruce, tamaracks, and some jack pine and white pine struggling to thrive.

There is something about a bog that is more distant and foreboding than any other wetland. This perception goes back to our hunter-gathering times on earth. We tend to think of a bog as alien, unfriendly, and hostile to life. But in reality, with our global warming approaching the tipping point, we are learning how bogs are critical to saving our planet.

Have you experienced a walk on a warm summer evening and felt a sudden and dramatic drop in temperature when approaching a bog? Peat bogs are nature's air-conditioning system. Bogs are the last ecosystem to warm in the spring and they repeat this heating and cooling process on a daily basis through the summer and autumn. Bogs are important local climate regulators that aid in giving us predictable outcomes in our weather. Bogs are also valuable as areas of carbon sequestration due to the formation of peat moss that grows at the top and dies at the bottom. This accumulating weight forces the peat deeper. Without light, the lower portions of peat die, releasing acids and tannins which halt bacteria from accomplishing nature's decay process.

Peat is sphagnum moss of which over thirty species are

known in North America. What makes sphagnum unique are the two types of basic cells: hyaline cells which are large empty cells that can absorb up to twenty times their weight in water when submerged but are filled with air when growing above the surface, and chlorophyll cells where the photosynthesis process occurs. The hyaline cells make peat a sought-after commodity for gardening soil. These same absorbent cells were used as a diaper fill by Native Americans and the plant itself contains a steroid with antiseptic properties.

No two bogs are alike, but generally bogs come in two types. The first type is a quaking bog, also known as a floating bog, whose surface appears as a turf or a saturated lawn that floats on water and gives one the sensation of walking on a trampoline. The second type is a static or grounded bog that displaces the water beneath and may extend to great depths. The only source of water for a true bog is rain and snow, but often one will find a typical northern bog surrounded by a poor fen where surface or ground waters enter bringing nutrients with them. It is around these perimeters of a bog where one will find sedge and other more diversified plant species in this lone mineral-rich area of a bog. Where this occurs there will normally be a moat or lagg around the outside edges of the bog. In a nutrient-poor bog where plants struggle for existence, such as leatherleaf and other members of the heather family, they have developed strategies to compensate for obtaining nutrients in this infertile zone by creating a mycorrhizal relationship (a fungus/root symbiotic relationship that aids in obtaining nutrients). Bog plants have developed unique strategies where plants in non-acidic environments have not. An example is the leaves of leatherleaf, bog rosemary, bog laurel, Labrador tea, and other bog residents which have adapted a tough and acidic taste in their foliage to repel wildlife.

If there is such a thing as a climax stage of succession to

a peat bog, it is a muskeg. Muskegs are grounded bogs that have black spruce and tamarack taking hold. A bog that goes the route of forming sedge peat or the fen stage rather than sphagnum peat will evolve into a rich cedar swamp. Spruce muskegs were the favored haunts of woodland caribou which were last found in Minnesota in the Big Bog of Pine Island State Forest in Koochiching County as late as the early 1940s. The Big Bog is a 300,000-acre peatland, fifty miles long and twenty miles wide, and is arguably the largest remaining true wilderness left in Minnesota.

A special treasure to be found in bogs is cranberries which ripen in the autumn. Wherever there is sphagnum, there will be cranberries clinging close to the surface. Cranberries are more than a condiment for Thanksgiving—they are powerful medicine, having compounds that can be used for a variety of health reasons. An oddity observed in bogs are reported sightings of strange lights referred to as "will-o'-the-wisp." These are caused by the release and ignition of methane gas. Bogs create and store methane gas.

Because of the conditions in a sphagnum peat bog that inhibit decomposition, the compacting peat forms a substance called black butter which is about 60% carbon. Over great periods of time, with further compression, organic activity, and loss of moisture, black butter will eventually become bituminous coal.

Russia holds the largest amount of sphagnum, estimated at 223 billion dry tons. In the United States, Minnesota and Maine have the largest remaining deposits of sphagnum peat bogs. According to estimates, approximately half of the United States' peat bogs have been drained with about ninety million acres remaining. Minnesota, which has the largest remaining areas of peatlands, has 7.5 million acres. Minnesota's peat bogs cover 14% of our land area and hold 37% of its stored carbon compared with only 3% of our state forests. Currently about three thousand acres are being mined for sphagnum in the Arrowhead, and another 820 acres in the Big Bog in Pine Island State Forest for garden peat.

Although peat bogs are the least diversified of Minnesota's eight wetland types, many conservationists feel their importance as climate regulators and carbon sequestration sites are too important to risk tampering with for such short-sited commodities as gardening peat or fuel for power plants. Plus, it could be possible for us to again have the sight of caribou browsing the lichens in the Big Bog country of northern Minnesota.

The ice goes out on Amik Lake sometime in April, which is always before the larger lakes in the area. When this happens, the lake is a haven for waterfowl and a bonanza for birders, or should I say just me, for the only time I see anyone else around Amik Lake is in the autumn when occasionally duck hunters will try their luck. The rest of the year, society might as well be off in another world as far as I am concerned, for my wife and I are the only human faces seen by the residents of Amik Lake.

There have been years when the ice goes off Amik Lake and neighboring lakes are still iced over, and the blue-winged and green-winged teal, shovelers, widgeons, gadwalls, mallards, wood ducks, hooded mergansers, ring-necked ducks, golden eyes, buffleheads, Canada geese and trumpeter swans are all present at the same time. And this is just ducks and geese; I am also blessed with a pair of nesting pied-billed grebes, nesting loons, frequenting sandhill cranes and an array of raptors. There are almost always a bald eagle, a red-tail and a marsh hawk present.

In northern Minnesota, we have had an increasing population of trumpeter swans (*waabiziig*). This species of swans was native to the state but was exterminated many years ago. In the 1960s the only population in the United States was in Yellowstone Park, which hosted a small population that migrated down in the winter. It was perhaps only in the last thirty years that trumpeters have made a remarkable comeback. When a flock of eight to twelve of these magnificent birds flies over with their four-foot-plus wing spans and with their loud French-horn-like blasts, it is a sight to marvel at. There is no other bird that can be mistaken for a trumpeter swan with their loud horn-like blast. When the trumpeter's cousin, the tundra swan, comes through here in the spring on their way to the far north and again in the fall on their journey south, their wheezy whistles are distinctively different from the trumpeter's.

A grand event for us was the summer of 2014. A cob (male) and pen (female) swan selected a small island of peat well out from shore and improved it by rolling what appeared to be mud, grasses and moss into rolls about the size and shape of a croissant. Hundreds of these were piled into a mound of about six feet in diameter and perhaps three feet high. There were five eggs laid, four of which hatched. The eggs were off-white to beige and were close to five inches in length. It was a great thrill to walk down to the pond one mid-summer evening and see four white cygnets with the parents. Hopefully, they will continue to honor us with their presence.

For perhaps six years now there has been an intact beaver colony on the lake. An intact colony means there are three generations of beavers residing here. I have counted up to nine and there easily could be more. A mated pair consists of the two dominant beavers in the pond, and when a third generation is born, the oldest offspring present will be driven out to find their own home.

I know that the lodge has been here for forty-six years for that is the duration of years I have been here, but judging from its size now and the size it was when I first saw it, I believe it could easily be at least one hundred years old.

Prior to the arrival of white men in the country north and west of Lake Superior in the mid-1660s, the Native people who lived here did not have a marketplace economy. Their economy was designed to provide for sustenance and giving and sharing for those who didn't have. Those who didn't have were provided for. Animals were hunted or trapped because they were needed for food, shelter, clothing and other necessities. They knew their survival was dependent on other life forms in a world where all were cohabitants. When the first white men arrived, they brought goods that improved the quality of life for Indian people such as metal cookware, wool blankets, tobacco, rifles, axes and steel knives, powder and lead balls. A marketplace economy of supply and demand was introduced to a culture that operated for thousands of years on an earth-based religion and cultural beliefs. These first whites were fur traders who saw fur pelts, especially those of beaver, as one of the most sought-after commodities of the day. These white traders brought steel traps and traded or gave them to Indians and told them if they continued to want these trade items, they needed to kill their animal deities, like the beaver, as a trade item. This was a dramatic turnabout in their culture. This marked the beginning of a changing attitude toward wildlife as a fellow partner in the travails of life on earth to a marketplace, supply-and-demand economic system that put a dollar sign on beavers.

The fur trade lasted for two hundred years and trapping continued as an economic necessity or as supplemental income for another hundred years and still lingers on today. The history of North America from the arrival of whites in the 1660s to 1840 is the history of the fur trade. Beavers were virtually wiped out on a continental scale. I remember listening to a state conservation officer explain that in the 1940s into the 1960s, protecting the residual beaver population was one of the state's wildlife priorities. Beavers were nearly nonexistent at that time. Of course, early in the trapping era the trade widened to any or all wildlife that had fur: deer, wolves, martens, fishers, buffalo, raccoons, bears, moose and more. Northwoods wildlife residents from beaver to buffalo were shipped off to Europe to make hats, coats, felt and other commodities of clothing. The fur industry in its day was similar in economic scope to the oil industry today in size and generating wealth. The millions of beavers decimated for top hats cannot be understated, and no one batted an eye as beavers and a culture were left in shambles.

For many trappers today, the price paid for a beaver pelt hardly makes the effort worthwhile. Today, the synthetic fleece that is made out of recycled plastic bottles is cheaper, lighter, and warmer than animal furs or even wool and this is the primary reason for the drop in price and demand for furs. The old trappers I know are merely going through the motions and going about their traps to relive what once was their history and tradition. They are not necessarily bad people, they just have an ingrained world view that is difficult to change. Their culture sees them as having dominion over all other life, and that the plant and animal communities were put here for their consumption. But then I must ask, isn't that the way our culture and every institution in our society thinks?

The arrival of a culture that took a deity, the beaver, and placed a dollar sign on it is not lost in its symbolism in today's culture and institutions with no ethic towards the land. In the Anishinaabe Teachings of the Seven Grandfathers, we are told we can be better people by observing the animals around us. *Amik* (the beaver) is the teacher of wisdom. In Larry Stillday's teaching lodge, he taught us that Wisdom was represented by *Amik* as one of the Seven Grandfathers:

> • To know and understand wisdom is to know that the Great Spirit gave everyone special gifts to be used to build a peaceful and healthy community.

- The beaver represents determination, strong will, gatherer, accomplishment.

- It uses its sharp teeth for cutting trees and branches, a special gift he received from the Great Spirit.

Perhaps these teachings are meant to be parables in teaching us or giving us examples from our co-tenants on earth and their life ways of how to achieve the "good way" in order to live in harmony with the plant and animal communities we depend on for life, but there is often more than parable symbolism to them. There is a degree of scientific truth to these teachings. As Larry Stillday taught, *Amik* represents wisdom because he had the wisdom to recognize the gift the creator gave him, which was sharp teeth. If the beaver should stop using his teeth, the hard upper and lower yellow enameled incisors would continue to grow throughout life and would grow into the roof of his mouth and into his jaw bones. The continual chewing of wood keeps them worn down so they do his mouth no harm. Understanding the gift of wisdom is what the beaver teaches us as he recognized this gift and uses this gift of sharp teeth for chewing wood, to build healthy and peaceful communities. He builds a solid and long-lasting lodge for his offspring and also shares this virtually indestructible dwelling with others such as the muskrat (*wazhashk*). *Amik* builds dams which impound water into small lakes, ponds, and series of ponds which create habitat for a much greater diversity of plant and animal communities. The gift of building these healthy communities keeps on giving generations later, as eventually over time they fill in and become soil habitats of greater fertility than before the beaver set his teeth and engineering skills into play. Even now, with climate change and prolonged droughts in the western United States, where beavers had been extirpated, ranchers and farmers are reintroducing the beaver as he is a proven entity in drought mitigation. The beaver will build a dam on a stream which impounds water into a pond, but they usually do not stop there. They will continue to build dams that eventually will become a series of dams, shrinking as they progress downstream with smaller and smaller ponds, all contributing to a supply of fresh water after drought has dried up other ponds. This truly is proof that the beaver is building healthy communities for the greater community of life.

The wisdom taught to us by *Amik* is that each one of us has been given a unique gift by the creator and it is up to each one of us to recognize this gift and do as *Amik* has done, use that gift to build healthy and peaceful communities.

If it be a summer's day and the sun is shining warmly and the wind is light or calm and if I put my canoe into Amik Lake, I get a classroom lesson in diversity and life from my neighbors. One of the first residents of the lake that quickly catches my eye is in the shallows near the shoreline. It is the bright golden flower of a horned bladderwort. This plant and its small but beautiful flowers are deceptive for it is a highly efficient carnivorous plant. It is rootless and the underwater fern-like foliage has many small bladders that, when they compress, empty themselves through small openings on the bladders, and then when the bladders expand they suck in microscopic zooplankton life which they digest. The presence of horned bladderwort is an indication that the water is clean and healthy. Also in the shallows are scores of wood frog tadpoles—the adult frogs are the first frog out and vocalizing in the spring and among them are mosquito larva, being fed upon by predators like dragonfly larva and up the food chain to water beetles, packs of whirligigs, water boatmen, water striders, and the *T. rex* of the insect world—the giant water bug. Every log, small mud island, or any protrusion has a painted turtle (*miskwaadesi*) sunning itself. Wood ducks, hooded mergansers and ring-necked females quickly lead their ducklings into the reeds and sedges to hide from the strange invader in the canoe (*jiimaan*). There is a great variety of water lilies, pondweeds and other submerged vegetation which harbors more life that is out of my sight in the depths. Dragonflies—aka mosquito hawks—number in the thousands above the water and hover and dart about in order to feast on the abundance of mosquitoes. Graceful and elegant swallows glide over the water snatching up other insects. Along the shore is a snag on which habitually perches an olive-sided flycatcher that darts out from its perch to snatch a meal then returns to the same snag to announce to the world his claim on this dead tree, calling, "quick-three-beers." I hear song sparrows and swamp sparrows still singing their spring songs, adamant about their claim to their place on earth. Perched high in an old white pine, and noticeably in sight is *Migizi*, the bald eagle. He watches me closely with his white head, yellow beak and yellow eyes. His head follows me during the entire duration of my visit. He shows no timidity of me as he remains there with an attentive eye.

Everything here seems so in balance and interconnected. Nothing is out of place here, not even me. On such a day as this, Amik Lake is a window which allows me to feel, see, and understand the interconnectedness of all life, both plant and animal, and the supreme importance of water. Being here brings me comfort, understanding, strength, and makes me a bit wiser as a man. I realize how lucky I am and want to share this experience.

To preserve and protect these special places on earth is to redouble our efforts at protecting all the watersheds, no matter where we live. Water is life and is sacred. All life has meaning and purpose. You do not have to live in a remote rural area to grasp this. Urban environmentalists have the same responsibility and task before them. As *Amik* the beaver, whose habitat is water, teaches us in the Seven Grandfathers, we need to be wise and search our souls for the unique gift we were given and use that gift, whatever that gift may be, as the beaver has, to build and protect healthy communities.

Migizi and the Trip to *Gichi Gami*

The first job of a citizen is to keep your mouth open.

—Gunther Grass

My late friend Larry Stillday told me that, "We learn to live with nature, be comfortable within it, and trust our instincts. Our animal guides can bring us messages of guidance and offer protection to shield us from negative energies. But we must be open to the animal spirits and the messages they bring. Every animal is different just like we are, each having their own attributes that gives them advantages in their daily life. Every experience we have with them has something to teach us. We may have a connection or attraction with a certain animal."

Maybe I have been living in the woods too long without

enough direct contact with human beings, but there is no doubt in my mind that we can communicate with animals. Of course this does not infer that we can sit down and carry on a conversation, but I do believe our actions, or their actions, can tell us something of value. Call it extrapolation, call it intuition, call it anything you wish, but I believe that interactions with wild animals can teach, communicate and intimate our thoughts and conduct.

I feed the birds. Every day I put birdseed in my feeders. Often the birds are fluttering above my head while I pour seed onto a feeding platform or into a feeding hopper. On a few occasions, I have had chickadees land on my shoulder as I go about filling a feeder. I can go out into my yard when there is a great deal of activity at my feeder with red squirrels and chipmunks below the birds, and they all carry on their business as usual, showing little or no concern of my presence. But as soon as a human stranger or visitor should be present, the birds and squirrels in the yard become scarcer. This tells me they are accustomed to me and know I do not intend any harm.

On a recent winter day, I snowshoed to my pond and a mature eagle was perched out on a limb in a large white pine that extended out in such a manner that I was able to stand directly below him. Normally they will fly off to another tree but this eagle stayed there while I stood fifty feet below him. We remained there for several minutes looking at one another. He had his head turned slightly to one side and tilted down at an angle so he could look directly at me. There was no exchange of words or mental telepathy, but I feel certain that there was, on his part, acknowledgement of me, recognizing that I intended no harm, and that I wasn't prey. He also seemed curious. On my part, whether there was any reception by him of my thinking, I felt admiration and joy that he was a part of my life and world.

There have been many times during my life in the woods

that I have been inspired by not only wildlife, but also plants. Anyone who has a deep appreciation and affinity for nature will understand this. Aldo Leopold wrote that pine trees gave him "a curious transfusion of courage." The times in my life that I have been inspired and uplifted by an animal, a tree, or just being within a wild and natural surrounding are countless.

In October of 2012, I was asked to speak at an anti-wolf-hunt rally in downtown Duluth above Lake Superior with an impressive view of the lake. It was a three-hour drive for me, so I left earlier than needed to allow extra time as my junker may not be the most reliable car in the state.

My drive took me through the Chippewa National Forest and several other state forests for the majority of the trip. This drive is a scenic and pleasurable trip through some of Minnesota's finest forested lands. Just after crossing the Mississippi River (*Misi-ziibi*) I saw something big on the shoulder ahead of me. As I approached, I recognized it as a large mature eagle sitting on top of a dead raccoon. I slowed down to perhaps 5 or 10 MPH because I have experienced eagles on roadkills before and know they will often fly up and out over the road surface, and the last thing I wanted to do was hit an eagle. Sure enough, just as I feared, the eagle flew out over the road in order to get airborne, and he lifted himself just above my front windshield with exerted wing beats so extraordinary I could hear the air rushing through his primary wing feathers. He was so close — no more than six to ten feet above my windshield — that I cranked my head over the dashboard to get a better look. His feathered legs and bright yellow talons were dangling below his body close enough to make out his deadly claws on each foot, and he too had his head cranked down and a bit off to one side looking at me with as much interest as I looked at him. Then the spirit-message from *Migizi* came, and as he looked down I conceived him to say, "I have been waiting here for you, you are the *gichi mookoman* (white man) who is going to stand up for my brother *Ma'iingan* (wolf)."

"Yes, that is me," I said.

"I will accompany you for a distance and help guide you on the journey you have chosen."

And with that, I kept my speed down and *Migizi* stayed above my windshield for perhaps a half mile or so before he veered off.

I was inspired by this event for the rest of my drive to Duluth. While giving my speech about the wolf, I felt the presence of the eagle with me. *Migizi* had lifted my spirits. As my friend Larry Stillday told me, "Our animal guides can bring us messages of guidance and offer protection to shield us from negative energies. But we must be open to the animal spirits and the messages they bring." He also told me that to reach the greatest spiritual attainment is through *Migizi*.

Migizi is one of the Seven Grandfathers and the teacher of love. Chi Ma'iingan (Stillday) told a story that I will paraphrase here. In the old times the people had become decadent and had turned their backs on the Elders and teachings that were to be their spiritual guide of good behavior. The Creator, *Gichi Manidoo* had become so disappointed with them that he considered wiping them out. Upon hearing this, *Migizi* paid *Gichi Manidoo* a visit and lobbied on behalf of the people. His words and love of the people were so convincing that *Gichi Manidoo* decided to give the people another chance, but told *Migizi* to warn the people that they were to pray daily and before each prayer they were to offer tobacco. As Chi Ma'iingan told me: "*Migizi* is the Grandfather and teacher of love because he so loved man." Below are some of Larry's teachings about the eagle:

• Love is represented by the eagle.

• To feel love is to know the Great Spirit, therefore, it is expected that our first love is to be the Great Spirit.

• Love given to the Great Spirit is expressed by loving oneself, if we can't love our self it is impossible to love anyone else.

• The eagle was chosen by the Great Spirit to represent this law.

• Symbolically, the eagle is the one who can reach the highest in bringing vision to the seeker.

• The attributes of the eagle are: divine spirit, clear vision, great healing powers, courage, sacrifice and connection to the Creator.

Bald eagles have become numerous in Minnesota. I see them every day, but never will I consider them to be ordinary. They have great spiritual power and enable us to find strength and reserve within ourselves through their spiritual power.

The Sugar Bush

When the maple tree begins to run and the little birds return after the hard winter, this is the New Year for the Anishinaabeg.

— Bob Shimek

The white man celebrates the New Year on January first — the Ojibwe celebrate it when the sap first starts to run in the sugar maples (*ininaatig*) in the early spring. The Ojibwe designation of their new year when the forest starts bursting forth life and producing sugar makes more sense to me than signifying the new year on January first when the hardest days of winter are yet ahead. Ojibwe Healer and Elder Larry Stillday (Chi Ma'iingan) told me the first run of maple sap, known in Ojibwemowin as *wiishkobaaboo* (sweet sap), combined with the process of making syrup or sugar from it, known as *zhiiwaagamizigan-ike* and *ziinzibaakwad-ike*, is the traditional Ojibwe renewal with the covenant of life. After the long hard winter of short days and long nights and the bitter cold and the deprivation of food and other necessities, when the sap starts to flow it gives hope to those of us who experience this change in seasons. Its significance cannot be understated. It is life beginning anew. The crows, which migrate south from the Northwoods during deer hunting season, time their springtime return with the first sap run in the sugar maple. Along with the crows, other early migrants include great flocks of ground-feeding sparrows such as juncos and fox sparrows. These small birds provided protein for Native people who had gone without through the long winters. It was a time that brought people and families together and all contributed their efforts in the sugar-making camp. The sweetness of the maple symbolized the renewal of life—the long hard winter was over, and people survived to see another year.

I recall reading an excerpt in Joseph Nicollet's Journal of 1836 about his trip to the headwaters of the Mississippi River while accompanied by guides Francois Brunette, Brunette's brothers, a Frenchman named Desiré Fronchet, and Shagobay with his small son who were from the Leech Lake Tribe. In that excerpt, while sitting around the campfire at night, one of the whites was noting the big dipper when Shagobay corrected him by saying that the constellation in question was *Ojiig* the fisher. Several years after I read that journal, Larry Stillday told me that the constellation was so named because during a long winter, *Ojiig* jumped into the sky and brought back the birds, which harkened the start of springtime and the beginning of the first maple sap run.

I often keep my maple syrup evaporator boiling all night, getting up at three-hour intervals to add wood and stir the sap. It is at this time, when the sky is clear, that I have a good look at the star-filled sky and Milky Way, and the first thing that jumps out at me is *Ojiig*. The story of this forest animal is recalled in my mind every time I go out into the darkness.

Odors of the outdoors trigger pleasant memories of past events and places in our lives. The smell of freshly fallen aspen leaves in the early stages of decay trigger in the brain memories of autumn, and the pungent smell of blossoming balsam poplar buds signals the mind that it's spring. These and more odors initiate emotions in my head, but one that perhaps stands above the others in my mind is the smell of maple sap boiling off steam over a wood fire. Standing next to a homemade evaporator with a red-hot wood fire and a stainless-steel pan filled with sap in a high rolling boil on a forty-degree April afternoon with juncos and fox sparrows scurrying about on the forest floor and returning geese in the heavens above – this is something that gets in my blood and makes me appreciate that I have lived to see another spring.

Making maple sugar or syrup, like so many skills of subsistence living, has been passed on by Native people. White people may have improved the utensils used, but the basic process remains unchanged through the centuries. An early account of a sugar bush was made by the fur trader Alexander Henry the Younger in 1763 in U.P. Michigan: "The season for making maple-sugar was now at hand; and, shortly after my arrival at the Sault, I removed, with the other inhabitants, to the place at which we were to perform the manufacture. ... On the twenty-fifth of April, our labor ended, and we returned to the fort, carrying with us, as we found by the scales, sixteen hundred weight of sugar."

What does one need to make maple sugar? First, you need some maple trees that are a minimum of twelve inches in diameter, and then you need a drill, taps, buckets, hoses recommended, good legs, a strong back, a homemade stove and a pan big enough to get thirty to forty gallons of sap in it. But most importantly, you need a big pile of wood,

preferably oak limbs, but any wood will do, and this prepa-
ratory work has to be done well in advance of sugar making
time. People who I give a bottle of maple syrup probably
have no idea of the work and preparation that goes into the
making of maple syrup or sugar, but I don't mind the hard
work because it's a love of labor and there is a high degree
of personal satisfaction when you have a cabinet shelf with a
dozen bottles or more of this gift from the maple tree.

My sugar maples are in a stand of northern hardwoods
of about fifteen acres in size. The canopy is dominated by
aging red oaks, but coming up below them are maturing
sugar maples. There are other hardwood species in the sub-
canopy and understory such as burr oaks, paper birch, red
maples, green ash, basswood, ironwood, black cherry and
aspen, but the sugar maples are more than holding their
own and patiently waiting for an opportunity to move
ahead for their eventual dominance. These different species
of trees are allies of the maples. Without them, if my sugar
bush were to be attacked by a disease or fungus that afflicts
maples, the disease would spread like a wildfire. These other trees—the oaks, basswoods, ash and others—will hinder
the easy spread of disease. Some commercial operations
have done just this, made a monoculture of their sugar maples, and many are now seeing climate change and other
factors killing their trees. Diversity of species makes a community stronger, not just in trees but in all facets of life. Diversity is stability.

A few of my sugar maples are nearly as tall as the red oaks
that compose 85% of my hardwood canopy. These larger
sugar maples can be found where a storm or disease has
killed an old oak, thus creating an opening where the sugar maple takes advantage of the increased sunlight. I have
sugar maples ranging in size from canopy height, to broom
handle size and down to trees only inches tall and so thick
in midsummer that with their foliage they blanket the forest

floor. The summer canopy of this hardwood forest is so thick that little or no sun reaches the forest floor. The thickly shaded canopy of this forest keeps the temperature much lower than most other forest types. The sugar maple has adapted to hang on for many years under the dense canopy of other species, being exceptionally shade tolerant, only to spring into rapid growth when an opening occurs. Once the sugar maples take over the canopy, they form the ultimate climax hardwood forest in these parts. They can live five hundred years and few if any other tree species can survive under the dense shade they make other than their own offspring. Once these maples reach climax status in forest succession, the only way this will end is a catastrophic event like a violent windthrow or fire.

I consider myself fortunate to have these maples of which many are large enough to tap. Here in these northern latitudes, the sugar maple is at the northern limit of its range. They have difficulty surviving temperatures of negative forty or colder. All my larger trees have frost seams on their trunks, caused by the extreme cold, and they appear like a long three-to-five-foot linear protrusion in the trunk as though it were pinched. To find exceptionally large sugar maples one has to go south, or frequent a sugar bush in close proximity to one of the large lakes in the area where a microclimate is more conducive to the *Ininaatig*. When people north of this range wanted to make maple sugar, they had to tap red maples or box elders (which are true maples), but the sugar content in other maples is much, much lower than in the sugar maple.

John Tanner (Shaw-shaw-wa-ne-ba-se), a white man who was adopted into an Ojibwe family in the early 1800s, spoke of making sugar in southern Manitoba where no sugar maples existed. "When the sugar season arrived, I went to Elk River and made my camp about two miles below the fort. The sugar trees, called by the Indians she-she-ge-ma-winzh, are of the same kind as are commonly found in the bottom lands on the Upper Mississippi, and are called by the whites 'river maple' [probably silver maple or box elder]. They are large but scattered and for this reason we made two camps." Tanner and his family had to work a lot harder than I do, because sugar maples average about one part sugar to thirty-five parts water, but the silver maples he tapped would have been around sixty or seventy parts water. I have read that people in Alaska have tapped birches as there are no maples there and make birch syrup, but a friend once tapped some paper birches and boiled the birch sap down and gave me this birch syrup to try, and I found the difference easily perceived. The birch sap was so inferior and had a flavor like molasses, and to me it would only make a suitable substitute if no other types of maple trees were present.

There is a great variation on the sugar content of the sap, the length of time that the sap runs, and the amount of sap that the tree provides each year. Even the sugar content will vary within a single season. The best ratio of sugar I have ever experienced was twenty-two parts water to one part sugar (22:1). The lowest sugar content I have experienced was 50:1. It is only through my own empirical experience, but the years with the highest sugar content seem to come after a drought year. It seems like the years producing the greatest volume of sap follow a wet year with a deep frost in the ground.

Every year is different. Some years when winter is short and spring advances rapidly, I have been hauling out sap by the first week in March. Other years things are not going good until early April. Some years end so soon that I am left wondering what happened, and other years can go on for almost two months, leaving me exhausted and tired from the full days required to harvest maple syrup and sugar. But during the months of March and April, there is not much else to do aside from cutting and splitting firewood.

The lakes are iced over, there is still frost in the ground, and the roads are breaking up, so it is a good excuse to be in the woods and feel the warm sunshine and take in all the smells and sounds of spring.

What causes sap to flow? It begins with the onset of winter which stops the sap flow. The sap left standing in the trunk of the tree becomes dissolved with the sugar and other minerals from the surrounding wood. The process of finding sap-dissolving sugar and other nutrients is temporary hence the limited time span of the sugar season. Springtime's warm and sunny days combined with freezing nights act as a pump to raise stored nutrients from the roots and get the sap moving. If the temperatures stay above freezing or below freezing in a twenty-four-hour period, this will stop the pumping process and halt the sap from flowing.

When I put out my taps, there will likely be twenty-four-hour periods early in the season when the temperature will not rise above freezing. These cold snaps will shut down the sap run. The inverse is also true: if the temperatures stay above freezing the sap will likewise stop flowing. This is probably why sugar maples do not produce sugar in more southerly climates. Once the season progresses to a span of ideal temperatures of twenties at night and forties or low fifties during the day, the taps can yield up to a gallon of sweet sap in a twenty-four-hour period. I usually put out sixty taps and find that is about the limit of what I can handle. With this number of trees tapped, I have hauled back as much as 450 gallons of sap.

Tapping trees needs to be done with some thought and care. Tapping a sugar maple can remove 15% of the stored carbohydrate reserves—it doesn't do the tree any good. Think of it as a person giving blood. Maples are also particularly vulnerable to soil compaction and air pollution. Trees that are too small—less than twelve inches at chest height—should not be tapped nor should larger trees have too many taps applied. I look over each tree before drilling the three-inch hole for my tap. I look for large enough straight trunks without any dead limbs in the canopy or other signs of disease. None of my trees are large enough for more than one tap. I drill a hole so it is at a slight upward angle into the sap wood and insert the tap soundly and securely, and then I attach to it a plastic tube with the other end going into a covered bucket. I try to put the tap into a different quadrant of the trunk from the previous year. I always check where past taps have been drilled first. The previous year's tap is easy to spot but taps prior to last season should be scarring over or completely scarred over and difficult to locate. If your tap holes are scared over by the second year, your tree is healthy.

We are a lot like trees in many respects. I think of my sugar maples when I think of my life as an environmentalist. To be an environmentalist one has to harden oneself in order to continue the fight for the struggles we pursue which usually end in defeat. When I look at the trunk of one of my maples for a spot to bore a tap hole, I see all the scars the trunk has and see how each tree has dealt with these wounds and how each wound has been compartmentalized. The sap flows around these compartments of scar tissue, rising from the roots to the top of the tree. It deals with its wounds by going around them and continues on with the struggle of living. I think of myself and how over the years of defeat and great disappointment I have learned to compartmentalize my own wounds or defeats which have enabled me to continue on. Without the healing, I would have given up long ago. I am reminded of what the naturalist Ernest Thompson Seton said: "Every tree like every man must decide for itself—will it live in the alluring forest and struggle to the top where alone is sunlight or give up the fight and content itself with the shade."

Once I have gathered enough sap to begin the sugar-making process, I start a fire in my evaporator which is an old fuel oil tank cut in half with four legs underneath to raise it off the ground and offer a comfortable working platform. There is a door on the front for feeding it wood, a chimney at the back end to keep a good draft, and an opening on top only slightly smaller than the dimensions of my forty-five-gallon stainless-steel pan which seats itself over this opening and in which I pour the sap. This evaporator is kept adjacent to a large pile of wood that has been gathered and placed here for maple syrup production.

Once I have filled my pan with sap it always amazes me how clear the sap is; there is no tint of any maple color to indicate it is more than water. The only way to confirm there is sugar in this clear sap is to dip your finger in and taste it — there is a faint sweetness to the water. Once the roaring fire in the evaporator heats the sap up to a high-rolling boil, large quantities of steam rise from the sap with a most unique and sweet odor all its own. This is the time-consuming process of making sugar. Depending on the conditions outside it will take five to eight hours to boil down forty gallons. If the water to sugar ratio is around 40:1, that means I will have to boil off about thirty-nine gallons of water. That's a lot of water that has to be removed. Friends have asked me if they can come over and watch this process of reducing sap to sugar. My reply is yes, if you find watching water boil all day fun, come on over. I keep several chairs handy, for myself and company, a good book, binoculars for migrant birds, and I also use this time to split firewood for the wood stove in my cabin. I do not finish it off outside over the wood fire because when it gets close to completion, one has to get it off the fire quickly or it can crystallize. So I pour it off when there is still a small amount of water remaining in the nearly complete maple syrup and bring it in the house for finishing on my gas stove where I can more closely control the temperature. It is here, under these more controlled conditions, that I can watch how the foam rises and settles with stirring so I know when to remove it from the heat. For me, the final determination as to whether the sap has all the water boiled off, or if it has to go back on the heat, is not to use a thermometer or other gauge but simply to taste it. I have learned most of this through a process of trial and error. More than once, on the following day I have tried to pour syrup out of a bottle only to find that it was too lumpy to pour.

There is much to learn from the plant community. They provide examples for us about life itself, they inspire us, lift our spirits and form the base layer on which all life rests upon. They have prepared the earth's atmosphere with oxygen so we animals can breathe.

Early in the sap run there is normally plenty of snow on the ground, often a foot or two in depth. This means the work is done on snowshoes and with a sled, but as springtime advances and the snowy season ends, I put the sled and snowshoes away and switch to boots and a two-wheel cart. I do the work by hand. Only when the ground has dried out enough will I dare drive my old four-wheel-drive truck, but I park the truck before I get into the sugar bush and there the legs and cart take over. I do not want to drive any vehicle in my sugar bush as the roots are prone to being damaged by driving over them at this sensitive time of the year when the frost is emerging from the soil.

The natural and unprocessed sugar provided by this magnificent tree not only yields the sweetness of our land but contains high quantities of minerals, trace elements, and amino acids. Recent findings have shown that maple syrup or sugars have antibiotic capacities. Besides an addition to our physical health, the trees display brilliant reds, yellows, and oranges in the autumn, and the fallen leaves enrich the soil with lime upon decomposition, further enriching the earth for other lime-loving plants and microorganisms. The prolific and abundant propeller-like seed production provides a valuable food source for deer, bear, squirrels, mice, birds, and a host of other animal life. The finished wood from this tree is very hard and exceedingly beautiful.

White-tailed deer are drawn to these northern hardwoods in which sugar maples prosper to drop their fawns. These woods seem to be a nursery for them. These hardwoods with their closed canopies and open understories are preferred by ovenbirds, scarlet tanagers, grosbeaks, red-eyed and yellow-throated vireos, chickadees, and black-and-white warblers. The dead snags provide a great many nesting cavities for woodpeckers such as the red-bellied, hairy, downy, and pileated, plus wood ducks, flying squirrels, gray squirrels, barred owls and many more, but the real celebrities of these haunts are the thrushes of which four species live in this forest: the wood thrush, hermit thrush, Swainson's thrush and veery. They nest here and grace these woods with their melodic song. They are the nightingales of the Northwoods.

I know the maple sap run is within a few days of ending when I hear the first wood frogs vocalizing. Soon after, there are thousands of wood frogs clicking away with their trill in my adjacent pond, and they are soon joined by chorus frogs and spring peepers signifying that the frost is out of the ground and the sap run is over. Even with the frogs marking the end, I often try to push the season longer than what it can do. When this happens, the sap will get a slight milky tint and have a funky, sour taste to it. All good things come to an end, but by the end I will have boiled down two hundred to four hundred gallons of sap that will equate to ten to fourteen gallons of maple syrup which will be our sugar for the coming year. There is no sweetener that rivals the maple tree. We relish it over cereal, wild rice, ice cream and with a good many other foods. There is no substitute for maple syrup processed over a wood fire through one's own labors.

The Ojibwe New Year (defined in part by the life cycle of the maple tree) is not only a celebration of our lives, it is a celebration of life on earth and its continual renewal.

The Land Where Food Grows on Water

This straw which I hold in my hands, Wild Rice is what we call this. These I do not sell. That you may not destroy the Rice in working the Timber, Also the Rapids and Falls in the Streams I will lend you to saw your timber … I do not make a present of this, I merely lend it to you.

— Ojibwe Chief at 1837 treaty negotiations.

When the moon is full in late August to September, this is the Ojibwe ricing moon, known as *Manoominike-giizis*. It is a very important time of year in northern Minnesota. Cars and trucks with canoes and push poles lashed to carriers are a common sight on the roads.

It has been my experience that when the rice ripens it is usually accompanied by beautiful summer days. My ricing partner and I prefer to find some small lake or remote stretch of river that is off the beaten path for our ricing locations. My partner, Karen, is not my wife but a friend that I have known for years. She used to be a bear hunting guide along the Canadian border and was known to help herself to the bait she used to lure bears in. She packed out a trophy-sized bull moose that her party shot in the Boundary Waters Canoe Area in the 1990s. On one occasion, as she and some friends were driving on a backcountry road, they came across a dead coyote that had been recently killed by a vehicle. Karen had the car stop and got out her skinning knife and skinned the coyote while the other passengers in the car looked on with incredulity as fleas could be seen jumping off the coyote carcass. When she had finished skinning the wild canid, she neatly rolled up the hide and placed it in the trunk and off they went.

She handmade her cedar ricing sticks — or knockers — known to Ojibwe as *bawa'iganaak-oog,* and I have crafted several twenty-foot-long balsam fir push poles with a duck bill on the ends. I have three canoes (*jiimaan-an*), but we use Karen's 17'4" Old Town Penobscot as it's more stable than any of mine. We tie down the canoe or *jiimaan* and pole to the top of my old truck, throw in a lunch, water, rice bags, string, a scoop shovel and voilà — we are off for the rice fields.

In Minnesota, you can only be in a rice bed between the hours of 9:00 A.M. and 3:00 P.M., six hours maximum. There are some regulations on the equipment, such as length and width of canoe, length and type of wood used for the sticks, but that's about it. Outside Indian reservations, it is up to the ricer to make sure they are in rice that is ripe. On reservations, the tribe announces when ricing can commence. On lands outside reservations, there is no preset start date nor is there an end date. All rice beds mature at different times. River rice generally ripens before lake rice, but it's all different, so regulations put the onus of responsibility on you to not be in rice that is unripe. All this is in the state regulations, but for many of us it is unethical to enter a rice bed that is not ready, and it's simply foolish to do so because knocking down unripe rice doesn't make sense. You can knock down a far greater volume of ripe rice in a much shorter timeframe than in a rice bed that isn't ready. Damage to the rice that is unripe can be done by entering a bed that is not ready.

The earlier opening dates for ricing in ceded lands is important to Native people for this rice was guaranteed to them in treaties and having access to these rice beds outside reservations has economic value as many people harvest rice to sell and this provides income for food, clothing, shelter and other necessities in life. I have an Ojibwe friend who said her parents used the income from their ricing to buy clothing and school supplies for her and her siblings. Ojibwe believe, and rightly so, that they have special usufructuary rights to *manoomin*.

We have been in rice beds when the weather is so accommodating that the ricing memories seem to blend together. Ricing can be a mystical experience, out in the sun with a gentle breeze blowing over your face, arms, and shoulders, which provides just the right effect to cool one down. The wind, the sun, a slight rattling in the rice stalks—it all makes the world seem in balance. I do the poling and Karen does the knocking. I stand in one end and Karen sits or kneels in front of me. It is my job to keep the canoe in the rice and as I am standing I keep my eyes in front of me, looking to where the most rice heads are. The water in a rice bed varies but is generally between one to four feet in depth. For me, the poler, I place the pole to my side and push, extending the entire twenty feet of the balsam pole out behind me. I try to maintain forward canoe movement that keeps pace with the knocker. The knocker gets into a rhythm of swish, swish, swish, swish. With a stick in both hands, she reaches out to the side and behind her, and with the stick in her left hand she pulls the rice over the canoe and brushes it with the stick in her right hand, then proceeds to do the same on the other side, reversing which hand performs which task. With each brush of the stick, heads of rice fall to the floor of the canoe making a sound like throwing sand or pellets on the floor. The sound has a welcome and pleasing effect to all ricers. It becomes music to our ears. As the dark rice heads with their beards fall in the canoe, they always position themselves with the beards up, and after they begin to build a pile, they resemble a bear skin.

It doesn't take long to get into a ricing rhythm which then allows me to take in all the beauty of this unique ecosystem. A rice bed is certainly not sterile or an area devoid of life. On the contrary, it is bubbling with activity. Starting from the small to the larger, a rice bed is a laboratory of insect life. There are the rice worms that can be found in unbelievable numbers. They resemble a kernel of rice in both size and color and time their maturity with the rice ripening. When in a rice bed with an abundant supply of worms, the rice knocked into the canoe will appear to be moving. They can also bite, or should I say nip, as the bite is not injurious but more of an annoyance. I prefer to wear only trousers or cut-offs, going bare chested, as I believe that the worms only bite when boxed in under clothing. My partner duck tapes the openings around her pant legs and shirt cuffs to keep the worms out, but for me that becomes too warm while exerting oneself with a push pole. The worms are only a part of the insect experience. There are rice spiders, rice beetles, rice fleas (not really fleas but likely some kind of springtail), and far more insect species than I can enumerate. Rather than be turned off by them, I see them as bearing witness to the fertility and diversity of life in a rice bed.

Besides the insects there are many varieties of waterfowl in the rice for it is a highly sought-after food. We are often flushing waterfowl with mallards and wood ducks topping the list. Last year while ricing on a remote and wild creek in Mississippi River headwaters country, we came upon two fully grown but immature trumpeter swans, or cygnets, as they are called. These two young birds appeared fully grown, but were yet unable to fly. They would flap their wings and scurry ahead of us until we caught up to them, and then they'd scurry ahead of us again. Another remarkable bird that favors rice beds is the sora rail which the Ojibwe call, along with other small birds in the rice, *manoominikeshiinyag* (rice birds). The poler, who is normally standing, is positioned better to see the rails running through the rice bed as though they could walk on water. With their big feet and small bodies, they scamper across lily pads so fast it appears they are running on the water surface. When they flush, which is always near to the canoe, they fly away weakly with their long legs and big feet dangling limply below their bodies. The old saying "thin as a rail" comes from this bird. Although it's not particularly small, it is very narrow in profile when being observed from behind or from the front.

Often Karen, who is seated or kneeling on the canoe floor, falls into a trance while rhythmically knocking rice in the mesmerizing summer conditions, but she is abruptly woken and startled from her trance when a big northern pike (*ginoozhe*) sunning itself in the shallows splashes and slaps its tail as it rockets off through the rice. But the real thrill while in the rice fields is *Migizi*, the bald eagle. Being on the water, and water being a favorite haunt of *Migizi*, there is almost always an eagle in sight. Once while we were stopped and eating our lunch, we counted five eagles directly overhead, soaring and circling above us, wondering what those *chi-mookomaanan* (white people) were doing in the *manoomin*.

Being in *manoomin* when the sky and the earth seem to meet in a most favorable fashion in the rice, it seems rather a blessing to be able to have this connection with earth. It is at such times that we realize how wonderful and beautiful the land is and how fortunate that northern Minnesota is to have this food that grows on water. It makes this region special. Being here makes me realize this is worth fighting to protect. And protect we must as currently there are attempts to run oil pipelines or begin non-ferrous sulfide mining projects that almost certainly will degrade or destroy these treasures.

There are already a number of oil pipelines running through northern Minnesota. Some go to the Twin Cities to the south, but many go to refineries in Superior, Wisconsin. The leaks from these pipelines are catastrophic. The largest was in Kalamazoo, Michigan, in which 850,000 gallons leaked into a tributary of the Kalamazoo River in 2010. Currently, they are still cleaning up that spill and want to run two more pipelines through the heart of headwaters country.

If you look at a map of the Mississippi River (*Misi-ziibi*) in Minnesota, the portion of the river in headwaters country is shaped like a shepherd's staff with the crook of the staff encircling headwaters country. The source of the Mississippi River is Lake Itasca in Itasca State Park. From the mouth of the infant river on the north end of Lake Itasca, the river feels the pull of the Hudson Bay watershed and flows sixty-two miles north and northeast to Bemidji, the first city on the river. It is on this first sixty-two river miles where one will find the last remaining wilderness on the infant Mississippi River. From Bemidji, its course gently bends to the east as though it is now drawn toward Lake Superior or St. Lawrence Seaway watershed. The furthest most northern point on the Mississippi is just downstream from Bemidji. By the time the river gets beyond Grand Rapids it gradually turns south on its 2,550-mile journey to the Gulf of Mexico. It is along this route in headwaters country within the crook of the staff that you will find some of the finest wild rice fields and some of the cleanest lakes in the region.

The proposed pipelines will cross the Mississippi River about twelve miles downstream from its source and then follow the border of Itasca State Park before traversing through the heart of headwaters country. After crossing the heart of lake country, it will cross the Mississippi again in the eastern portion of headwaters country after the river has turned south below Big Sandy Lake. A spill anywhere along this route would be devastating to wild rice fields, wetlands, lake country, Itasca State Park, the infant Mississippi and everything downstream.

A public hearing was held in January 2015 in Bemidji by the Minnesota Public Utilities Commission (PUC) to get citizen input. This was not the first public meeting on the issue. Thus far, a pipeline project has never been stopped in Minnesota; all have been approved. Environmentalists hope the result will be different in this fight, but the issue is far from being resolved.

I attended this public hearing and made verbal testimony on this pipeline project. The hearing was chaired by an administrative law judge, had three members of the PUC in attendance, and had seven representatives from the Canadian pipeline company, Enbridge. People were only given four to five minutes to speak. In that short period of time it was difficult to make a strong argument against the project. As I was speaking, I saw a look of impatience on the judge. I opened up with a short story and then stated that I was here to speak for those who cannot speak for themselves—the animal and plant communities that will be directly impacted by this pipeline. I could see by the look in this judge's eye that he did not get what I was saying. He urged me to make my point, which I was trying to do but my testimony did not have the desired effect. I may as well have been speaking in a foreign language as the panel of PUC and Enbridge folks did not seem interested in what I was talking about. Allotted time periods go by quickly and my time was up before I got to the meat of my message. Maybe that was just as well as what I wanted to say would likely have gotten the judge hot under the collar.

I had intended to draw a comparison between extractive industries such as big oil, big mining, and big timber, and big Ag and the Ojibwe *wiindigoo* – a cannibalistic ghoul. (*Wiindigoog* are human-eating monsters that victimize Indian people while weakened in the lean winter months when supplies are getting low.) I wanted to show how *wiindigoog* have transformed themselves from ghoulish monsters with insatiable appetites to extractive corporate industries with the same insatiable appetite that can never get enough. *Wiindigoog* always want more and more until there is nothing left, only this time they are not consuming people, they are consuming the resources of earth. But I decided it was best not to use this analogy with an unfriendly administrative law judge who was already displeased with my message that dealt with life forms of little consequence to him, he and the commission being of a mindset to wrap their brains only around economic thinking and not complex interconnectedness of plant and animal communities. Maybe the judge, the oil representatives, and the Public Utilities Commission staff were like what Chi Ma'iingan told me: "When man is separated from nature, his heart hardens." Aldo Leopold wrote over sixty-five years ago that we need to "quit thinking about decent land-use as solely an economic problem. A thing is right when it tends to preserve the integrity, stability, and the beauty of the biotic community. It is wrong when it tends otherwise."

Close to twenty years ago while my wife and I were running a small Ma & Pa business in a small northern

Minnesota community, I got a call from the Headwaters Canoe Club out of Bemidji asking me if I could guide a film producer on the headwaters of the Mississippi River. I have spent most of my life exploring the watery backcountry in the region and had developed a reputation as being good in a canoe and knowing my way around in the bush. I agreed, and met the producer and her assistant representing Monadnock Media from Massachusetts, and the photographer, Allan Moore, who does most of the photography for Ken Burns' documentaries. They were making a film of the Mississippi River for the Mississippi River Museum in Dubuque, Iowa. One of the first things I asked the producer was, "What about northern Minnesota is most impressive?" I assumed her answer would be the lakes. Her answer was the wetlands. She said she had never seen wetlands in such abundance. I agree, we are blessed with the preponderance of wetlands, for they are the pumps and kidneys of our state. They keep the land healthy by filtering the water, flood control, renewing the aquifers, offering habitat for diverse plant and animal communities, and providing wild rice.

There is too much at stake here to allow pipelines to cross our land, or to permit mines to start extracting sulfur deposits within this water-rich region. A leak in one of the pipelines would be catastrophic. Repeatedly, response time is horrendously late, and cleanups never finish or restore the land to its original state. Copper mining companies that are pushing the state permitting process have a track record which demonstrates sulfide mines have a 100% probability of contaminating surface and ground waters for generations. There are currently over one hundred exploratory permits issued to copper mining companies, and the two current applicants would be operating mines that are in the watersheds of the Boundary Waters Canoe Area Wilderness, the largest wilderness area east of the Rockies, and the St. Louis River, which is the largest tributary of Lake

Superior. So again, people who care about the land are pitted against the powerful interests of corporate greed. The rice beds in this region are of far greater value to its people than the short-sighted oil production or the sulfide mines which are under review.

Anishinaabeg:
The Keepers of *Manoomin*

It's not about Indians, it's about people ... the overall philosophy is to reconnect all people to nature and inevitably to themselves.

— Chi Ma'iingan

The staff of life to the Anishinaabeg people who occupy the forest regions of Minnesota and Wisconsin is wild rice (*manoomin*). Treaty rights preserve their rights to hunt, fish, and gather from lands they ceded to the whites. Through the exercise of these rights, Anishinaabeg people obtain their food, clothing and shelter. Even today when many Anishinaabeg people rely to one degree or another on manufactured goods, many of these manufactured goods are purchased through the sale of rice they gather or fish they take from the lakes. These rights were guaranteed to Native people. These treaties are contracts. But besides the economic value of rice to the Anishinaabeg, there is a deep history and connection to *manoomin* and the land, and although white people are late arrivals, their early history also has its roots directly connected to *manoomin*.

Being a resident of headwaters country of northern Minnesota, I am often asked, "Where is the best place to find wild rice in the nation?" My reply is, "You are standing on it." There are more acres of rice fields in northern Minnesota than anywhere else on this continent. In fact, not only are there more rice beds in Minnesota than anywhere else, there are more genetic strains of rice here than anywhere else.

The importance of *manoomin* to the Anishinaabeg cannot be understated. To the Anishinaabe it is a sacred food and has great spiritual meaning. In their Seven Fires Prophecy which describes the purpose for their westward migration and foretells of each stopping place, the Sixth Fire (fire being a stopping place) will be where food grows upon water. "There will be seven stopping places along the way. You will know the chosen ground has been reached when you come to a land where food grows on water." (As told by Edward Benton-Banai, Midewiwin teacher and Grand Chief of the Three Fires Midewiwin Lodge.) Obviously, "where food grows on water" is *manoomin* or wild rice.

Prior to the arrival and dominance of the Ojibwe in northern Minnesota in the early 1700s, this area was principally controlled by the Santee or Woodland Dakota. Wild rice was a principal staple in their diet. Sometime in the early 1660s (the exact date is still questioned) Pierre-Esprit Radisson and Médard Chouart, Sieur des Groseilliers visited the Dakota near the vicinity of Prairie Island near Red Wing, Minnesota. There, Radisson described eating wild rice and its harvesting: "Our songs being finished, we began our teeth to work. We had there a kind of rice, much like oats; it grows in the water in three or four foot deep." (*The Explorations of Pierre Esprit Radisson,* Arthur T. Adams, Editor.)

Even after the Dakota-Minnesota War of 1862 in which most Dakota people were driven out of Minnesota and into the Dakotas, wild rice remained so culturally important to them that on or around 1895 the Black Hills Dakota designated the month of September as the moon when they dry rice and October as the moon of dried rice.

Prior to the Dakota in Minnesota there was the Blackduck Culture. Some archaeologists believe that the Dakota came out of the Blackduck Culture. This would have taken place in what archaeologists refer to as the Woodland Tradition which is dated from 800 B.C. to A.D. 1700. Prior to the Woodland Tradition was the Paleo-Indian Tradition which is dated from 10,000 to 8,000 B.C. In this period we find the retreat of the glaciers, and the people who lived in this time were nomadic big-game hunters who killed mammoths, mastodons and giant bison along the retreating ice of the Wisconsin glacial movement.

During this period in headwaters country great ecological changes were taking place due to the glacial melt. Rivers and lakes came to dominate the country along with greater forest diversity of both deciduous and coniferous biomes combined with the influence of the prairie biome. During this Woodland Tradition period the archaeological record shows Indian people becoming reliant on wild rice.

By the Late Prehistoric Period between A.D. 900 and 1700, there was more of a shift in village locations from river to lake sites. This took place due to more reliance on *manoomin,* both in diet and culture. So when we look at the association of Native American peoples in headwaters country to *manoomin,* we are looking at thousands of years of influence. This was not something that happened overnight; *manoomin* shaped their lives in all facets over a great period of time.

Not only was it their staff of life, it was important spiritually and culturally, and in a very real way also became the fabric of their being.

In 1836 Joseph N. Nicollet traveled through headwaters country on his way to survey the source of the Mississippi. When he entered what is now the Leech Lake Indian Reservation in the region around Big Rice Lake and Laura Lake he noted, "Here also begin what the natives call 'their gardens,' where they gather abundant crops of wild rice."

The history and spiritual importance of *manoomin* to Ojibwe people is demonstrated by their placing *manoomin* in spirit houses to sustain the deceased on their journey to the spirit world. These practices are not recent but go back to ancient times. In Thomas Vennum's book, *Wild Rice and the Ojibway People,* he cites archaeological records in Michigan where wild rice was a mortuary offering as early as 400 to 600 B.C.

When we enter *manoominike-giizis* the rice heads begin to ripen. The plant is an annual and does not sprout from last year's roots. It can only grow by reseeding itself. The seeds are heavy and sink to the bottom. There is a long barb on one end that always stands up whether it has fallen to the bottom of water or the canoe floor. Over time, the mass of rootage in the soil at the bottom of the plant can impede rice germination, so proper aeration is not only beneficial but necessary. In Vennum's book, he cites an anecdote made by a bush pilot who spotted a moose feeding on aquatic vegetation, and buzzed the moose, causing it to flee through the shallows with much "churning and splashing." The next year the pilot flew over the exact spot where he had frightened the moose to find a lush green swath of wild rice.

Water quality is vital to rice. It must have unpolluted waters and will not tolerate any water that is compromised.

It is particularly intolerant to sulfates and will not grow in waters exceeding sulfate levels of fifty parts per million.

When the rice kernels germinate in May they appear like submerged ribbons waving in the water. As the leaves grow, they reach the surface sometime in late June, which is important because if they do not emerge to the surface of the water by then, the lack of sunlight reaching these submerged leaves will result in a poor yield. Once the leaves do reach the surface, they lay prone until they get about a foot or more in length, and then they stand erect. As the standing plants mature, the stem, which is segmented like a bamboo plant, grows above the leaves and forms a panicle. The panicle is composed of the flowers. The *manoomin* plant is a bit different from other plants in that the male flowers grow below the female flowers. The female flowers become the rice grains. The pollen is very light and can be lifted for self-pollination purposes, but fertilization is more likely to be from windblown pollen. When near a rice field at this time of year, the first thing to look for is reddish-purple color in the seed heads. This means that the female flowers have been fertilized. The rice then takes between ten and fourteen days to ripen. It goes through a series of stages, the first one being the milk stage when the seeds are of the consistency of a thick salve, in which case you shouldn't be there because rice is sensitive to human contact until fully ripe. The next stage is the dead-ripe stage in which it is ripe enough to harvest, followed by the shattering-out stage in which the fully cured kernels separate from the stalk and fall into the water and become *manoomin* plants next year. Much damage is done to rice stands by people entering these beds before the rice is ready. This lack of patience by many white people has been a grievance to Indians for a long time.

When in a canoe on rivers or lakes laden with rice, especially during the mid-summer phase when the rice is just starting to stand erect, there is a unique smell that pervades rice beds so noticeably that I am confident if I were blind and had just been awoken from a long sleep and placed in a canoe, I could tell you what time of the year it was by the smell of *manoomin*.

Rice is vulnerable to dramatic fluctuations in water levels. When it is in the floating stage, the short spongy roots are subject to uprooting when water levels rise suddenly. If water levels rise even gradually after the floating stage, prolonged submersion of rice prohibits exposure to the open air and sunlight, which will cause the size and amount of rice kernels to be low due to the plant having put too much energy into plant growth rather than flowering and seed production.

Getting into a rice bed for harvesting before the rice enters the dead-ripe stage can cause harm to the plants. Harmful weather factors can damage a harvest before the rice is ready; storms, strong winds, rain and other natural events can greatly harm the rice if it is near ripe. This is why Ojibwe people had a "rice chief" who told when the rice was ready, where to go, where ricing camps would be set up, and provided other oversight in order that everyone got their opportunity to harvest this food without harming the rice bed and with equality to all harvesters.

Beginning in the 1880s, the Army Corps of Engineers began building dams that impacted headwaters country for water control management, development and navigation. They confiscated Indian land and inundated thousands of acres of rice beds and villages. The rice harvests at many traditional Ojibwe ricing locations became a mere fraction of what it was before the dams were built.

As to Anishinaabeg beliefs in the origin of *manoomin*, the Lac Courte Oreilles Band Elders in Wisconsin tell that the first *manoomin* was found in the Red River of the North, and from there it was scattered and planted eastward until it arrived in Wisconsin. Many other Indigenous people believe that you cannot plant rice, only the Creator determines where there will, and where there will not, be rice. I have thrown rice into my own little lake and a few seeds germinated, but they failed to reseed for the next season, and repeated attempts also failed. I have talked to others who have tried to reseed rice where it did not formerly grow and had the same results. There are great mysteries in life and *manoomin* certainly has its mysteries. Maybe it's a good thing that we don't understand this facet about *manoomin*, for some mystery is a good thing. It keeps us a bit more humble when we know that we don't know everything.

The Historical
Importance of *Manoomin*
to *Gichi Mookomaan* (White Man)

I believed, as the waterthrush that foraged at the mouth of Min-
nehaha Creek, where the rippling current joined the mighty Mis-
sissippi ... To be free as a wild creature, not having to shoulder hu-
man cares, able to climb, run, jump, swim, lie on an embankment
in the sunshine — these gave a release to the young spirit that may
be perhaps described as primitive, but nevertheless exquisite in the
most elemental sense.

— Calvin Rutstrum

Having made the point of the supreme importance of *ma-*
noomin to Anishinaabeg people, *manoomin* also has its place

in the history of white men. In Minnesota and Wisconsin the first white men to arrive were fur traders. These rugged men were French-Canadian and were called *coureurs de bois* — wood-runners — and as the fur trade became established and taxed by the Governors of New France (Quebec) the term *coureurs de bois* became a term for unlicensed traders — traders operating outside the law. The trade became organized, and as possession of Canada and the colonies came into the hands of the English, it rose to become one of the most important financial enterprises in that period of history. Fortunes were made in the fur trade. Many of these trading posts in the Great Lakes region such as Grand Portage, Fond du Lac, and Fort William became household names in Europe. Although American history for many white Americans brings to mind stories of the West, cowboys and Indians, and manifest destiny, it is important to note that those parts of our history only lasted for about fifty years. The much greater span of our recorded history was the fur trade.

The fur trade began in the mid-seventeenth century and fizzled out in the mid-nineteenth century. Although there was much in this era that was shameful in the way fur traders exploited Indians, it was as close as we've ever been to so-called halcyon days in white-Indian relations. The principal trading companies were the Hudson Bay Company, the North West Company, and later, the American Fur Company.

The division of labor in the fur trade was divided into different groups. The *bourgeois* were the partners, men who ran the companies from Montreal. The men who ran the fur posts in the Northwoods were the *commis*, or clerks, and the workmen or muscle of the trade were the *engagees* or *voyageurs*, who paddled and portaged canoes, traded goods, and manned the posts during the winters. The relationship of these fur trade men to the Anishinaabe was a partnership in the trade. The Anishinaabe were the procurement factor in the trade—they trapped and acquired furs and in turn traded them to these fur men in exchange for cast-iron cookware, guns, black powder, steel traps, tobacco, wool blankets, apparel, sewing needles, and many other goods which improved upon the quality of their life. Alcohol was used as a trade item which was a blemish on the whites, and they also implemented a system of credit with the Anishinaabe that was fraught with high interest rates, unethical credit and other ways that traders exploited them. Before the first whites and the fur trade, Anishinaabe people lived in a communal economy. After the fur trade, a supply-and-demand marketplace economy altered Native life and pushed them to exploit animal resources for goods and other items of economic value.

During this two-hundred-year span in our history, white people, for the most part, did not want Anishinaabe land or the resources there, they only wanted wealth from furs. Most whites understood that this was Indian Country and they traded, married, and interacted only at the pleasure of First Nation Peoples. This relationship began to change in 1837 with the first land acquisition in Minnesota, and the change would be profound in how it altered lives and land.

Many historians have elevated the importance of pemmican in the fur trade to a level that I do not believe it deserves. Pemmican is dried and pounded buffalo meat stored in animal skins with fat and often dried blueberries or rose hips. Pemmican, dried peas, and corn were to the *voyageur* what freeze-dried foods are to modern day canoeists and backpackers. The most vital food item to the fur trade for the greater part of the year was *manoomin*. If it was not for *manoomin*, the fur trade would have flopped. The traders and their *engages* would have starved to death if it had not been for Natives and *manoomin*.

The importance of wild rice to the existence of the fur trade is repeatedly described in the journals of fur traders.

Fur posts were built not only near Anishinaabe communities, but close to substantial rice fields, and these journals describe the abundance and immensity of the rice fields. In 1823 when explorer Stephen H. Long and his travel companions were traveling down the Red River of the North, he wrote, "arrived at a considerable river called Wild-rice river and crossed it about 9 miles from its mouth. It has its rise in a Lake about eighteen miles in diameter, and from the abundance of wild rice growing in it, is denominated Wild Rice Lake. The supply of this article of food yielded by the lake is said to be inexhaustible. At the outlet of the lake was formerly a trading establishment belonging to the NWC (North West Company)." (*The Northern Expeditions of Stephen H. Long*, Stephen H. Long.) When Long arrived on Lake of the Woods, traveling from west to east on August 26, 1823, he notes, "We have seen but very little Wild Rice till our arrival at the Lake of the Woods, but in the coves and recesses of the lake it is abundant. It is now in a mature state and the Indians are engaged in gathering & preparing it for their winter subsistence."

As early as 1775, Alexander Henry the Elder, while making camp on Lake of the Woods with a brigade of *voyageurs*, canoes, and outfit on their way to the Saskatchewan River Country, emphasized the importance of *manoomin* to the fur trade: "In a short time, the men began to drink, while the women brought me a further and very valuable present, of twenty bags of rice. This I returned with goods and rum, and at the same time offered more, for an additional quantity of rice. A trade was opened, the women bartering rice, while the men were drinking. Before morning, I had purchased a hundred bags, of nearly a bushel measure each. Without a large quantity of rice, the voyage could not have been prosecuted to its completion."

In 1802 at Rainy Lake, the meticulous and accurate journal keeper and North West Trader Daniel W. Harmon noted that wild rice is "gathered in such quantities, in this region, that in ordinary seasons, the North West Company purchased, annually, from twelve to fifteen bushels of it, from the Natives; and it constitutes a principal article of food, at the posts in this vicinity." (*The Journal of D. W. Harmon*).

Fort Folle Avoine on the Yellow River, a short distance below Yellow Lake in Burnett County, northwestern Wisconsin, and a tributary of the St. Croix River, has historically been known for its prolific rice fields. The French name "Folle Avoine" is "fool's oats," named after a plant of similar appearance in Europe. The XY Company trader Michel Curot noted in his journal in late August 1803 a letter which he received from a fellow trader that said, "there is no wild rice this year, he was obliged to go the River au Serpent [Snake River in east central Minnesota] to trade." (*A Wisconsin Fur Traders Journal, 1803-04*, Michel Curot.)

In Editor Douglas A. Birk's *John Sayer's Snake River Journal, 1804-05*, Birk writes, "Reaume's diet on the Snake River in 1803, like Sayer's the following year, consisting mostly of venison and wild rice. The Ojibway were the chief suppliers." Birk goes on to write that the North West trader Joseph Reaume "returned to the Folle Avoine [on the Yellow River in northwestern Wisconsin] to buy and stockpile wild rice. After buying 42 bags on the Snake River, he probably went to Nami-Kowagon [Namakogen River] or some other point east or northeast of La Prairie's Yellow River post."

The importance of wild rice should be no secret to those studying the fur trade. In John Tanner's narrative, he notes while in the employ of the American Fur Company he "was made to paddle by myself a canoe heavily loaded with wild rice, and to submit to other laborious employments which I did very reluctantly ... The winter had now commenced, and Mr. Cote sent me with one clerk, four Frenchmen, and a small outfit of goods, equal to one hundred and sixty dollars in value, to trade among the Indians. We were furnished with no other food than wild rice at the rate of eighteen quarts per man." (*The Narrative of John Tanner: "The Falcon,"* John Tanner.)

Even in the year 1848 after the demise of the golden days of the fur trade, Henry Rice wrote to the famous, experienced, and gigantic African-Ojibwe trader George Bonga at Leech Lake, "Your rice you must purchase with ammunition & if the Indians will not pay rice for it, let them go without. You must be sparing of it until winter for if you are not the first thing you will know you will be out." (*Henry Rice & Family Papers, Box #1*, MN Historical Society.)

At the time of this writing, the future of *manoomin* and the approval of oil pipelines and the sulfide mining projects are in review. The protection of these treasured and unique resources is in our hands and the hands of state regulatory agencies. An outpouring of public comments and a strong resistance has been and is being made by Anishinaabe people, white environmentalists, organic farmers, and people who simply wish to keep their treasured water pure, their rivers free, and their lakes pristine.

Snags, Disease, Cavities and Dead Trees

Soon after I bought my woods a decade ago, I realized that I had bought almost as many tree diseases as I had trees.

— Aldo Leopold

Maybe thirty years ago while deer hunting from a tree stand on my land in northern Minnesota, I heard a rustling and commotion behind me. I turned around and saw a goshawk lift itself up from the snow-covered ground to the top of a ten-foot-high jack pine snag. This particular jack pine, about eighty years old, had its crown snapped off in a strong wind the previous summer. The adult goshawk perched on the top of the snag and turned its head from side to side while peering down to the ground. Then the hawk spread its wings and fluttered down to the base of the tree where I lost sight of it, but I could hear rustling and shuffling in the snow and leaves. Several minutes passed, and then the goshawk lifted itself up to the top of the snag again and began scanning the ground with great interest.

The goshawk repeated this up and down from its perch on the jack pine snag to the ground below it a half dozen times for perhaps a half hour before it gave up and flew out of sight. My curiosity was piqued by what had caused the goshawk to do this up and down routine, but I waited in the tree stand as it was still early in the morning and prime time to have a deer come by. As I continued to hunt, I heard the explosion of a ruffed grouse behind me and immediately turned to see a large, red-phase-colored ruffed grouse fly away, coming from the base of the jack pine snag in which the goshawk had spent so much time.

When I climbed down out of the tree, I walked back to the jack pine snag to see what this was about. The tracks in the snow on the ground told the story. Immediately below the snag was the crown that had broken off from the main trunk. Most jack pines are loaded with branches up and down the trunk. When it fell, the upper trunk with its many limbs had impaled themselves into the ground, providing a predator-proof bomb shelter for the grouse. The tracks of the grouse in the snow showed that he had been moving back and forth among all the stout limbs impaled in the ground. The hawk could not quite fit between the many impaled and sheltering limbs, nor did it have the quickness and dexterity of the grouse. The hawk's tracks moved along just outside the downed top while the grouse tracks were all in the interior of the impaled limbs. The red grouse owed its life to this jack pine top.

I was lucky to find this land I now live on as it contains multiple forest types within eighty acres. In the central part of this land are some large red and white pines nearing old-growth status. Some of the white pines are well in excess of one hundred feet tall with large crowns. During 2005 and 2006 this region experienced severe drought conditions. I believe this drought weakened some of the big white pines by making them more susceptible to disease and insect infestation. My most treasured and largest white pine lost its crown during severe winds. I was heartbroken that this old giant was gone, but I suspected this would happen as I had observed a large mass of white pitch encircling an area about six feet wide and about fifty feet up in the tree. The area of the pitch was an indicator that there had been an insect infestation in this tree. The huge felled top covered a large area on the ground making a mess of trunk, branches, limbs and needles. Some of the limbs on this massive trunk were the size of a small tree, and I could walk on the limbs of the downed top like a bridge or scaffolding with relative ease. In most places the ground below this mass of limbs, branches, and needles was completely concealed. Within days, cottontail rabbits, red squirrels, chipmunks and many other small mammals and birds made their forms, nests, and sanctuaries below this blowdown.

It used to be that when a tree like this fell, I would get my chainsaw and clean it up. I saw it as unsightly, a mess that I had to clean up because it was detracting from the beauty of the forest. I had read Leopold's masterpiece but it hadn't soaked into me. It was only through years of experience witnessing the value of blowdowns, dead trees and diseased trees and seeing how they fit into the scheme of things that I realized my idea of esthetics was different from my animal neighbors.

In 2012 the red oaks in this neck of the woods had a bumper mast crop (abundant acorn production), so I restricted my bow hunting to a stand of mature northern hardwoods. In this stand, I found a clump of three red oaks that were over one hundred years old and provided me an ideal place to put up my portable tree stand. I noticed as I was securing the stand that one of the three oaks had a four-inch cavity.

Like in any healthy hardwood forest with an oak component there will be a good supply of gray squirrels, or *misajidamoog*. While hunting in these woods in the autumn one almost continuously sees a gray squirrel moving about, either in the treetops or on the ground, finding and burying acorns. While back in the tree several evenings later as it got closer to sundown, I noticed several gray squirrels approaching the clump of oaks I was in. One of them cautiously climbed the tree, staying on the backside away from my attention. As it was adjacent to the cavity hole, it peaked at me from around the backside of the tree. My first reaction was to scare it off as I feared it would start chattering and alert any deer to my presence, but I remained motionless and the squirrel quickly scurried into the cavity. The second squirrel repeated the same precautionary care until it too felt safe to enter the cavity, followed by three more gray squirrels, five in all, fitting into the cavity and out of sight. I could hear them in the tree scurrying around, but they were safely out of sight. Every night that I was out in this clump of oaks, at sundown, the same five squirrels scurried into the tree, each time getting more accustomed to me. By November, they no longer paid attention to me on their way into the tree for the nighttime.

Although I could not see them, I knew they were curled into a ball with their large bushy tails wrapped around the mass of squirrels to keep themselves warm. That winter proved to be tough, with many low temperatures of thirty to forty below zero with a total of ninety inches of snow. On many of these bitter-cold winter nights, I thought of these five squirrels and felt good knowing they had their warm tree hole and a good supply of acorns stashed away.

When in a stand of mature hardwoods, whether hunting, sugaring, birding, or just out for a walk, I now see a plethora of cavity holes of many shapes and sizes. They were always there, I just couldn't see them. Having learned their value, I now see them all over this forest.

Many cavities owe their existence to woodpeckers, others to a dead limb. An example of how this happens would be a dead branch. First it absorbs moisture, then fungi and bacteria enter the woody branch and decay begins, then a gray squirrel will start chewing on the decaying branch. The chewing or drilling of a woodpecker will begin to carve out the branch and into the trunk. Once in the interior the decaying heartwood allows for further excavation. Soon they have a hole large enough to permit a squirrel, woodpecker or other cavity-dwelling creature to set up housekeeping. Squirrels continue to chew around the opening to prevent them from closing up as made evident by the build-up of scar tissue around the hole.

I have seen barred owls nest in tree cavities, and when one of these hoot owls chooses a tree hole they may use it for a lifetime. Another owl that uses tree cavities is the diminutive saw-whet owl that is not much larger than a plump robin. More than once while visiting my hardwoods I have heard the whistle of a wood duck which caught my attention, and looking in that direction I have seen the stunningly beautiful male perched on a limb adjacent to a cavity with its mate sticking her head out. If the cavity is close enough to the water it may be graced with the most handsome hooded merganser.

We do not normally think of cavities in association with fishers (*ojiiig*), but they are vitally important to these large members of the weasel family. Female fishers need large enough cavities in older standing timber — often eighty-year-old aspen trees — and will frequently move their young from one cavity to another during the youngster's development.

These cavities are of vital importance to a wide array of wildlife. Like Leopold, I now see the diseases and other calamities that have afflicted my woods as having impacts that transcend the commonly held beliefs about esthetics. When looking deeper into and observing nature more closely, we see them as part of what Leopold calls a "mighty fortress."

Canoes and Snowshoes
(*Jiimaanan* and *Aagimag*)

Mountain men, desert men, canoe men, they are the same the world over – only the land differs. ... The country has done something to these men, given them calmness and imperturbability, the mark of the wilderness.

— Sigurd F. Olson

For thousands of years the canoe has been an integral part of life in North America. It was here in the Great Lakes region, where the paper birch trees were in abundance, that Native Americans first engineered the canoe, which they called *jiimaan*.

The paper birch and cedar trees were spiritually important

to Ojibwe people. With the bark from the birch tree, combined with rails and planking from cedar, along with roots from spruce or tamarack and pitch from pine trees, they had all that was needed to make a canoe. Our modern canoes use different materials, but little else has changed from that first birchbark canoe.

Blessed as our region is with a network of rivers and lakes, the canoe is probably the most functional and utilitarian creation given unto the resources and the people that gave it birth. With its mobility and lightness, there is virtually no area in northern Minnesota and the Great Lakes region that isn't accessible to the canoe. With only a minimum amount of skill, young and old can paddle and portage their canoe on the same ancient trails traveled by Esk-ke-bug-e-coshe (Chief Flat Mouth), Ozawindib (Yellow Head), Bagone-giizhig (Hole in the Day), Zebulon Pike, David Thompson, George Bonga, and Joseph N. Nicollet. Early Minnesota history and the canoe are inseparable. The canoe was the ultimate "do-all" creation. When the first Native American placed the first canoe into water, he transformed his and all other lives to come. Used for hunting-gathering, war, exploration, travel, and communication, the canoe became the ultimate in versatility.

But aside from all the practical uses intended for the canoe, there is one that is perhaps the most important of all, and that requires the human spirit to unlock it. It is the ultimate gift of the canoe. When one seats him or herself in a canoe, low to the water, takes paddle in hand, strokes that paddle in the water, and feels how intricately the canoe responds to their slightest touch, they become transformed and feel a connection with the natural world that perhaps they have never felt before. This is the real magic in a canoe. Maybe this is best expressed by Sigurd Olson when he said, "The movement of a canoe is like a reed in the wind. Silence is part of it, and the sounds of lapping water, bird songs, and the wind in the trees. It is part of the medium through which it floats, the sky, the water, the shores ... A man is part of his canoe and therefore part of all it knows."

Skill and artistry are part of canoeing. Only another skilled wilderness canoeist can appreciate the demonstration of skill and artistry when two partners are rhythmically paddling in sync, when each has the canoe stroke down to its ultimate efficiency as they cruise across a big lake within some wilderness area with a smoothness that can only be described as graceful. They arrive at a portage and disembark from the canoe so smoothly and adeptly, and almost in the same motion, hoist their canoe and packs on their backs and dog trot across the portage and load everything up as neatly and efficiently as when they took out. All this being done so in sync, that it hardly slows them down. To arrive at this skill level it takes time spent in a canoe, learning to paddle with another, and physical fitness with a strong back and good legs. When you reach this level of ability it gives one pride that you have mastered this means of travel and the satisfaction that you are carrying on a tradition that has existed here far longer than the gasoline combustion engine.

Joseph Nicollet did not forget that the canoe and paddling skills he acquired were originally provided by the Anishinaabeg. He was a French surveyor, geographer, and mathematician who traveled to the Mississippi headwaters in 1836, and he noted this level of skill while traveling upstream on the Mississippi when he encountered a group of Ojibwe women and children just below what is now known as Little Falls: "During my travels in America, I have often admired the precocious skill with which the children of the natives living along the shores of lakes and rivers maneuver their canoes; but I have to admit I did not expect as much on a river as the Mississippi. Only yesterday, it was evident how afraid I was, although it was the women who manned the canoes. But this is what one observes every day and at any time of the day on the Mississippi wherever Sioux and Chippewa Indians are to be found."

Northern Minnesota is blessed with having large blocks of public lands, networks of lakes and rivers, and wild and semi-wild areas as opportunities for humans to perpetuate these primitive modes of travel. Aldo Leopold talked about this very thing and cited canoe travel and pack train travel as being, "as American as a hickory tree; they have been copied elsewhere, but they were developed to their full perfection only on this continent."

Another form of wilderness travel is snowshoes (*aagimag*). Snowshoes appear to have come about simultaneously in both North America and Asia, but the traditional snowshoe that is still used today was developed in North America by the Huron and Algonquin people.

It seems plausible that the development of the snowshoe came about by human observations of other animals and how they move about on the surface of deep snow. The ruffed grouse that prospers in deep snow has developed numerous tentacles around the outside of its feet to enable it to stay atop the snow. The snowshoe hare has exaggerated feet which allow it to run across the surface of snow while its pursuer sinks into the snow as the hare escapes. The lynx too has over-sized feet that allow it to keep up with and sometimes overtake the snowshoe hare. Many forms of wildlife have adapted in one way or another to deep snow. Native people observed animals on a daily basis and learned from them better ways to live in harmony with nature.

One of those adages attributed to some unknown American Indian says; "The white man always attempted to avoid the snow or skirt it, whereas the Indian always looked for the best way to walk on it and live in harmony with nature."

The traditional snowshoe design has an ash frame (ash being resilient wood) with rawhide lacings and leather foot bindings. There are numerous models that are designed for different terrains, trails, snow depth, and forest density. Some of the models are called the Alaskan, Huron, Bear-Paw, Ojibwe, and Green Mountain Bear-Paw, and then there are the high-tech shoes that were originally designed for snowshoeing in the Pacific Northwest mountains.

When studying the traditional snowshoe the frequent question is, how can the rawhide lacings that have so many openings keep one up? How this is accomplished is that when walking in loose fluffy snow with traditional snowshoes, there is greater weight dispersal, and as the snow compresses the entire square foot area within the ash frames, regardless of the openings between the lacings, acts as a solid surface on the slightly compressed snow. The ability for snowshoes to keep one up on the snow is called "float."

Without snowshoes a person would not be able to get around in the woods during the winter months. With them, you can go anywhere. Yes, there are winters in the northland when the snow doesn't get deep enough to require snowshoes, but normally they are the only way to get around off trail and in the woods. Even during many maple-sugaring seasons, the snow is too deep to get around without snowshoes. They are a required item of equipment when the snow is a foot deep or deeper.

Snowshoeing is a way that allows me to get around in the woods, when without them, I would be grounded. Cross-country skis are a great way to get a cardiovascular workout, but on snowshoes, you are able to keep your eyes watching what is going on around you and not on the trail ahead of you as when skiing. The big woods around me are frequented by hunters from mid-September to early December. Until recently, the spring and summer months rarely had other people enter these woods, but that changed with the advent of off-roading by ATVers and ORVers. But in the winter, all the woods that I can walk are mine alone and without snowshoes this could not be done.

Snow conditions vary from day to day. Often the snow we get in November is the base layer until next spring. Snow settles and twelve inches on the ground today will be less tomorrow. Though the settling will not be great, it will nonetheless be somewhat shallower. A new snow depth of twelve or more inches that fell during cold temperature conditions such as fifteen degrees will be fluffy and light. When one snowshoes in these fresh and dry snow conditions, you will sink 30% to 40% of the total snow depth. The reaction is to ask, "Are these snowshoes really helping?" If you take off your snowshoes and walk you will immediately see the difference. Even with less snow depth, when you think snowshoes would be of no value, taking them off you find that walking in less than ten inches of snow is like walking in loose sand on a beach. Your foot slides and there is no traction in order to push off on your feet.

In the spring, with rising temperatures and thawing conditions, the snow will develop a crust that will not support body weight in just boots, but put on a pair of snowshoes and you can scoot around anywhere as though you were walking on plywood. Even when you find crusty snow conditions that will support body weight, you will still break through on every tenth or twentieth step. This can be so disturbing and disrupting to your pace that you will be inclined to put your snowshoes back on in order to enjoy yourself. Besides, breaking through crusty snow can be injurious to your shins and cause hyperextension of joints.

Sometimes the first primitive designs can't be beat by modern technology; the canoe and the traditional snowshoe are two examples of this.

Tonics of the Wilderness

We have to stop treating our soil like dirt.

— Wes Jackson

We have a large garden and gardening is a real challenge at this northern latitude. We can expect there to be frosts into June, and often we have our first frost in early September. In 2004 we had a killing frost on June 19 and we replanted only to have another killing frost on August 19, which means we only had a two-month growing season.

I have learned which garden crops are more suitable here and which are not. We have a large patch of asparagus, potatoes, raspberries, and a large fenced in area for cold crop delectables such as cabbage, carrots, beets, Brussel sprouts and up to eight different varieties of lettuce. Our asparagus, which has all been started from seed, usually starts emerging sometime in the second half of May. When the asparagus is up, we eat five to six meals of it a week, even making sandwiches out of it. It is the first green harvested in our garden, and I look forward to these greens after the long cold winters in the northland. The potatoes we plant do very well here. We plant up to a half dozen varieties which keep well in our root cellar. Depending on the year and my ambition, we have harvested from two hundred to five hundred pounds of potatoes. Our potato harvest gets us through the year to the next potato crop. Rarely do we have to buy potatoes, and we also supply family members with them. Our soil is a mix of clay, sand, some black loam and I add manure that I get from neighbors who have horses or cattle. I also add some leaves, compost and wood ash from my stove. We have two large raspberry patches of different types, both being varieties that do well in the northerly zone where we are. But greens are something my body craves after a winter of eating greens out of a can. The various lettuce seeds I plant are generally not large enough to start harvesting until late June. During this period before my lettuce gets going, I go into the woods to get my greens, and the plant I eagerly seek is stinging nettles (*Urtica dioica* and *Urtica gracilis*) or, as it is commonly called, "itch-weed."

Warning: bring gloves as skin contact will cause extreme itching, pain, and rash. Stinging nettles are covered—stalk, stem, and leaves—with thousands of stinging hairs. It is abundantly found in alder swales and black ash lowlands. This often-cursed plant has a plethora of uses: it's edible, functional, and medicinal. The thousands of tiny hairs on the plant act like hypodermic needles that inject formic acid. Formic acid is what bees and wasps inject when they sting you. It is this formic acid, which is almost pure protein, that makes nettles so healthy to eat. Boiling the young plants renders the formic acid harmless and the result is that you have a dish of greens that are arguably the highest in protein, iron, other trace elements, and also rich in vitamins A and C. I find this dish excellent when topped with butter, a dose of Italian oil, and salt and pepper. I drink the broth as a tonic. Whether it's psychosomatic or not, I feel a sense of invigoration after a dose of nettles. It is not bad tasting and after eating nettles for a week or more I develop a taste for this healthy herb.

During the first half of spring, after the long winter, I often feel anemic, tired, and with a general lack of energy. The effective remedy for this is to eat liberal amounts of itch-weed for a week or better, and after doing so, I have an amazing turn around in my physical and mental wellbeing. Itch-weed for me is a tonic.

When I am out in the woods collecting itch-weed, I also pick other young greens popping up out of rich woodland loams, such as wild lettuce, violet greens, young dandelions, cleavers, and jewelweed. The aromas in my pail after a day of harvesting is truly a magnificent woodland potpourri.

Functional uses of *Urtica* include using the tough hemp-like fibers of the plant to make string, twine, and fish nets as done by the Iroquois and Hurons. The use of plant fibers for clothing dates back to the Bronze Age and they were used for this purpose as recently as WWI by the Germans as fabric for tents and army uniforms.

Medicinal uses include treatments for hair conditioning, coagulation and hemoglobin formation, intestinal bleeding, and depression of the central nervous system, among many other disorders.

I was telling an Ojibwe friend of mine about my springtime nettles escapades, and she related a story of her grandparents eating itch-weed in the spring for the same reasons as I.

Euell Gibbons wrote and proselytized about the joy of harvesting wild plants for both food and medicinal uses, what he called, "reaping what he did not sow." Unfortunately, he became the brunt for many jokes, but Euell Gibbons was not the freaky health food nut as often portrayed. He liked his whiskey and even enjoyed a Big Mac. Euell saw industrial society as taking a toll, and he believed people were beginning to suspect that they had paid a high spiritual price for our plenty. Each person would like to feel he is an entity, a separate individual capable of independent existence, and this is hard to believe when everything we eat, wear, live in, drive, use or handle has required the cooperative effort of millions of people to produce, process, transport, and, eventually distribute to our hands. Man must simply feel that he is more than a mere mechanical part in this intricately interdependent industrial system, and that we are in danger of losing all contact with the origins of life and the nature which nourishes it.

But itch-weed is not the only wild plant we harvest for food, medicine, or other practical purposes.

Cattails are so abundant that some ecologists, though they are native plants, view them as invasive. They are very aggressive so don't feel like you're doing harm when gathering them.

The prized edible parts of the cattail come in phases from early May into July. The first stage is called "Cossack asparagus," named after the Cossacks on the Russian Steppes who relished it. Watch for this development when early shoots rise above the water about six inches to several feet in length. Just grab the plant with your hand below the surface and pull and twist until it breaks off neatly from the root stalk. Peel off the tough green outer leaves and you will have a tender stalk, edible raw or cooked. I would describe the texture and taste as a blend of celery heart and asparagus. Our preferred way to eat them is steamed and served with butter on top, as you would asparagus—they are super delicious!

The second phase is cattail corn on the cob. Watch for this to begin around mid-June. This will be when the immature flower spikes are enclosed in a green sheath like the husk on corn. Cut them just before the spikes burst through the sheath. Peal the green sheath as you would corn. You will have before you cylindrical green rods about the diameter of a pencil. If you pinch off a bit of the green surface, a bright yellow content is revealed. Prepare and eat these spikes as you would corn. They are delicious, high in carotene, and when done, the "cobs" will resemble small, plastic knitting needles.

The third phase concerns the pollination. Around the fourth of July the flower spikes will have burst out of their sheaths. The upper part is the male flower and the lower portion is the female. The male portion produces gobs of bright yellow pollen. The best time for gathering is early on a calm dry morning. Just go around the wetland in a canoe or in waders and shake the flower heads in a bag. You will be surprised to find it doesn't take a lot of work to gather a sizable amount of pollen. Mix this bright golden pollen 50/50 with your favorite pancake (or muffin) mix and you will be eating the tastiest pancakes you've ever had.

Euell Gibbons called the cattail the "supermarket of the swamps." I think you'll agree.

There are many books written on this subject but I find that none measure up to Euell Gibbons' field guides, such as *Stalking the Wild Asparagus*. They are not only informative in the edible category but also provide useful and interesting info on the lore of each plant. Much other information that I have about wild plants has come from Native people and some of the early homesteaders in the region, but I must emphasize the importance of knowing what you are eating thoroughly before ingesting. There are many plants growing in the woods that are deadly poisonous. I have done my share of mushroom gathering but not until I was thoroughly educated on the subject. An old saying among mushroom hunters is, "There are old mushroom hunters and bold mushroom hunters, but there are no old and bold mushroom hunters." This adage is worth remembering when gathering any wild plant.

Arguably the most poisonous plant in this region grows in association with stinging nettles, and that is *Cicuta maculata*, also known as spotted water hemlock and spotted cowbane. The French call it *Carotte de Moreau* (the name of a *voyageur* who mistook it for wild parsnips and died from eating it). This is not the same hemlock that Socrates drank though it is related. The hemlock that killed Socrates was supposedly a painless death, while *Cicuta maculata* is an excruciating death.

The leaves of *Cicuta maculata* are twice or thrice compound, coarsely toothed and often of reddish tinge. The rather flat cluster of white flowers is in a loose umbel and, when ripened, resembles dill seeds. Probably the most surefire way to identify it is by the vertical purple streaks on the stout stem. Its favorite habitat is damp ground, preferably in alder lowlands. It is in the carrot family. A peanut-sized nodule on the root is toxic enough to kill a full-grown cow. It is a prolific and common plant in its favored habitat. All parts of the plant are deadly poisonous.

Death from this plant is extremely painful and an agonizing way to die. Ingestion is almost certain death. Those who have survived suffer from nervous system damage for life. DO NOT mistake this plant for wild parsnips or wild celery, as it closely resembles them. Know what you are doing before foraging for wild plants. This plant has been referenced as more poisonous than the deadly *Amanita* mushroom. Thousands of pioneers died from a sickness called the "milk sickness"—this was from drinking cow milk of cows that ingested *Cicuta maculata*. The mild sickness is what killed Abraham Lincoln's mother, among many other pioneers.

Not just forbs and herbs contain food and medicine, but trees as well.

There is a time in late spring when the Northwoods air is laden with the aromatic and somewhat pungent smell of the balsam poplar. The air is heavy with its scent. If I had awoken from a Rip Van Winkle nap with no knowledge of the date, I could tell you what month it was and even the exact time of the month we were in by the smells of the forest. Woodland bedstraw, basswoods flowering, the bacteria from decaying leaves in the autumn, all of these trigger specific responses in my mind.

The balsam poplar is a tree worth getting to know. Another name it goes by is "Balm of Gilead" which is really a misnomer; the real Balm of Gilead is a cypress that grows in the Mideast. But the balsam poplar is every bit as miraculous as the Balm of the Mideast. First of all, the balsam poplar (*Populus balsamifera*) is in the Salicaceae family of trees whose name is derived from salicin, which is contained in all parts of the tree. Salicin was the pain killer ingredient in aspirin before chemists could replicate these natural ingredients. A side note to this is that salicin is in all poplars, such as trembling aspen, which is a favored food of beavers, so I presume that beavers never get headaches.

In the balsam poplar, the part of the tree that is most useful for healing is the buds. For any cut, sore, abrasion, rash or other wound, just go to your local Balm of Gilead and pick one of the large sticky buds and squeeze it between your fingers and sticky yellow-green ooze will come out in rather copious amounts. Now spread this on the wound. Its healing capacity is amazing and it smells good. My wife had large, open cracks that afflicted her fingers in the winter from cleaning solutions when we owned and ran the motel. She tried every commercial salve and ointment that she could find and nothing worked. I went out into the winter woods and picked a branch off a balsam poplar and she applied the ooze from the buds as directed and overnight her hands had begun to heal. Its healing capacity has never failed us, and grouse and other wildlife like to browse on it, and it makes the late spring air of the woods especially fragrant.

There are so many other interesting members of the plant community in the woods that it would take up volumes of space to describe them. The four that I wrote of only serve to remind us of the great and diverse communities that still exist in our beautiful and extraordinary world. The plants are indeed our relatives, and I mean this in the truest way.

Black Wolf

We have respect for animals. We don't keep them in cages or torture them, because we know the background of animals from Distant Time. We know that the animal has a spirit – it used to be human – and we know all the things it did. It's not just an animal; it's lots more than that.

—from a Koyukon Elder

For the three decades I have lived on these eighty acres, it has been the home range of wolves. The home range of wolves is normally considered to be quite large, up to hundreds of square miles, but the principal determination to the size of their home range is directly related to the prey density within their range. In the region of northern Minnesota where I live, the deer herd is large. From my experience as a deer hunter, living in the woods, and staying in touch with game surveys, it is safe to say that the deer population is at a minimum of twenty deer per square mile, but deer habitat can change at any given locale within this region depending on varying ecosystems. I and others of like-mind who live and get out in the woods within this region share information and experiences, and I believe it's safe to say that the average range, or territory, covered by wolf packs around here is forty to sixty square miles.

Minnesota is blessed with large amounts of public lands. Our state forest system of over four million acres is the second largest in the nation; only Alaska has more. We have two national forests, Chippewa and Superior, that total nearly four million acres. Our county administered lands (CAL) are expansive. St. Louis County, which is Minnesota's largest county, has 900,000 acres of county managed lands, and within Superior National Forest we have the Boundary Waters Canoe Area Wilderness, the largest designated wilderness east of the Rocky Mountains. All these public and semi-wild lands give Minnesota a haven for wildlife.

I live in an area where public lands are primarily state or county managed. These two government entities demand greater volumes of wood be logged, and in this area the soil make-up is more conducive to a general group of tree and plant species, and there is a greater presence of small cattle operations with fertile hayfields that support a larger deer population. If you were to travel twenty miles to the northeast you would be on federal lands, Chippewa National Forest, where in this part of the Chippewa soils are sandier, timber harvesting occurs with less intensity and logging practices are more species targeted, and there are far fewer farms. Keep in mind the fact that while deer are adaptable to almost any habitat, they thrive in far greater numbers in disturbed environments, such as logging sites. Deer are creatures of edges rather than the deep and dark coniferous forests. This in all probability accounts for the reasons why I have a healthy and vibrant wolf population: ideal habitat and lots of semi-wild public lands. I cannot think of two more important requirements for a healthy predator-prey combination.

The pack size in my neck of the woods has varied from year to year. During the early 1990s when my wife and I operated a motel in a nearby small town, the slow tourist months of winter gave me the opportunity to throw my snowshoes in the truck and make the half-hour drive to my eighty acres, where I would roam the forest and observe wolf activity and sign. Snowshoeing throughout the vast public lands surrounding my eighty enabled me to make a good survey and census of the resident wolf pack.

Female wolves enter estrus in February, and wolves seem to become more territorial then, patrolling their territory and marking it with urine, sometimes making the trails look as if they were emptying bottles of orange juice on any noticeable rock or stump along the perimeters. During this same decade in the nineties, this pack dug out a den on a south-facing hillside in a stand of conifers. The den was approximately a straight-line distance of one mile from our cabin, and in May my wife and I could sit alongside our pond in the evening and listen to the yipping of the pups. I should note that subsequent to locating this active den, I found two other abandoned den sites, and one den site that was abandoned before completion, all within a half mile from the active den. It may also be interesting to note that the hillside with all the dens was the bank of a glacial tunnel valley which was created by a river below the glacial ice ten thousand or more years ago.

All three dens had an entrance that was higher than their width. A short tunnel of perhaps three or four feet led to a chamber area that was smaller than I would have expected, barely large enough for one adult and a good-size litter of tiny pups. By late May or June, the pups were removed from the den and relocated at a rendezvous site on the opposite side of our pond where we could hear the juveniles and adults on a regular basis through the summer months. When the adults went on the hunt, a particular wolf, probably a subordinate female, would remain behind with the pups. Often we would hear an adult howl about a mile to the north. Late on summer evenings we would hear another adult east of our lake, most likely the guardian female, followed by the yipping of pups. It is said that a pack will group-howl prior to a hunt, but from what we experienced, howling functioned as communication in a wide number of ways. This activity in close proximity to our cabin went on for a decade. The pack abandoned the rendezvous site when the youngsters were big enough to run with them.

We had a first-hand experience of how wolves can be protective of their young in early September of 2004. I had a neighbor that lived within a mile west of me who had a black and chocolate lab that he allowed to run free. They often would be seen chasing deer on my land and would go as far as the woods to the east side of my pond where the wolves had set up their rendezvous site. I had tried to warn him of the danger in this without informing him of the exact location where the wolves were. On this particular evening, which was quite calm and beautiful, we heard the screaming of one of the dogs near the edge of the lake. While one lab was making the most horrendous cries, we could hear the second lab barking as it was running west, towards its home. I remember telling my wife that either the dog was killing something, or it was getting killed. I assumed it was the latter.

The barking continued for fifteen or twenty minutes and I tried to make my way around the pond, but it became too difficult in the brush and darkness. The next day it rained, so I stayed home, and on the following day I had a friend coming who I had permitted to hunt on my pond during the early goose season. As he carried a bag of decoys, I carried my canoe for him to use for retrieval. When we arrived at the pond's edge, we noticed a big white pine on the opposite side that had a great many turkey vultures and ravens in and around it. Rather than ruin his goose hunt, I waited until the next day to investigate the birds of carrion and found the completely cleaned bones of the chocolate lab. He and his partner had gotten too close to the wolf rendezvous site with adults present and the wolves chased them. The black lab had gotten around the lake, but the other dog got trapped too close to the lake and the wolves had caught up to him in a quartering angle and killed him. The bones were so clean and devoid of any hair or tissue that the only way I could confirm the identity was a few hairs left between its toes.

This extraordinary experience with breeding wolves came to an end in early 2005 when some human residents living in the area went off-roading on a large ATV early in the denning season. They were riding within twenty yards of the den site which resulted in the wolves abandoning their long-used dens and rendezvous site near our home, and since then they have moved to an unknown location. That was the end of a most enjoyable and interesting experience. This is only one of thousands of incidents where ATVs, dirt bikes, and ORVs have damaged habitat and displaced wildlife.

By June of 2004 we sold our business and made the cabin our permanent home. Wolves had become something that we heard, observed sign of, and saw. We were living with wolves and they added interest and excitement to our lives.

The largest pack size I observed was during the winter of 1996-97 when I had counted seven sets of tracks on my pond. This winter and the previous were the severest winters northern Minnesota had experienced for many years. Both winters had snow totals exceeding ninety inches, and the winter of 1995-96 set record low temperatures. The deer numbers plummeted during these years. Winter has always been the chief limiting factor of deer populations in northern Minnesota. Wolves did very well those two winters but I do not see wolves as the primary cause of deer deaths, but rather as agents for their decline due to the cold and harsh winters. One needs to consider that winter is the season of preference for wolves. There are no biting insects and no ticks — the cold temperatures are something our native stock of wolves have evolved with. They get around with ease compared to their prey, so hunting is at a premium in the winter, and these two winters were a boon to wolves. There is not always this perfect simultaneous balance in nature, it is more often a dynamic equilibrium with predator and prey, a teeter-totter of back and forth that balances out in the end, and in the case of extreme winters, this is often how it plays out. By 2000 to 2008 the deer herd had rebounded to record high populations and a deer hunter, when purchasing his regular deer license, was then allowed to buy up to five additional licenses for antlerless deer. Between my bow and rifle, I was taking four to five deer every autumn during these years. This growth in the deer herd all played out with over three thousand wolves living in northern Minnesota. At this time the wolves were covered under the Endangered Species Act, which also helped to spread their range into Wisconsin and Michigan. It should be noted that during this same period, chronic wasting disease was spreading in Wisconsin which was attributable to an overpopulated deer herd. Chronic wasting disease was also due to Wisconsin allowing the baiting of deer, in which an exchange of saliva on corn used as bait transmits the disease from animal to animal.

As a deer hunter, I have always kept a close eye on the general condition of deer going into the late autumn. I have directly correlated their general health to the abundance of certain foods that they rely on, or lack of them, such as the mast crop of oaks, the condition of forage in the understory due to adequate rainfall, or drought. In November of 2007, a large deer herd went into the winter in bad shape. I could see this by a lack of heavy tallow on the backs of adult deer. Generally fawns will not have the thick layers that adults have, but this particular year, when sawing through the leg bones of fawns, the marrow was the color and consistency of strawberry jam, which translates that they were already malnourished before the onset of winter. This was compounded by a record snowfall in northern Minnesota of forty-eight to fifty-six inches during the month of April. The previous record snowfall in Minnesota for the month of April was thirty inches. This hit the deer herd so hard that I found dead deer in the woods as late as June, and they were not wolf kills, they were walking skeletons that had just keeled over. Many surviving does had aborted their fawns.

Following this disastrous April of 2008, the predictable happened. Many deer hunters blamed the wolf and took it upon themselves to do something about it. It was within two years of this April storm that my woods were without wolves. With all the snowshoeing I do during winter in the woods around me, I saw only one or two sets of wolf tracks, and neither one of those were seen with enough regularity to confirm they were resident wolves and not just transit animals moving through the area.

Later that season I talked to an old deer hunter who hunts the public lands around me, and he told me that he had heard of foul play by a local group who had been responsible for the disappearance of wolves. What they did, how they did it, or if they did it, I'll never know for sure as I was never able to ascertain any more information about it other than the wolves were gone. Whoever did it got away with it. This was not the first time that this sort of deed had been done around here. Maybe a decade earlier, a pack of wolves had been wiped out and the culprit was bragging about what he had done while intoxicated in a bar in Walker and was reported. He was convicted and punished though I do not recall what consequences he suffered, but he did not get off lightly.

During the winter of 2011-12, I regularly saw a single set of large tracks in the snow. A lone wolf, who I suspected was a male by the large size of the tracks, had stayed around all winter. It was in February of 2012 after the wolf had recently been delisted by the U.S. Fish and Wildlife Service that I was out for a winter walk and had paused by my small lake and noticed down the shoreline were two eagles perched in an old aspen with some raven activity. I sensed immediately that a wolf kill was the result of this congregation of eagles and ravens. I walked up along a brink line that was forested by northern hardwoods. The brink paralleled the pond and I headed in the direction of the eagles. It wasn't far before I saw a very large wolf track in the snow headed downhill towards the lake, but when I looked for the track path, I could not see any more tracks. I had to get off the game trail I was following for perhaps seven or eight yards before I found his track again. I then realized the great distance between his tracks and that told me this wolf was running, moving with great leaps and bounds as he was hot on the pursuit of a deer. As I was moving downhill and was being impressed with the distance between his great stride and the extremely large size of his prints, I kept raising my head to glance downhill in case there was something there I needed to see. When I was within fifty feet of the bottom I could see the downed deer and blood on the snow. It was so fresh that neither a raven nor eagle had landed. The only tracks were of the wolf, the deer, and the scuffle. There were only several small amounts of hair and flesh removed from the deer. I began to suspect that the wolf had been at the carcass while I was first observing the two eagles in the aspens. The wolf was probably flushed away by my approach. I was taken by the skill and speed of this wolf.

Before the end of February I was regularly seeing two sets

of tracks: one large set that was most likely this big wolf, and an average-sized set that I hoped was a female. I have two game cameras out for photographing all types of wildlife, and I began to capture photographs of a big black wolf, big enough to make the tracks I had seen.

That summer following the wolf-kill incident by my pond, and on a week that we had our granddaughter staying with us, my wife and granddaughter were walking to the mailbox which was a half mile away on a rural gravel road. As they came to the end of our driveway and began the trek on the old township road, a large black wolf walked out of our property and onto the township road about a hundred yards in front of them. He stopped and stood broadside, turned his head and looked at them, then casually turned and went back into the woods where he had come out. My wife had seen wolves before and her initial comments were that he was particularly large, with long legs and a noticeably bushy tail. Later that summer I set one of my two game cameras on an old logging skidway and captured three juveniles in the darkness of the night, one after the other as they passed the camera. The third one stopped—probably the camera's dim red flash caught his attention—and he looked at the tree on which the camera was attached as if posing. He was a fine young male with a healthy coat, big black tail, and his head and ears looked so large and out of proportion to his six-month-old body. I still today, as I did then, take great satisfaction knowing that wolves had come back to these woods. As I write this, I smile with the knowledge there is a mated pair with young and healthy wolves on the move, traveling the forests of the north, representatives of the Creator's supreme success. I could not help but think of how the return of the wolf has made the Northwoods complete and whole, and thinking back forty years when I would never have dreamed that the day would come in my life when the wolf would recover and I would be living with them. The big black male had filled the void, a female met him, and they formed a pack, but my history with this black wolf was not over.

I continued to catch him on my game cameras set in the big block of public lands surrounding me. In early September of 2014 as I was preparing for a canoe trip to the Boundary Waters Canoe Area Wilderness (BWCAW), I pulled a camera that I had set by a salt lick within seventy yards of my cabin. I had the camera here all summer in order to photograph the deer population that frequented my land. When I viewed the footage I was surprised to see a photo of the black wolf within four feet of the camera, and judging by the direction he was moving, he was coming into my yard. I am certain the lingering smell of deer around the lick was something any healthy wolf could not resist. I left for the BWCAW with that wolf on my mind, and knowing he was still here in my woods made me at ease.

In the early summer of 2015 I had my camera set about a mile from my cabin and captured a good looking gray wolf without any white, black or other markings, but completely gray. The only exception was the long gray tail hairs were tipped in black, making this wolf easier to recognize. This photo was taken in the rain and her guard hairs were visibly wet, but even wet, she looked big and healthy. About a week later, I captured her image again, but this time she was right behind the big black male. I am now certain she is his mate. I was beginning to feel that I knew these wolves.

In mid-July of 2015 I was preparing to make a journey to Baraboo, Wisconsin for a wolf conference partly sponsored by the Ho-Chunk Nation. Two days before my departure, on a rainy morning, my two dogs and I took a walk. We were walking on a heavily used game trail along the edge of my pond. When we got on a point jutting out into the lake and surrounding wetlands, I stopped to scan the opening for wildlife, and as I looked out over the bog on the south end of the lake I saw something moving and knew by its shape that it wasn't a deer. I took my small day pack off and dug around for the binoculars, but by the time I found them and got a focus, I could no longer see what it was I wanted to identify. As I stood there looking out over the bog with a faint veil of fog and humidity hanging over the pond on this wet morning, I had a feeling that this was a wolf. As we continued on the trail, in the direction where I had the unidentified sighting out on the bog, Babs was at my feet and Rodney was a few yards out on the grasses on the edge of the wetland. Most of the time I kept Rodney on a leash as the hound in him made him want to run off on scent trails. As we were on a section of the trail that was within several yards of the lake opening, my attention was grabbed by movement—it was the black male. The first thing I noticed about him was he was soaking wet, like us, and then he saw me within a second after I saw him, and I think he was as surprised as I at this chance meeting. Then Rodney saw him and barked and took off running toward the wolf. The wolf turned and ran from Rodney and they both disappeared behind a clump of shoreline alders. I called for Rodney and ran out behind them as they both disappeared. I heard no breaking of brush, no growling, no fighting, nothing but silence. I continued to walk ahead, calling for Rodney to no avail. I was afraid for him, thinking that, although he is a big dog, he would be no match for this big wolf, or possibly even the presence of more wolves than the black wolf. They seemed to have completely disappeared, no indication of anything. I knew if Rodney was okay, he would come home, so that's what I did—I went home. I felt guilty and knew if harm came to Rodney it was my fault because I should have known that Rodney would run after him. Within ten minutes after I got back to the cabin, Rodney returned completely untouched. We were all happy that no harm had come to him.

In early October of 2015, after a windy couple of days, I and my little springer Babsy walked out from our cabin on a grouse hunt. The trail that we chose went around the north end of my pond, and in a low grassy area with the trees set back from the trail corridor. As I rounded a bend in the trail I noticed something out of place. I walked this trail often and was intimately acquainted with it and there was something in the trail that didn't belong. My first thought was that it was a top in one of the trees that blew off in the recent winds, but the forest edge was set back too far. As I stood there pondering what I was looking at, with Babs off in the trees sniffing around for a grouse, the object that I was studying moved slightly, and then suddenly and almost magically appeared in great clearness and detail of vision to me, as if she had just materialized out of thin air. It was the big gray female wolf with the black-tipped tail. She blended in so well with her surroundings on this overcast day that even while scrutinizing her at a distance of no more than twenty-five yards she was no more than a gray ghost. Once she knew that I had her pegged, she turned and loped off with a certain elegant ease and disappeared around the next bend. Never did I feel any danger or threat; it was a chance meeting with no more surprise or fear than meeting a deer. Babsy never saw her, but once the wolf had trotted off, Babs moved on with me until she reached the point on the trail where the wolf had stood, and then Babs smelled her big wild canine cousin and came back to me, leaning on the side of my leg and looking up at me with her big brown eyes as if to say, *Dad, that big wild dog is back, what should I do?* As the hunt continued on, Babs stayed near me for about one hundred yards or so, and then she picked up the fresh scent of the feathery rocket, a ruffed grouse, and any lingering thoughts of the wolf vanished and onward we both went, resuming our attempts to chase grouse around the township.

The next news I had of the alpha pair was a game photo that a deer hunter shared with me of three wolves: the black male, his mate and another wolf. There could have been more but the camera lens only had enough room to get the three. Big Black was in the lead. I have seen numerous tracks since then but cannot confirm if any are of the two alphas.

I have come to feel an intimate knowledge of these two wolves in the five years that they have established their territory in this big block of land that includes my home. This black male has more importance to me than any wolf I have encountered. He moved into these woods after it was made wolf-less and has, with the gray female, reared an undetermined number of wolves. To me, the black wolf is proof of the ability of nature for renewal if given a chance; this is nature flexing her muscle. The first sign of him in these woods occurred at the same period when the U.S. Fish and Wildlife Service announced its delisting of the eastern gray wolf in 2012. Immediately the Minnesota Department of Natural Resources announced they would have a hunt, and that hunt would be held after the firearms deer hunting season. However, when the state legislature went into session, the Minnesota Deer Hunters Association, with legislative support by northern Minnesota politicians, moved the hunt up in time so it coincided with the firearms deer season. Over four hundred wolves were killed that first year.

Few issues in Minnesota involving a natural resource have done more to polarize the citizens of this state than the decision to kill wolves. There were and will most likely always be, for generations, a small segment of the population that hates wolves to such an extent that they will resort to any means to kill, torture, and inflict some of the worst methods of cruelty on the wolf. I often refer to this group of wolf haters as the environment's version of the Ku Klux Klan. When reflecting upon the situation that delisting put us in, I think of a commentary in a widely read Minnesota sportsman publication done by the paper's editor on a trip he took to a sportsman's writing convention somewhere in Montana during one of the first rounds of the back and forth of wolf delisting and relisting. He wrote about the grumbling he heard from many writers from the western states about their fear and anxiety of wolves and their impact on game herds and livestock, and I recall the Minnesota editor musing about the unnecessary panic and fretting by these westerners about wolves and how they were no big deal, that Minnesota had great hunting with a healthy population of wolves present and the entire issue of wolves had died down in Minnesota. The Minnesota Department of Natural Resources had kicked a hornet's nest, as they would soon find out.

The delisting of wolves by the U.S. Fish and Wildlife Service, combined with the Minnesota DNR's rush to have a hunt, has done more to unsettle Minnesota's outdoor-loving citizens than anything the DNR has done in my lifetime. This also has done more to degrade the image of the DNR to many of its citizens. What it has also done, and maybe it was time for concerned citizenry to have their eyes opened, was to demonstrate to the citizenry the role that politics and the marketplace play in decision-making within the Department of Natural Resources.

As a devotee of Aldo Leopold and his "Land Ethic" I often wonder what he would say or think of natural resource agencies today both on the state and federal levels. First of all, Leopold wrote, "Unless there be wilderness-minded men scattered through all the conservation bureaus, the societies may never learn of new invasions until the time for action has passed. Furthermore, a militant minority of wilderness-minded citizens must be on watch throughout the nation and vigilantly available for action." I have always liked this quote but the question today is, what kind of men are scattered in all the "conservation bureaus"? Wilderness-minded citizens seem few and scattered far between. I have often seen my role as an environmentalist as having had to fight a conservation bureau like the DNR in order to protect wildlife and our state lands. As contradictory as that sounds there is solid proof of it.

About fifteen years ago, I was told by a retired MN DNR wildlife manager that early in his career there was a fifty-fifty balance between politics and good land stewardship in the decision-making process within the DNR. He went on to tell me that he feels the balance is currently more like eighty-twenty or ninety-ten, with politics over conservation. More than seventy years ago Leopold, in a subsection of his essay the "Land Ethic" entitled "Land Health and the A-B Cleavage," got to the core of the tug of war between these two camps. The A and B are the two schools of thought that he categorizes in the conservation thinking of his day. Leopold describes group A as regarding land as a commodity with principal concerns being board feet, numbers of pheasants and trout harvested, and bushels per acre and group B as regarding the land as a biota with complex ecological interconnections, its function much broader than what group A sees as sustainable land use. Leopold advocates that forestry, wildlife management and agriculture needs to look beyond economic goals and manage the land for the health of watersheds, diversity of plant and animal communities, wilderness areas, threatened species, and the role of predators. Leopold as a trained forester harshly criticizes his own field as it "feels no inhibition against violence; its ideology is agronomic." Seventy years later, we have not yet progressed in our thinking and, in fact, may have moved backwards.

Yes, we have had some great successes in wildlife conservation with the passage of the Endangered Species Act in 1973, but we have also seen some great losses, and I would argue that the successes have come more from ordinary people who have taken it upon themselves to fight for what is the right thing rather than from those people administering conservation bureaus. Thus far in protecting America's environment, commerce is the winner.

At this point, I think it is of particular interest to consider Leopold's use of language when he said it "feels no inhibition against violence" in his description of type A forestry practices. I do not think he is specifically citing the word "violence" in a singular manner; I think he is using it in a broader way as when thinking of a timber sale or a broader scope impact on the land like mining. I remember visiting with an Ojibwe friend who told me that when she was a little girl and she and her family would leave their home in a car and saw a big logging truck coming out of the woods loaded with logs, her mother told her that those trees, cut down and piled onto that truck, reminded her of Jews being murdered in mass in the Nazi concentration camps. I have always tried to be careful in not condemning extractive industries to an extent and to be mindful in public to acknowledge the importance of wood, minerals, and oil in our everyday lives, but when mulling over the statement made by my friend about mass killings of trees and equating them to people, it made me think. When I was preparing a plan for timber harvesting on my own land I spent a great deal of time marking different trees to be saved for my own reasons, whether I saw them as habitat, cover, food sources, or nesting. With public timber sales they generally neglect the impact on other species, both animal and plant, that reside in a community. We see wildlife as being animate but often fail to think of trees and plants as living beings. I think what Leopold meant when he wrote "it feels no inhibition against violence" is that we need to think in broader terms with consideration given to the interconnection of all life. My Ojibwe friend's analogy has stuck with me.

In my lifetime I have seen a shift in the DNR from a balance between group A and B to an agency that is guided more by politics and economics rather than what is good for the health of the land. And with the rise in power of special interests and corporate America, the DNR often performs its tasks more as an agent to industry than an agency looking out for the health of the land. When I was growing up, the Minnesota Department of Natural Resources was named the

Minnesota Department of Conservation. The shift in name is more than symbolic to many of us.

In the summer of 2012, prior to the first wolf hunt in Minnesota, the DNR held an online survey to ask the Minnesota public their opinion on holding a wolf hunt, and 79% of respondents opposed a wolf hunt. Anti-wolf-hunting groups formed, rallies were held, the Governor's Mansion was placarded, ads opposing the hunt were in newspapers and television, and all fell on deaf ears to the governor, the state legislature and the DNR. A lawsuit was brought against the DNR and Minnesota state courts ruled in favor of the DNR; the ruling was appealed to the state supreme court and again ruled in favor of the DNR. During the court proceedings, a DNR interoffice memo sent by the chief of wildlife became public, which got to the core of the reasoning behind holding a hunt: "However, after giving it considerable thought over the weekend, I have come to the conclusion that we owe it to our primary clients, hunters and trappers, and to livestock producers as secondary clients, to do what we can to establish a legitimate harvest opportunity now that the wolf is under our management authority."

It should not be the job of the Minnesota DNR or any other resource management agency including the federal government to make game farms out of the Northwoods.

The Minnesota Supreme Court ruling validated the DNR's intentions of following the wishes of their clients: hunting, trapping and cattlemen's associations rather than what is good for the land.

It would be wrong to lay the entire onus of blame on the DNR as our state legislature has mandated commerce-orientated land policy upon the DNR through legislation, and this doesn't apply only to the wolf, it applies to timber harvesting, mining and other related land resource issues.

Having been actively involved in environmental issues in

Minnesota for more than twenty years, I am reminded of President Eisenhower's farewell speech to Congress in 1961 in which he warned the country of a growing "military-industrial complex." It seems apparent to me with the power and influence of corporate extraction industries, the rapid growth of off-road vehicle manufacturers, and sporting goods commerce that we now need to beware of a "recreational-industrial complex," and our public lands have become their marketplace, and whether it is for timber, oil and precious metals, or as places for off-road vehicles, our public lands and wild places are under siege. We as environmental ists need to acknowledge the value of these resources today. Often it is corporate greed which supersedes sustainability and our needs, but these lands are not corporate lands; they are public lands, our lands, not lands specifically intended to be solely resources for extractive industries to plunder for greed and profit. These lands are essentially our commons and we should maintain the fact that a right to use is not a right to abuse.

Seldom does the business sector view our public lands and wild places as anything but something to make profits from. This point of view also manifests itself in all our institutions: political, economic, educational, and religious. Leopold's land ethic gets to the core of this issue and people give Leopold and his essay accolades but seldom put his ideas into practice. In the traditional Native American community, a world view exists almost identical to Leopold's land ethic in their relationship to Mother Earth, but it is pervasive in their traditional culture, and rather than using academic language it is portrayed spiritually. They recognize and worship not only all life on earth but water, air, even the rocks. They see man as being utterly dependent on all the animals and plants he shares earth with—they see all other life on earth as not needing us, but we need everything else to survive. Every living thing is a relative and the animals that live around us can be observed and important lessons are taught that can guide us to be better humans by simply observing life around us. The wolf that has been the target of so much hatred and persecution by descendants of European ancestry for thousands of years is a deity among many Native tribes. Among the Ojibwe the wolf, or *Ma'iingan*, is one of the Seven Grandfathers.

My friend, the late spiritual leader of Red Lake, Larry Stillday (Chi-Ma'iingan, Big Wolf) taught at his Ponemah teaching lodge in August of 2012 that *Ma'iingan* is one of the Seven Grandfathers, and the wolf is a teacher of Humility:

- To be truly humble is to recognize and acknowledge a power greater than ourselves whom we call the Great Spirit.

- It is understanding that in the eyes of the Great Spirit we are all equal [all life is equal].

- What makes us equal is the sacred breath of life the Great Spirit gives us.

- The wolf represents: loyalty, perseverance, courage, stability, teacher, and intuition.

- The wolf bows his head not out of fear but out of humbleness, he humbles himself in our presence.

- A wolf that has hunted food will take the food back to the den to eat with the pack before he takes the first bite or he regurgitates all he has for the pups.

- *Ma'iingan* is an animal guide for true teaching.

During the ongoing battles in the political arena to protect the wolf, especially in the political front and within society, we as advocates of the wolf have had to look within ourselves; so much of our reaction to wolf-hating legislators, hunters, cattlemen, and individual members of society was to rant, scream, and behave in a reactionary manner, often appearing to be a bit irrational. When having conversations with Larry about this, he calmly told me that the way to win this effort for the wolf was to be the wolf. He went on to tell me that the opposition wants us to jump up and down, scream, and act like children. Being the wolf means to act with humility, not to show weakness but to show strength by acting with civility, showing respect, using intelligent information and data, and making ourselves look good. If we do this, Larry said, the opposition will be the ones to look bad, and then he would share a story told by Elders in a manner to bring his point home. I cannot say with all certainty that we achieved the level of humility that Larry advised, but some of us did, and I would like to think that "being the wolf" has helped us win the battles we have, though the war has not yet been won.

After one of Larry's teaching lodges, a close friend of mine was going to get a spiritual name from Larry in a naming ceremony. My friend's name is Michael Meuers, and both he and I are mutual friends of Larry. Michael has worked for the Red Lake Band of Ojibwe for several decades. The person receiving the name was to ask a number of persons to be present as "namesakes" or *wey ah or niiyawen'enh*.

As the naming ceremony commenced, Larry told of the Great Spirit—*Gichi Manidoo*—and the creation story and that man was the last created. As man looked around and found he was alone he asked *Gichi Manidoo* if he could have a brother, and *Gichi Manidoo* gave him the wolf as his brother. Man and the wolf roamed the earth and named everything. In their journey they became very close as brothers. Once all creation had been named by them, the Great Spirit said they were to now follow separate paths and that on this path they would have parallel fates, what will happen to one will also happen to the other. I tell this to emphasize the importance of the wolf to Ojibwe people and their cultural difference to white society. To Ojibwe people, the wolf is not a demon; he is revered and looked upon truly as a brother.

When I ponder this wolf-and-man-as-brothers story, and its origin in the naming ceremony, I cannot help but wonder if something similar did not happen to European-Americans in our history in the Cro-Magnon era as we love dogs and millions of us have dogs living with us in our homes and as part of our families. We use dogs as partners in work, hunting, rescue, and as companions. We are intrinsically linked to dogs and dogs may be our mystic connection to wolves.

In a gathering at Bemidji State University to teach the importance of *Ma'iingan* to Ojibwe people, a song was sung by Floyd "Buck" Jourdain, Jr. (Tribal Chair of Red Lake Indian Reservation). After singing the song in Ojibwemowin, Buck translated the song's story into English. The story-song as I paraphrase it is:

A man went hunting to feed his family and relatives. A bad storm came up with freezing temperatures and blinding snow. The hunter became lost as he could not see in the blizzard and he sat up against a tree. With hypothermia setting in, he leaned his head back against the tree and closed his eyes, knowing that death would soon be upon him, and he faded into unconsciousness.

Sometime later he regained consciousness and found his body warmed. Everything was dark and he thought he was in the spirit world, but then he put his hand out and felt that there were furry bodies covering him. He struggled a bit and then realized the fur was the body of wolves laying upon him—warming him—and then he saw a very big wolf who spoke to him: "Brother, do not worry, we will not harm you." The wolves allowed him to lay in their den to heal, and they brought him food and kept him warm. As he regained his strength, the big wolf told him that it was time for him to return to his people and the hunter said, "I am lost and know not where my people are." The wolf replied, "We will bring you there." The man and the wolves walked a great distance until they came to an opening that the man remembered, and then he saw the smoke coming from the lodges of his people and the voices of the women and children laughing — he was overjoyed to be home, thanks to *Ma'iingan.* The wolves then told him to go, cross the opening to his people, as they could go no further. The man thanked them and crossed the opening and when his people saw him, they celebrated his homecoming as they too thought he had died. It was then that the man looked back and saw the wolves were gone, but then he heard them howl — long and deep howls coming from his brothers.

Wolves are so spiritually important to Anishinaabeg people that in the summer of 2010, Buck Jordain, with the advisement of the tribal council and Elders, made Red Lake Indian Reservation a wolf sanctuary, and among many points cited by the Elders of Red Lake, one of particular notice is the following:

> The wolf represents a "minor" Clan of the Red Lake. Tribal Spiritual leaders and elders speak of the parallel fates of wolves and native people. Many believe that if wolves prosper, the people of Red Lake will prosper, and if wolf populations suffer, so will the Red Lake Nation. Thus, management of wolves on Red Lake lands shall be driven by the great respect that the Red Lake Band of Chippewa have for this important tribal resource. Red Lake lands shall remain a sanctuary for wolves, with management scenarios designed to promote and preserve them.

So here we arrive at the realization of two cultures with diametric points of view about the wolf. One culture honors him as a brother, a Grandfather, one of the Seven Grandfathers who teaches humility, with a clan named after him and the cognition that the wolf plays a role in the natural scheme of things and is a powerful spiritual presence. The other and dominant culture sees the wolf as an evil killer, reducing our deer herds, killing our livestock, and the villain in our folklore and fairy tales. Where did our attitude towards the wolf go wrong? I believe it was thousands of years ago.

There was a time when people of European descent were a hunter-gather culture with an earth-based religion. The cave paintings in Lascaux beautifully depict people who worshiped earth and the creatures whom we shared it with. That changed as cultigens and agriculture redirected our culture towards Christianity. I have nothing against Christianity, but Judeo-Christian beliefs generally ignore the natural world and focus almost entirely upon human beings with no recognition of the plant and animal communities who support us. Understanding the different perspectives of the wolf helps us to arrive at that right place in life and our world. The wolf is more important than just a listing on the Endangered Species Act. He symbolizes our struggle and journey over thousands of years in trying to arrive at an ethic in which we can live peacefully with all life on earth. He is far more than a controversy; he is at the vortex of our struggle to find that land ethic.

I have gone full circle from the day that black wolf appeared in my wolf-less woods, and I am aware of his struggle and determination to exist, find a mate, build the pack, and survive where he rightfully belongs. There is no free lunch in a wolf's life; it is a continual struggle from the day he is born to his last day, and humans have compounded that struggle to live. Whether he is still alive today as I write this, I cannot know. But I do know that his will to live, the powerful spirit he transfuses into my world and the world of every living creature in these woods, is felt every minute of every day. He will not know of my affection for him and what he means to me, but I am aware of him and I owe him, and so do a growing number of people who want our land to retain the powerful spirit he instills into it. The greatness of his spirit and the wrongs we have inflicted on him come down through the ages. It is time we let him be.

Makwa:
Grandfather of Courage and Healing

The last word in ignorance is the man who says of an animal or plant: "What good is it?"

– Aldo Leopold

It was in June of the first summer we became permanent residents of these woods. My two dogs woke me up with boisterous barking at one o'clock in the morning. I was certain as to what had caused my two springers to go bonkers, so I got up and grabbed my flashlight and shined it out the backdoor towards my bird feeder, and, as I assumed, a bear had pulled over my bird feeder and was lying comfortably on the ground while eating the spilled sunflower seeds. It was dark but I could identify this bear as bigger than average by the size of his head and the relatively small size of his ears to the big skull. This was not the first time bears had visited my yard and bird feeder, and I was in the habit of going out, making a lot of noise, or shooting over their heads to scare them off. My mind told me to not let them get used to doing this, so I stepped outside dressed only in shorts, stood on the small deck just outside the backdoor, only armed with my flashlight, and started to yell at the bear: "Go bear! Go bear!" After yelling at him for several minutes, and with the bear completely ignoring me, he finally started to get up very slowly, reminding me of a sloth in the extreme slowness of his movements. This bear was bigger than I expected. When he got on all four feet, he started to slowly turn away from me as if he was going to leave, then suddenly and unexpectedly he spun around with lightning speed and made several lengthy leaps towards me with such alacrity that I found myself petrified. It happened so fast that there wasn't time for fear. The bird feeder was fifteen yards from where I stood, and the bear charged so fast that had I been standing there with a rifle pointed at him, the bear would have gotten me before I could have pulled the trigger. He skidded to a stop only a few feet from me by extending his front paws and legs directly in front of him like putting on the brakes. He began to huff at me and then started his sloth-like turn again, only this time he went back to the bird feeder and finished consuming the birdseed. I went in and sat for some time before I could regain any composure while the bear finished its meal at my bird feeder.

The bear (*Makwa*) taught me three valuable lessons that night. First, I live in his home. Second, the bear is one of the fastest, strongest, and most powerful spirits in the forest. Third, late May and June is the mating season for bears, so males are on the move and in a territorial mood.

Every spring and early summer I hear and read complaints from mostly nearby landowners about bears coming into their yards, getting into their garbage cans, and raiding their bird feeders, some of which are on their decks near their windows and doors. The newspaper stories will have a remark by some wildlife specialist noting that natural foods are in short supply, or that we are in a mild drought, or a number of reasons given for the sudden appearance of bears in people's yards. The reason for this as I see it is that it is mating time and male black bears will travel great distances in their search for females or food. I have had a lot of direct experiences with bears in the wild, and when males are in the breeding urge of May and June, they are a bit more aggressive and territorial than they would be any other time of year. It is simply a case of bears being bears.

Since that first summer we have gotten to know a large number of bears. Our home in the woods is on the regular travel itinerary for local bears. I may be able to slightly decrease the number of bear visitors we get by shutting down the bird feeder, but we enjoy the summer grosbeaks and finches and the amount of birdseed that we put out each morning is only a half-gallon or less of sunflower seed. I believe that if we did not feed the birds, there would still be enough odors coming from our normal everyday living that would attract any bear traveling downwind. A bear's sense of smell is so acute that it is beyond our understanding. We have come to enjoy their visits from late April to September. We have learned that rule number one about bears is giving them their space. It's very wise to stay indoors when they are here, but if you have to go out, acknowledge their comfort zone and stay outside of it. An excellent example of this is at my wife's hummingbird feeders, which have been damaged by the bears. If we awake in the middle of the night to find a bear is at our sunflower seed feeder, I go out with my headlamp and a step ladder and gather the hummingbird feeders. The bear at the bird feeder on the north side of our cabin typically ignores me while I am on the south side collecting the hummingbird feeders. As long as you give them their space and show respect, they will not bother you.

I have many times encountered bears in the woods on foot during daylight in which they act nonchalant and walk off until out of sight. Nothing in nature is true 100% of the time, but I find daytime bears showing more timidity than nighttime bears. Bears at night show far less fear of humans and are more determined to follow through with what they want. On numerous occasions, we have had bears in our yard or in a campsite in the dark and have watched them as they move about, comfortably, checking out whatever strikes their interest, appearing like black shadows, almost ghost-like. It is astonishing how fast a four-hundred-pound black bear can move through a thick forest in silence and stealth. Their padded feet are like moccasins further muffling their footsteps. It is at night, when a bear is in your company, that you can feel the powerful spirit and strength of the wild.

In the Teachings of the Seven Grandfathers, *Makwa* is one of the Grandfathers and is the teacher of courage. Larry Stillday provided this bullet-point to teach us about *Makwa*:

- To have the courage of the bear is to overcome our fears that prevent us from living out our true spirit as human beings.

- To have courage is to have the mental and moral strength to listen to our heart.

- In the natural world the bear shows us the spirit of courage.

- By nature it is gentle, but if you show any sign of approaching a bear cub it will display total fearlessness in defending her cub.

- The bear represents power, industriousness, instinctive healing, gentle strength, introspection, dreams and the heart-living spirit.

• The bear is very close to the land and brings many medicines to our people.

• When we have a hard time in our life, whether it be something we're going through or a decision we have to make and we are afraid, we can call on the spirit of the bear to help us have the courage and strength to do the right thing for our life.

• The bear is the part of the self that needs to retreat into its own space, hibernate and heal itself.

• It is comforting and protective and a common animal spirit for mothers.

Frances Densmore spent much of her life in the early 1900s with the Ojibwe tribes in Minnesota documenting language, culture, and use of resources. Concerning the Midewiwin (Grand Medicine Society) and the training of the Mide, or participants in the Midewiwin, Densmore recorded what her Indigenous friends and teachers told her. As to the important role of the bear in the Midewiwin she wrote: "Medicinal use of herbs has been handed down for many generations in the Midewiwin. It is said that members of the Midewiwin 'follow the bear path' in proceeding from a lower to a higher degree in the society and that some of the best Mide remedies were received from the bear. ... In this connection we note that the bear was highly esteemed by the Sioux medicine men." (*How Indians Use Wild Plants for Food, Medicine, & Crafts*, Frances Densmore.)

White cedar foliage is one of the four sacred plants to the Ojibwe and they used it for a variety of medicinal reasons. Whenever I walk in a cedar swamp, I always find large strips of bark pulled up and away from white cedars. All the sign indicates that this was done by bears. I believe that they do it after coming out of their winter slumber to get to the inner bark where the cedar sap and cambium medicines are. Another name for white cedar is arborvitae, which translates to "tree of life." The other part of the tree where medicines are found is in the scale-like foliage. It is in the evergreen foliage where oil is found that has antiseptic and also heart-stimulant properties that can be toxic if used in a pure state. Bears have the innate ability to recognize medicines by detection with their acute sense of smell.

Bears travel great distances for food sources. Though bears are thought of as carnivores, they are opportunists and will eat whatever is available. Early in spring after leaving their dens, bears will eat early greens, raid ant mounds, carrion, and stalk fawns in June. I have observed bears eating calcium-rich water plants, young grasses and clover, and I once watched a bear high in a black ash in mid-May eating the young blossoms of the ash's flowers. The bears in my area generally disappear in mid-July. The reason for this is because the soils around my home are clay based and do not favor the sandy acidic soils that blueberries do well in. About fifteen miles west of me is found such sandy soils where blueberries and jack pines thrive. When we make the drive to this region to pick blueberries on the public lands found there, it is not uncommon to bump into a bear doing the same thing. Once the blueberry crops have been exhausted, the bears disperse in search of the various species of wild cherries that are spread throughout and about to ripen. Five miles south of me is a state forest that has extensive stands of mature oaks. In the autumn, bears will travel great distances, especially from the north, to fatten up on the acorn crops found here. Bears, like other resident animals, are far better acquainted with their home range than contemporary humans. During the summers of 2005, 2006 and 2007, we were in a drought. We saw very few bears those three years. I was certain that our bears traveled to greener pastures.

Prior to sometime in the late 1960s or early 1970s, the black bear in Minnesota was classified as vermin and could be killed day or night year-round. By the mid-1960s I was an active deer hunter and seeing a bear was a rare occurrence. Bears are secretive animals in their habits, but the incidences of bear encounters in those early days were few and far between. As the bear population grew and the DNR established a designated hunt for bears from September first to mid-October, a culture of bear hunting developed in Minnesota.

Many of my hunting friends became bear hunters and, as I owned land in northern Minnesota, I was asked to permit bear hunting on my land. In 1997, I bought a bear license and went out once but my heart wasn't in it. A number of friends took turns hunting bears on or near my land. Historically, bears were an important source of food for Native people and white folks prior to the mid-twentieth century. The historical record of hunting bears is well established. Bears were hunted with dogs (dog hunting was never permitted in Minnesota) and also trapped, but the most common and almost exclusive method used today is baiting. Baiting was generally done by placing food which attracts bears, such as pastries, grains, molasses, syrup, etc., on the ground or in a shallow hole and covered with logs. The hunter would put his stand in a tree overlooking the bait.

Since I have become a year-round resident in the woods and have had so many different bears come into my yard, most of which were entirely peaceable in nature, and since we have gotten to know so many of these bear-people, I no longer participate in bear hunting nor do I permit bear hunting on my land. Many wildlife managers would accuse me of being a worst-case example of anthropomorphism, but I see animals differently than they. The bears that visit me are all of different temperament; each has his or her own personality.

Observing bears when in my yard, it's easy to recognize

their intelligence. It was during my time assisting bear hunting friends with baiting that I first became aware of the extraordinary intelligence of bears. When this baiting method caught on it was quite successful, especially when the natural food sources were minimal. Questions about fair chase and ethical hunting concerning baiting were discarded because most hunters felt that by just going out into the woods and having a bear come by randomly seemed too unlikely to happen. As bear hunting progressed, the commonly used baiting method became less effective. Bear guides and aficionados would recommend this or that kind of food to entice a bear to a bait site, but the growing problem for bear hunters was that bears who were regularly visiting baits and wiping out all the food put there were doing it at night, well after legal shooting hours ended. We experienced this too, and put timing devices on cover logs. When a bear came and removed a log, the timing device would stop, thus indicating the time the bear or bears came. As was the case with the majority of hunters, the bears would come to the baits around a half hour to forty-five minutes after shooting hours ended. This habit of bears waiting for the hunters to exit the bait stations became, more or less, standard procedure in the bear community. I believe most bear hunters would agree that female bears are passing these learned traits on to their young. Bears have learned to wait until the hunter climbed out of his tree stand, walked out and started his truck. Bears became so adept at this that some hunters would have another individual walk in with them, then the second individual would walk out, theoretically making the bear think the hunter had left, but as many hunters learned, bears could also count.

Baiting was widely condemned by anti-hunting groups as an unethical way of luring a bear in and then killing it, but the reality of baiting is that it is only minimally effective and getting less so every subsequent year. Another factor working against the bear-baiting hunter is the natural food crops.

I have had firsthand experience of how an active bait site can go dead by the appearance of a natural food source. Acorns are of great value to a wide array of wildlife: bears, deer, squirrels, jays, chipmunks, grouse, and many other species. The baiting season in Minnesota for bears starts in mid-August and the bear hunting season starts on September first.

The only two species of oaks that inhabit the forests in northern Minnesota are burr oaks and red oaks. The burr oaks drop acorns earlier than the acorns of the red oak group and the burr acorns are generally not as prolific as acorns of the red oak group. Where I live, in the Mississippi headwaters area of northern Minnesota, is approximately at the northern edge of the oak range. Oaks have trouble tolerating the cold temperatures this far north. The red oak acorns drop in early September, and when the red oaks have an average year to a bumper mast crop, bears will abandon bait sites that they have been using for the protein and fat-laden acorns. Bears know that there is more food value in acorns than there is in prime rib scraps and candied apples.

As popular and nutritious as acorns are to bears and other wildlife, the hazel shrub and its fat-filled nuts are another food sought out by bears in late summer and early autumn. The hazelnut, sometimes called a filbert, is over 50% fat content; the rest is protein and carbohydrate. Acorns and hazelnuts are of paramount importance to bears that have to put on lots of fat in order to get them through the long sleep ahead in the cold northern winter. Fruits like blueberries, raspberries, and juneberries ripen in July and August, but chokecherries and pin cherries are late summer and early fall, coinciding with the bear hunt, and finding bear scats on forest trails that are soft and of a purplish tint with scores of pits is common. Bear hunting is like deer hunting, grouse hunting, or any other hunting; if you want to be successful, know what's happening in the plant communities — the plants will tell you where to have a successful hunt. Plants are cyclical in nature. A good hunter will do the necessary scouting and observe what the plants, from a small herb to a one-hundred-year-old oak, are doing and who's having a good year and who is not. The forest talks but a good hunter only hears it by learning its language.

In today's hunting culture, the chief operative word is profit. With bear hunting and the baiting method, an opportunity was created for hunting guides. Guides understood that the baiting method took time, labor, and preparation for an average Joe from somewhere else who wanted to come up to northern Minnesota and kill a bear as a trophy and have its head mounted with angry, bloody fangs snarling on his wall, or have the hide made into a rug as a memento of the risk he put his life in. I know bear hunting guides who have hundreds of bait sites throughout the region, all or most on public lands where they then charge a handsome fee for some hunter to lease and hunt. Many of these guides have hired help to service the large number of bait sites, which are accessed by use of ATVs they ride roughshod over the land. The damage I have seen done by bear guides on ATVs is bad enough in itself to halt this practice. The principal problem is too many bait stations. The DNR is trying to limit the number of bait sites, but it gets back to just about every environmental issue we face, especially with hunters and fishermen, which is letting the genie out of the bottle. It's a lot easier to let the genie out than to get the genie back in the bottle, or, simply put, once you create an economic niche upon the land, it's extremely difficult to end it, no matter the ramifications on the land.

In 2015, the Minnesota DNR estimated that there were 20,000 black bears in Minnesota. That may be true, but in my empirical experience living in the woods, I would say 20,000 is on the low end of the estimate. If the 20,000 population estimate is accurate, one way of looking at it is that for every wolf in Minnesota there are twenty bears, or a 20:1 ratio of bears to wolves. But to use this estimated number for a hunt quota is misplaced, as bears, like wolves, do not need to be hunted to control their populations. Both these predators control their own numbers and there has never been a study which proved that populations of wolves or bears need to be managed by humans.

The hunting success rate for bear hunters in Minnesota has been in decline. Too many bear permits are issued causing a plethora of crowded bait sites, some so close I have had hunters tell me they can hear another bear hunter coughing from his stand. Although an occasional big bear is killed, it is generally younger bears taken. She-bears teach their cubs to only approach bait sites well after the darkness of night settles in and these teachings are passed on from one generation to the next.

Most of the bears killed are very young. One conservation officer I spoke with in the early 1990s told me the average size bear killed by hunters was eighty pounds. I recently read an article about a successful bear hunting guide in northern Minnesota who stated the average size bear killed through his services was 130 pounds. A 130-to-150-pound dressed weight bear is at best only three years old which makes that bear immature. Occasionally you will read of a four-hundred-pounder that will be killed during the hunting season, but bears killed that size are few and far between.

From my study of American Indian history and the fur trade history, if bears were seen, they generally were killed. The exception to this would be if the Ojibwe hunter was of the Bear Clan. Big game like deer were not nearly as prevalent two hundred years ago in northern Minnesota as they are today, so bear meat was taken when the opportunity came. Once in a while a bear would be seen swimming across a lake by a canoe brigade of fur traders and would be shot and cleaned for the meat, but most of the bear killings were from incidental meetings or involved dens. An interesting account of an incidental bear killing in a hibernation den is found in the story of John Tanner or Shaw-shaw-wa-ne-ba-se (The Falcon). Tanner was a white boy who was abducted by Shawnee Indians from his Kentucky home in May of 1789, and later adopted by a kind and loving Ojibwe woman. He lived for thirty years with his adopted Indian family before returning to white society. His story or narrative as it was dictated to Dr. Edwin James, *A Narrative of the Adventures of John Tanner During Thirty Years Residence Among the Indians of the Interior of North America, residing at Sault Ste. Marie*, has become one of the best depictions of what day-to-day, feast-or-famine, real life experiences of Native American life was like. Tanner became a great hunter and many of his hunting episodes would likely be offensive to people today, but the following story is told with great humanity and passion.

In Tanner's first bear kill the youthful hunter relates how it all came about in his adopted mother's, Netnokwa's, dream. The circumstances surrounding the dream and the family were that they were in starvation mode in winter. Netnokwa awoke Tanner, and her biological son, and informed them of a dream she had:

> "My son, last night I sung and prayed to the Great Spirit, and when I slept, there came to me one like a man, and said to me, 'Net-no-kwa, tomorrow you shall eat a bear. There is, at a distance from the path you are to travel tomorrow, and in such a direction, a small round meadow, with something like a path leading from it; and in that path there is a bear'"

Tanner later continued by recounting his events of the following day:

> "At length, I resolved to go in search of the place she had spoke of, and without mentioning to anyone my design, I loaded my gun for bear and set off on

the track. At length, I found what appeared at some former time to have been a pond. This I thought must be the meadow my Mother had dreamed of; and examining it around, I came to an open place in the bushes, where, it is probable a small brook ran from the meadow; but the snow was so deep that I could see nothing of it. My Mother had mentioned that when she saw the bear she had, at the time, seen smoke rising from the ground. I was confident this was the place she had indicated, and I watched long, expecting to see the smoke; but wearied at length with waiting, I walked a few paces into the open place, resembling a path, when I unexpectedly fell up to my middle into the snow. I extricated myself with difficulty, and walked on; but remembering that I had heard the Indians speak of killing bears in their holes, it occurred to me that it might be a bear's hole into which I had fallen, and looking down into to it, I saw the head of a bear lying close to the bottom of the hole. I placed the muzzle of the gun nearly between his eyes, and discharged it."

As cruel as this may sound today, Netnokwa's dream and Tanner killing the bear provided them with food during a time of want. Bear meat is not fat as many have remarked, it is lean. The surplus of bear fat is outside the meat. The meat is as good as any wild game I have eaten and it has a peculiar blue tint to it, and the fat has many uses.

The black bear is well equipped for living a solitary life. As a predator, besides having an impressive mouthful of teeth, he has large claws, impressive bursts of speed for short distances, and an acute sense of smell. Plus, the added advantage is that bears can climb trees. I have heard that large white pines serve as nursery trees for cubs, with sows sending cubs up the trees for their safety. After a long period of rain in June, I took a walk in the woods. On a game trail that crosses a wet swale, I came to an old-growth white pine with an immense crown that towered above all neighboring trees and was within a quarter mile of my cabin. On the carpet of pine needles below the tree, there were nine large piles of bear scat. During this rainy period, I was having bear visits every other night. I thought it somewhat peculiar that these visits would be this regular due to the rain. When coming upon these scats below the pine, I realized what was happening with this bear; he would go up into the densely foliated white pine and find a crotch of branches in which to relax, which also gave him protection from the steady rains. The bear learned that being among the thick limbs and foliage prevented him from getting into a good position to excrete, so he would climb down and take care of his business on the ground, and then climb back up into the shelter of the dense covering of pine needles.

I sense that I am one of the lucky ones to live with bears; they have taught me much and have given me hours of enjoyment. Observing these majestic creatures living free and in balance with the natural world has been a gift that I will always appreciate.

In sharing some of my thoughts with Larry Stillday by email, he remarked to me, "You are right, our relatives the animals do much better than we human beings who think we know more or better, our animal relatives simply live with the rhythm of the universe as compared to us that think we can dominate or control the natural laws."

The bear taught me one of his messages of living in rhythm with the universe on a beautiful May afternoon. I was on the phone talking to my friend Wade, who formerly had been a bear guide. He knows as much about bears and their habits and behavior as anyone I know. He gave up being a bear hunting guide perhaps fifteen years ago over doubt and guilt he had for being culpable for the death of so many bears for all the wrong reasons. I mention him in regards to the timing of what happened on that phone call and his former history with bears.

As we were talking, I was sitting by a window on the south side of my cabin and noticed two bears on the south end of my yard about forty yards from the cabin. I was perplexed at the sight of two good-sized bears being so casual together. Bears are solitary creatures and having two males together at this time of year would be rare. It was May 23 and this is the breeding season when males can get quite nasty to one another. I assumed that both bears, being rather large, were males. I told my friend that I would have to hang up and would call him back. I got my camera and watched the two bears circle round the east side of my opening in the woods to the north side of the cabin. The smaller one, who appeared three hundred pounds plus, came in on my bird feeder first and pulled it over and calmly lay down by it and started to eat the spilled sunflower seeds. Once it had toppled the feeder and lay down, the larger bear came in behind, and that's when I realized how big this bear was. He was the largest black bear I have ever seen. At this time of the year, bears are about as lightweight as they get, and this bear could easily have been 550 pounds. By September, this bear could be 150 pounds bigger, making him well over six hundred pounds. After he came in behind the smaller bear and took a drink out of my bird bath, then laid down and calmly watched the three-hundred-pounder finish the birdseed, the bigger bear got up and approached the smaller bear and put his massive arm under the smaller bear and lifted it up. That's when I realized what was going on. The three-hundred-pound bear was a female in estrus and the big bear was courting her.

Mister Big acted so courteous and nonaggressive during the first part of the episode that I became even more perplexed. He lifted her to all fours, and then he mounted her. After he completed this first round of business he dismounted her and grabbed her by the back of her neck with his teeth, though rather gently, and pivoted her around 180 degrees and tried to mount her again, but this time she sat on her hind end. All the while this was going on, I was standing on a small deck just outside my north door filming it. At first I was taking still photos, but as soon as I realized this was two bears in the act of making more bears, I switched the camera to video. He did a lot of sniffing and body contact with her, and then they both left the yard together by the same way they came into it.

It took me some time before I realized how privileged I was to be an observer of this act. I continue to ask myself why. Why did these two bears feel so comfortable mating while I stood there, filmed, and watched? They had thousands of wild lands where they could do this in complete seclusion. It would be indeed a rare occurrence for bears this size to come into my yard, and even more rare for this to happen during full daylight. Was there some kind of bear karma in my yard, or did they just happen to rendezvous here? Maybe the reasons were as simple as what Larry told me: "When people are balanced and in harmony with our Earth Mother, the animals know that. What the old people used to say is the animals are talking to us, sometimes they use sound, but most of the time they use their behavior, and it's therefore up to us to be able to read what they are acting out."

I have had dozens of different bear visitors at my home, from females with cubs, to 120-pound youngsters in their first year away from Mama, to a four-hundred-pound male with an attitude we have named Scarface, to brown and cinnamon colored bears, to Mister Big who is so big and dominant that he can afford to be gentle. They have become neighbors with personalities I am closely acquainted with. I could no more kill one of these bears than I could my dog. As Larry taught of the bear in the Teachings of the Seven Grandfathers: there is more to the teaching of courage than to protect the young, though this is one of them, but also "to have courage is to have the mental and moral strength to listen to our heart." The bear has taught me of the many ways I can use courage to live the right way, in harmony and balance within the universe.

As I penned this essay on my experiences with *Makwa*, it was early January, in the midst of winter, and the bears were asleep in their dens. Winter has become for me the time of year for sleeping in the long nights, taking walks in the cold silence, reflecting on myself and loved ones, and getting my mind right. It is the bear within me, or as Larry said, "The bear is the part of yourself that needs to retreat into its own space, hibernate and heal."

Economy

Gigaagiigidotamaagom, maada'ooyok gaa-miinigooyeg — You are speakers for us now, share what you have learned.

— Chi Ma'iingan

In my life thus far of sixty-seven years, I was born into a low-income family in rural South Dakota, and while still young, I moved to a big city and was a poor student, a troublemaker, and barely got out of high school. I met my wife-to-be in 1973 while living and working in northern Minnesota, and we were married in 1976. I had jobs ranging from factory worker to logger, from mid-level management of a trading business to a small business owner along with my wife. Much of my past is something I would not brag about as I sowed more than my share of wild oats, but by the time I was in my late twenties, and after getting over some bumpy roads, I settled down to an existence of being part of the groupthink of American institutions of getting-and-spending and doing my best to be a conformist.

In the late 1960s, I went to a two-year college and studied history and was fortunate to have had a teacher who encouraged me to think broadly in interpreting history, plus I was exposed to a more liberal version of history that one seldom receives in high school, which enabled me to think for myself and outside of society's box. But by 1970 I, as the country, was in a troubled time, and I dropped out of school. I appeared to be the prodigal son who couldn't find his way back home.

By early 1974 I was getting my personal behavior in order, living in the big city and working for a large commodity trading business: the Minneapolis Grain Exchange. My job as Chief Weighmaster was to oversee a staff of thirty to forty men who were stationed throughout the many grain elevators in the Minneapolis-St. Paul area. We acted as a third party to ensure that all grain sales, which were based on weight, were legitimate and correct. We were, in a way, the grain cops. I was head of a department that often dealt with mid-level management people from big grain firms. My experiences with them began to give me second thoughts about the ethics and justness of our economic system. Often my job required that I serve as a punching bag for these corporate managers. I would have to listen to their rants about how they are businessmen and they didn't need the weight oversight we provided, nor did they want the costs our service incurred. I began to have serious concerns about the business environment I was working in. These so-called businessmen were, to me, nothing but corporate bureaucrats with no monetary investments of their own other than a driving force of ambition, power, and greed. Soon, my dissatisfaction with our economic institution began to permeate into all our institutions.

Always having a deep and abiding love for nature and wild places, and wanting to return to the north land, we waited until our two children graduated from high school, and then my wife and I bought a small motel in northern Minnesota as a way to escape from the crowds, sprawl and business world of the big city. I thought that a life as a small businessman in a rural setting would give me a relative degree of freedom from the corporate entanglements.

What we found at the motel was another dimension of commerce that was, in its way, as cruel and dehumanizing as what we had left. The only redeeming factor was that we lived in the country where in a five-minute drive I could escape the helter-skelter world of getting-and-spending and find solace in the woods.

What we found at the motel was that our loan from a local bank had become in a sense our parole papers. The bank and the Small Business Administration became parole officers and infiltrated our lives in a multitude of ways, including personal manners. I began to feel like Thoreau's townsmen when Thoreau said, "I see young men, my townsmen, whose misfortune it is to have inherited farms, houses, barns, cattle, and farming tools; for these are more easily acquired than got rid of."

After operating the motel for ten years, the banks had decided they didn't want anything more to do with us. The small-town bank that mortgaged us would not refinance us when we wanted to remodel our rooms, and when we decided to sell, none of the banks would consider loaning money to a prospective buyer no matter how much money they had to put down because, as the banks informed us, the region isn't a tourist community anymore but is now a retirement community, and they were not interested in small businesses like motels or restaurants. They left us with only one option, a contract for deed, which we did twice before finally freeing ourselves of ownership. Up to this point we lived the life of consumers, with mortgages, credit card debt, and with our lives literally owned by banks. Now that we had rid ourselves of the debt and burden of home and business, car debt, and credit card debt, we could start to look forward to a life free from the worst aspects of the American economic system. Living in poverty without debt is more attractive to me than living under the burdensome life of bearing the weight of too many material possessions and too much debt; at least I could feel a sense of independence and freedom.

Thoreau said 150 years ago, "In short, I am convinced, both by faith and experience, that to maintain one's self on this earth is not a hardship but a pastime."

I was becoming tired of the accepted ways of society and wanted to sever as many ties as I could, knowing full well that I would never be able to sever them all, but I felt I could sever enough to live on the outside while still being able to look in. I remember reading in one of Sigurd Olson's books about men who couldn't live within society, but he did not refer to them as hermits but rather as "perimeter men." I did not want to be a hermit, and for sure my wife didn't, but I felt I could get as close to that definition of a "perimeter man" as possible while my wife could retain all the necessary outside contacts she wanted with family, friends, and society. I didn't want to be a recluse but rather a well-connected recluse. People say that everything has a purpose. Maybe it does, or maybe it doesn't, but I have always had an affinity for nature and have always wanted to live as close to it as possible in every respect.

In the spring of 2004, we got rid of the motel and moved to our sixteen-by-twenty-four-foot garage kit that we call our "cabin," which I built in 1987 for five thousand dollars. At that time, we were not at the end of the road but beyond the end of the road. When I say road, I mean something you can access without a four-wheel-drive truck. Though I have had this land since 1970, the only amenity that I put in was a well with a hand pump. There was no electricity, no phone line. The sixteen-by-twenty-four-foot building had two eight-foot sliding glass doors, one on the north side and one on the south side. The cabin has three small insulated glass windows and a single outside door. When it was built, I put in a cinderblock chimney with tile inserts for a wood stove. The walls have two inch insulation and the ceiling has four inch insulation. The walls have wood paneling and the floor is a floating cement slab. I have an outhouse and a small steel shed.

One of the tasks we had before moving from the motel was to get rid of as many possessions as possible. After we finished the move and had everything we owned on site, we were finally able to relax. I often thought about all the furniture and appliances we formerly had. I wondered about what I had done and how long I would be able to live like this, with few material possessions, in relative poverty, with little or no income, and in a home so small that we have had kitchens in the past that were bigger than our present entire living quarters, but as time went by, I began to feel a sense of liberation. Liberated from having too much. I have friends that have pole barns in which you could put three or four buildings our size under the same roof. Thoreau on Walden Pond and the single dwelling he built was ten feet by fifteen feet with a garret, closet, a large window on each side, two trap doors, one door at the end, and a brick fireplace. The cost for Thoreau to put up his building in 1845 was $28.12. The cost for me in 2004 was a little over five thousand dollars. Thoreau did his stint on Walden from July 4, 1845 to September 6, 1847. His time span living there alone was two years, two months, and two days and was meant to be an experiment. We moved in on June 4, 2004, and it will be twelve years this summer and counting. Our intentions are that our time here is not an experiment; it is a way of life. Thoreau had a smaller living capacity by 134 square feet, but he didn't have a wife, two dogs, and a cat.

Although the way of life we have chosen is of our choosing, there is also an economic bearing to it. When we sold the motel, we got it back with a horrendous amount of damage and had to borrow money to make the necessary fixes which took a big bite out of what we thought would be a margin of profit on the sale, so when we got here we only had a small amount of money. Long before we got here, I had cut and peeled numerous large red pine logs that I had taken off this property, and with the money we had, I had a basement put in, raised the log walls and put a roof on it. I covered the window and door openings with plastic and used it as a storage place as the money ran out before finishing it. For the first few years here we were living on a very small pittance, odd jobs, some speaking engagements, and a small amount in an IRA. When we turned sixty-five, we both started to collect social security to a total sum between us of slightly over $1,700 a month. Since then, the small IRA has been exhausted.

Our essential living costs are for things we cannot sever and must have in order to function in the limited scope we do amidst society: property taxes, small insurance coverage on our building and possessions, auto insurance as we own a small gas-efficient car and an old four-wheel-drive truck, and a monthly phone/internet bill from a local co-op that ran in fiber optic cable over a half mile for only fifty dollars. Other than what I have already mentioned, the land we live on and surrounding resources provide us with food, heat, and shelter. I often tell people that if I did not own this land, we would be living in a cardboard box under a bridge somewhere. And it needs to be emphasized that we wouldn't be able to do any of this if we did not have our health. Taking care of your body and overall physical health is of vital importance in pursuing this way of life.

Our Heating

One of the items we invested money in when first settling in our home in the woods was to get rid of our barrel stove and purchase a solid, cast iron, efficient wood burner with clean-burn technology. Though we had to fork out over one thousand dollars for this stove, it was well worth it. The stove burns wood with incredible efficiency which means I do not have to cut as much wood as I would with a more inefficient stove. This stove technology also emits a much lower amount of greenhouse gases and pollutants. In the early 1970s I worked in the woods for a year for a local logger and log home builder, and I became proficient with a chainsaw and I now cut all my wood. I have a stand of mature hardwoods and am able to access it with my small Toyota 4x4 truck which enables me to haul the wood back. I do all my own splitting with a splitting maul. Aside from the gas and chain oil, there is little overhead in my wood-collecting procedures so in essence we have no heating bill. I try to stay a year ahead with my wood piles, and when they are stacked and covered, I draw great satisfaction to stand beside them and look upon the results. I call this stacked and drying wood pile my version of pre-buy.

Our Food

Prior to living here fulltime, we had a small garden, but upon settling in, we improved and enlarged the garden to approximately 150 feet by 75 feet. Within this garden area, not all the ground is in production. There are three solar arrays for our electricity and an area about fifteen feet by twenty feet that is solely used for wild flowers that are pollinator attractors. Through trial and error and advice from others, we have learned to grow vegetables that are hardy for this northern climate, and provide the best results for our labor and time.

We have two large asparagus patches in which we relish the harvest. We have two large raspberry patches, one Boyne's and the other Latham's, both of which do well in the north and take little maintenance. We grow lots of potatoes: reds, whites, and golds and sometimes some fingerlings. Our yield of potatoes is normally between two hundred pounds to five hundred pounds annually. We give a lot of them away but keep enough to provide us with taters until the next harvest, and also some seed potatoes for replanting. We have a fenced in area seven feet in height and about twenty feet by forty feet dimensionally in which we plant a wide assortment of lettuce, cabbage, carrots, Brussels sprouts, peppers, peas, and other green leafy plants that deer and rabbits would like to get at. We also plant heirloom tomatoes but normally do not can or preserve them. What we get from the tomatoes is highly variable from year to year. Mid-August is the earliest we have gotten ripe tomatoes and often we have killing frosts in early September.

Gardening is a challenge here in the north land. In 2005, we had a killing frost on June 19 and again on August 19 of the same season. The year 2005 was a sixty-day growing season for our warm crops. Thankfully we had a lot of cold crop veggies.

As much as our garden provides for us, we do as good or better foraging off the land. In March or April, I put out as many as sixty-five taps in my sugar maples. Some years we have made as much as fifteen gallons of maple syrup. We not only use this sugar for topping on pancakes or ice cream but also use it as a sugar substitute. My wife makes a maple syrup pie that will knock your socks off. The wood that fuels my evaporator, in which I boil off the water from the sugar, is obtained from my land. It is the tops from the dead oaks that I cut as firewood.

By May and before my garden is producing greens, I get an intense craving for greens after the long winter without. This is when I grab a bag, leather gloves, and set out into the woods to pick the first stinging nettles, wild lettuce, cleavers, dandelions, violets, and other edible greens. I may eat these five days out of every seven as an essential part of my diet and continue to do so until my garden is providing more greens than I can handle. The feeling of invigoration and health from these wild greens is an immense satisfaction.

By September, my ricing partner and I load up our canoe, push pole, ricing sticks, bags, and head out to one of many ricing beds where we collect wild rice every year. During an average season we can knock down over five hundred pounds of rice in four to five days. After processing this rice, we each end up with over one hundred pounds of edible rice. This is more than enough rice for my wife and I as we eat it anywhere from two to four times a week. Wild rice, or *manoomin*, is extremely nutritious and full of beneficial trace elements.

When mid-September arrives, this means the start of the hunting season. I bow hunt until November when I switch to rifle hunting. Between what I may get with my old stick bow, and what I get during the rifle season, we are provided with good, lean deer meat. We do not feel that we need a lot of meat and eat less now than we formerly did. About a half pound of venison in a stir fry of garden onions, green peppers, and cranberries over a bowl full of wild rice is as good a meal as any man could ask for, and knowing that it was grown, harvested, or shot by your own hands adds another level of appreciation. Another source of meat is ruffed grouse. I do not hunt them as hard as I used to, but if I can bag about six to eight a season I am happy as they are the best tasting fowl I have eaten.

Our Water

In 1987 I started to drive a well by hand. I had forty feet of 1¼-inch well pipe, a sand point, couplings, pipe wrench, and a sixteen-pound sledge hammer. I had driven the forty feet of pipe down and had not yet hit water. I realized it was futile to continue, for if I kept going and hit water, the water would have to rise in the well pipe to within twenty feet from the surface. If the water wouldn't rise that high, a hand pump and priming would not be able to raise it to the top. Under ideal conditions, water has to be within twenty-five feet of the surface in order to pull it up with an old-fashioned hand pump, so being able to get the water up as high as I would need it to rise did not look good. I hired a local well driller and he pulled my forty feet of 1¼-inch pipe out and drilled further until he hit a good water vein at sixty-five feet with a two-inch pipe and stainless-steel sand point. The water rose to within thirty feet of the surface, and he then dropped the 1¼-inch pipe with an attached cylinder inside the two-inch pipe. This allowed me to pump water year-round without priming the pump. The principal action for getting water to the surface was all in the cylinder, which fit snuggly within the two-inch pipe and actually lifted water as I raised and lowered the pump handle.

Every morning of every day, I pump water. I tell people that I do not pump iron, I pump water, and I do lots of it. I do not mind it as it reminds me how valuable water is to life. Several years ago my cylinder cracked, which resulted in not being able to get water out of my well. This was in the winter and the morning lows were in the negative thirties, and my local well man could not do anything until it warmed up due to the extreme cold not allowing his hydraulics to operate. So I had to go over a week without water. We had to drive to neighbors that were over a mile away and fill our five-gallon jugs with water. During this period I had written Larry Stillday about our water situation, and he wrote back: "Hey, it's good hearing you got your pump working, of course as you know that is one of the elements that we depend on, we need the water it does not need us, just like our Mother the Earth, she doesn't belong to us, we belong to her and to her we go back. We live in an interconnected and interdependent world, how sadly we forget that, or even more sadly is how we can think we can change that perfect system the Creator put in place, which by the way is very simplistic. He made everything so simple, until he created the human being, and that's the reason things start to go out of balance and how man puts the blame on our relatives the animals to justify his mistakes."

Our Electricity

Long before I became a permanent resident of the woods, I envisioned myself as someday living with sun-generated electricity. Selling our small business didn't make any big profit for us so it became questionable whether we would be able to afford the installation of a solar power system, and I was totally ignorant about solar electricity. I contacted the local electric cooperative and they came out, measured the distance from the nearest electric grid to my building, and gave me an estimate of four thousand dollars to run grid electricity to a post near my cabin. This estimate was based on the fact that they would go the first thousand feet free, and then charge so much a foot after that. This was in 2004, and since then they have eliminated or reduced the free distance and raised the cost per foot.

At this time, most electric co-ops were rather disdainful of people like me. I had a friend who was on the grid and had installed a number of solar panels which required he sign a contract with the local electric co-op to have his panels wired to the electric meter in order that he could take advantage of any subsidies that were available. When he was making solar electricity, the meter would be reversed as his electricity would be going into the grid. When a co-op representative came out to inspect and do the formalities, he was somewhat contemptuous to my friend, treating him as he was some kind of nutcase for taking the renewable path. When the electric co-op came to estimate the costs for me to be connected to the grid, and I realized they had a poor attitude towards people like me, I reassessed the notion of being connected to the grid at all, and tilted my thinking more favorably to being independent from power companies and to have the sun as my sole provider.

I contacted a renewable nonprofit in the area and they were able to obtain for me the solar panels and components I would need to have a stand-alone solar power system, or in other words, an electric system independent from the grid. The solar panels were discontinued models made by British Petroleum and available for one hundred dollars, which indicated to me that BP knows full well the future of solar. The panels were small by today's standards, only a maximum of 45 watts, and I bought twelve of them. Much of the labor I would provide myself. I built the solar arrays out of two-by-eight-foot jack pine boards that I had cut here in my yard from my own trees. I made two arrays, each with six panels attached to them. The nonprofit was also able to get me the necessary components needed for a stand-alone solar power system such as a charge controller, which regulated the flow of electricity from the panels to the house and batteries. They also were able to get me a battery meter and an inverter which converted the DC current from the batteries to AC current. I learned that you lose approximately 15% electricity in the inverter process, but to use DC current means one has to buy DC appliances and electric fixtures and the greater costs of DC household products outweighed the costs of buying an inverter and using AC lights and appliances. Then there were eight, 6-volt deep-cycle batteries that I bought and two utility boxes which would contain four batteries each. My battery storage system was wired so I would have two 24-volt lines, or a 48-volt system of battery storage.

The cost of all this including the twelve solar panels, wiring, PVC conduit, circuit breakers and box, lightning rods, charge controller, battery meter, inverter, eight batteries, and two utility boxes, plus all nuts, bolts, and various hardware, was seven thousand dollars. This would be a three-thousand-dollar difference between the co-op and my solar system. And the co-op would only bring electricity to a post seventy-five feet from my cabin; I'd have to wire the electricity to my cabin. Plus, there'd be the additional monthly fee if I used the co-op service. At my seven thousand dollars, the solar power system is complete from sun to cabin and will incur no regular monthly service charges.

I also had to buy a generator and charger large enough to generate 20 to 30 amps of electricity during extended cloudy periods. The generator cost over six hundred dollars and the charger was two hundred dollars. Initially, there were some wrinkles I had to smooth out in a live-and-learn process. We originally bought a small nine-cubic-foot electric fridge, but soon realized that the compressor on the fridge sucked too much electricity in the short days and cloudy periods in November and December. We ended this problem by buying a good, used propane fridge from a friend who lives a similar lifestyle. Since the initial installment, we have added six more solar panels that are identical in manufacturer and size to the original twelve.

We have converted all our lighting to LEDs and our TV and laptop computer are also LED lighting. We have five light fixtures, a 21-inch TV, a radio/CD/tape player, a vacuum, and many other minor electric-appliances. Our fridge and stove/oven are propane. We have a 105-gallon propane tank which we need to fill twice a year.

It is important to note the efficiency of solar electricity in such a northerly location as Minnesota. Most people still subscribe to the belief that solar works okay for places like southern California, New Mexico, Arizona, or Nevada, but not in the cold north. This is completely erroneous, as the nature of solar panels and what they are made of (silicon) works more efficiently in cold. The colder it is the more electricity solar panels produce. Yes, in northern Minnesota, we can get some long durations of cloudy periods in November and December, but when we are in the bone-freezing cold of winter, the sun is shining, which is primarily the case from mid-December through the remainder of winter. I can produce, on average, 150 watts more of continual flow in winter than I can on a comparably sunny day in any summer month. Cold sunny days outside produce warm sunny days when it comes to solar-generated electricity.

Living with an electrical system where the sun is the provider means learning to live rhythmically with the sun. During long periods of overcast, I wait for the sun to shine before using the vacuum or other electrical appliances that require high voltage. Living rhythmically with the sun fits in nicely with a lifestyle that desires to be in harmony with the natural world.

Our Outhouse

When we became year-round residents I recognized that our seasonal outhouse would not be sufficient for our 365-days-a-year usage, so I dug a seven-foot-deep hole of four-feet by four-feet length and width. I made the outhouse quite roomy—room enough for a two-holer. I learned that it was best to not add any decomposers that were marketed to speed decay. The best thing is not to put anything down the hole other than feces and toilet paper. The natural bacteria in the soil will do a sufficient job of decomposing, and any marketed decomposers will only hamper nature's own recycling.

The worst time of year for the outhouse is the winter and not summer. In the winter everything freezes and can get rank. In the summer, the decomposition works so well that there is normally no odor. There are pluses and minuses to using an outside toilet, especially in a region where the air temperature in winter gets down into the negative thirties and forties. When it is that cold, you do not take the time to read the newspaper. And year-round, you will have visitors, mostly deer mice and red squirrels. The pluses: you don't have to clean toilets, nor work on plumbing, and when you are done with your chores, there is no stink in the house— you leave it behind you.

There are a great many books in circulation about living in the woods on a dollar a day, or about this person's or that person's struggle for existence with the elements, but that is not the reason I moved to the woods. I came here to experience the real world first hand and to learn what it had to teach. What I have done is definitely not for everyone. Here I am aware of the beauty and importance of the diversity of life in a healthy ecosystem, and the interconnected and interdependent nature of all life, and how those interconnections of life are what supports and maintains human beings, clean air, clean water, and the land from which we extract a living.

It is an urban society in which modern nations find themselves, and my message of living with the land is mostly meant for urbanites as they form the greatest majority. It is not that people living in cities are less connected to the land than country folk, as I know many people who have been born, raised, and spent their entire lifetimes in rural America, and who only see the world in which they live as an adversary. So many people who have their origins in rural America and never left those locations have not had the chance to appreciate their surroundings. The majority of advocates for wild America are coming from the cities, and that is where they should come from as people in cities are in most need to be reconnected to nature. Urban people who are able to experience natural settings, state parks, and wildlife refuges, etc., become the people who best advocate for them as they realize the need for these wild lands to charge their batteries, batteries that are drained from too much sprawl, concrete, and concentrations of humanity.

I remember when I was an urban person and my need to get away from it all. On many a Sunday afternoon, I would drive to the University of Minnesota and visit the Bell Museum and walk the halls of their wildlife exhibits and sit and gaze into their dioramas. These dioramas were paintings of actual scenes in Minnesota by the famed and beloved Minnesota nature artist, Francis Lee Jaques. I recall scenes on the North Shore of Split Rock Lighthouse, with wolves in the foreground, a bull moose on Gunflint Lake, or a beaver lodge on Nicollet Creek in Itasca State Park. I would sit for hours by these scenes and enjoy the artistry and taxidermy. I believe that just being there and pondering the images of real places soothed my soul and my need to be physically in nature. I also know how much I appreciated the nature centers in the metro area such as the large wetlands of Wood Lake Nature Center in Richfield. I would often visit this place where I could see wood ducks, geese, muskrats and other wildlife that helped recharge my battery. Whether it was the T.S. Roberts Bird Sanctuary between Lake Calhoun and Lake Harriet, or being down along the Minnesota River in Bloomington, both places allowed me to be among wild things and temporarily forget I was in the city.

My journey started simply enough with a love for nature, but evolved with the input of people like Henry David Thoreau, Aldo Leopold, and Chi Ma'iingan into an awakening and understanding of the relatedness and interconnectedness of all life on earth. This is what I am and what defines me.

I have friends and family who feel sorry for my condition, living in what they would define as poverty and with few assets and not much of an economical future, but it is I that feel sorry for them, for they have not seen or experienced the wonders and miracles of the natural world. And there have been many who have told me, "You missed your calling." I smile when I hear this, but in my heart I know I have not missed my calling, I heard it loud and clear.

For the last twenty-five years of my life I have been what was often called an "activist." While actively trying to save some special place on earth, or a particular animal or plant, or promoting a way of thinking about earth in order that people would be more respectful, many times I have questioned the efficacy of what I do. I had talked about this subject with my friend Chi Ma'iingan and he told me, "Hey you know what? There will be those that will care, quite often we don't see those we have made an impact on as we walk our own walk, there are people out there that notice and want very much to be able to walk the path we walk, yes even those that imprison themselves with all the material things, they most of all are the ones that envy those of us that walk the simple path." Larry would often tell me to, "Just keep walking, if you missed it the first time, you'll come to it again as life is a circle. And what we must always do is practice honesty in its best essence of meaning."

In the Teachings of the Seven Grandfathers as Larry taught me, the Grandfather of Honesty is *Masaba* (Wilderness Man, Bigfoot):

- The *Masaba* represents the essence of honesty and innocence.

- Honesty means being an honorable person free from fraud or deceptions.

• Honesty means to refuse to lie, steal, or deceive in any way.

• The Elders say the highest honor that could be bestowed upon anyone is the saying: "There walks an honest person; he can be trusted."

• Honesty to the Elders means being true to yourself.

• Never try to be someone else: live true to your spirit, be honest to yourself, accept who you are and the way the Great Spirit made you.

Bird Relatives

*For the animal shall not be measured by man. In a world older
and more complete than ours they moved finished and complete,
gifted with extensions of the senses we have lost or never attained,
living by voices we shall never hear.*

— Henry Beston

There is no group of animals that occupies more niches in
my world than birds. Only insects could be argued to have a
wider range of existence. Birds occupy habitats from below
the water surface up to the clouds. They occupy every level
of the forest between the soil to the tops of old-growth trees.
They nest in the ground, on water and every level on and
inside trees: kingfishers and bank swallows in soils, loons
and swans on water, and innumerous birds in vegetation

at every level in the forest. They vocalize for a wide array of purposes: territory, attracting a mate, and recognition. They excel in sight, hearing, and smell and they have the gift of flight. Birds are truly miraculous. They inspire us, add song to nature, dazzle us with myriads of color, and raise our spirits. Life without birds would be intolerable. A world without birds would hardly be worth living in. Here are only a few of the birds in my world.

Ravens

You know, raven don't hunt anything for himself. He gets his food the lazy way, just watches for whatever he can find already dead. Like in the old story, he always fools everybody so he gets by easy.

—Richard Nelson

When my wife and I moved into our humble abode for year-round residency, we noticed a group of eight or more ravens were hanging around and flying low over our small opening in the woods. Normally I would associate this amount of ravens in close proximity to having wolves nearby, but these ravens seemed entirely focused on us. They would land in pines, fly low, and were more vocal than even this talkative bird normally is. This lasted for a week or more before they went on their own way. I can only assume that they were interested in the new squatters in their territory—us.

Ravens, or *gaagaagiwag*, are highly intelligent birds. In fact, I would have to rank them in intelligence with bears and wolves. Often, when walking in the woods, and I see or hear a raven, I will simulate a raven call and the raven will respond. Almost always they will deviate from their direction of flight to circle back and fly low over me which allows me to start a conversation in which ravens will almost always interact with me. They have a wide vocabulary ranging from guttural croaks to an abrupt loud "gaak." In the autumn, groups of mostly juveniles will do acrobatic flying maneuvers. These aerial acrobatics are yearling ravens establishing their dominance in raven society.

I often tell people that I know when wolves are in close proximity, such as within a one-mile radius, when I first step outside in the morning. If there is a higher than normal number of ravens to be seen or heard, I know the wolves are in the area. Ravens follow wolves, not in such a close sense that they are directly overhead but in the general area as they benefit from wolf kills. In the winter or early spring when there is snow on the ground and I come upon a recent wolf-killed deer, the first thing that grabs my attention is all the raven tracks in the snow. Once wolves have pulled down a deer and have begun to feed, the ravens will almost immediately join in. Wolves seem to tolerate the raven's perpetual presence and may benefit from the raven's presence as a type of alarm warning them by announcing when man may be approaching. The only wolf kills where I have not seen a preponderance of raven tracks and scats are those that are so fresh, the ravens have yet to drop in. The snow around wolf kills tells who also partook in the feast, and that may be eagles, foxes, weasels, and even shrews, but the raven is the main dinner partner for the wolf. There are many different and unusual relationships and partnerships in the wild, and the raven-wolf relationship is inseparable. They are a bird and a mammal, perhaps two of the most intelligent and powerful spirits in the woods, living together in a rather symbiotic mutualistic relationship. It is difficult for me to think of one without the other.

About once every three years a pair of ravens nest in a one-hundred-foot-high red pine within sight of my cabin. The nest is a conglomeration of sticks and branches about three to six feet below the top, but when standing underneath the tree it cannot be seen through the dense foliage of pine needles. When they do nest in my vicinity, it is always in the same tree and using the same old nest with some necessary improvements being made. I know by February if they are going to nest near my cabin as I will regularly see the ravens carrying sticks. When the eggs hatch in late spring or early summer, it becomes a noisy place, and as the nestlings mature the level of noise increases. On a warm evening in late June when all windows are open, I am often awakened at one or two in the morning by the squawking of young ravens.

Before I learned that the peat bog bordering the north and south ends of my small lake had cranberries, I would hear and see ravens on the bog, especially in late autumn or early winter. This aroused my curiosity as to why the ravens were landing on my bog. I wondered if there was a wolf kill out there or some other carrion. I went out to see for myself and discovered a plethora of ripe, bright-red cranberries lying on the green sphagnum. Ravens can be moody. Early one spring, well before breeding, I was on the bog and noticed a raven get up out of the moss and leatherleafs and fly low towards me. He kept coming and I assumed he was playing games with me and would veer off at the last minute. He didn't, but rather came and pecked me directly on the head. If I didn't have the cap on, he may have taken a piece of my hair or even scalp. He came back and I kept waving my hands and got off the bog.

Snowshoeing back to my cabin one cold and bright winter afternoon, a large raven was perched in the tip of a balsam, and as I approached I gaaked at him, and he flew off down the trail in the direction of my travel and landed, again, high in a balsam. I gaaked at him again and he responded in kind, and we continued this walking-talking conversation all the way back to my cabin. It is such an experience as this that supports Larry Stillday's opinion that the animals of the woods can and do talk to us, we just have to pay attention to the calls, body language, and other behaviors they use.

Many Native American cultures hold the raven in high esteem. The Koyukon tribes of northern Alaska recognize the raven, or as they call him *T'seek'aal,* as their creator. Most Native cultures have a trickster figure who is a powerful spirit and creator. In Ojibwe culture this trickster is *Nanaboozhoo* and is at the vortex of many creation stories. In Koyukon culture, their *Nanboozhoo* is *T'seek'aal* or the raven, and as such he holds a most important position in their beliefs.

To all Native American cultures, they see a select few animals holding positions of powerful spiritual influence. In almost all of them, the bear, wolf, eagle, and large members of the weasel family such as fishers and martens, to name some, are held in special regard. Living with ravens as everyday neighbors who I see and hear, it is no wonder to me that they, too, are intelligent and powerful spirits.

Owls

Tyger! Tyger! burning bright

In the forests of the night

—W. Blake

When I read William Blake's poem, I do not think of the big cat, but I do think of what in North America is sometimes referred to as the "winged tiger" or "tiger of the air," the great horned owl. This owl may be the most powerful and fiercest raptor in North America. I have read of this owl stealing food from bald eagles and even driving them from their nest. Although this large owl only weighs about three pounds, it is known to have carried off eight-pound skunks and adult house cats. Some museums have stuffed great horned owls several generations old that still retain a faint skunky odor. Though this bird has radar-sensitive ears, its sense of smell is extremely poor. There are numerous reports of humans who have been attacked by this bird when getting too close to its nest. Some bird books have called this owl the "fish owl," due to its habit of snaring fish in shallow streams with its powerful talons.

An important physical trait of all owls is that their primary wing feathers have a saw-toothed fluting on the edges which allows them to fly with complete silence which, coupled with their powerful and deadly talons, makes their silent attack even more deadly.

On a March night many years ago, I heard some strange and unidentified cackles and screechy noises coming from near my cabin. The next morning I investigated as to what could be the source of these mysterious sounds. Within seventy yards of my cabin I found two fluffy immature great horned owls in a dead jack pine. Upon discovering the young birds I then found the large nest of sticks and branches in the crotch of another jack pine. The immature birds were still in juvenile plumage but were actively walking about on the limbs of the jack pines. I was not residing at the cabin fulltime, only a temporary visitor, and the next time I was at the cabin, the owls were gone. Since then I have not had a great horned owl nest on my land. I have read studies that indicate this notorious owl has been in decline. This troubles me, as of all the owls, the great horned has reached the pinnacle of success in the owl world. This owl's size and strength, with its radar hearing, sharp night vision, silent flight, and large piercing talons, make it a high achievement in evolution.

On a recent evening drive with my wife in our old truck on returning home from a visit with a friend, and as we were coming down a remote forest road, we saw a large winged creature fly out from the woods and turn and glide low over the dirt road and then bank its wings and soar up and land in a large overhanging branch. It was at dusk, but slowing down to a stop by the overhanging limb I could see it was a great horned owl by its eared feather tuffs, and it had some large black and white prey in its talons, either a magpie, hairy woodpecker, or pileated woodpecker. When stopping and looking at the perched owl, he stared back at me with his large yellow eyes in a most contemptuous and defiant glare as though to let me know that he was the tiger of the night equipped with the "fearful symmetry" to make him burn brightly in the forests of the night. His look indicated to me that he was not worried by my presence and that I had nowhere near the faculties of survival that would put me in a position to judge him or even further consider his fearful symmetry.

The great horned owl may be in decline, but the most commonly seen and heard owl of the northern forests is the barred owl, and which is presumably the owl who many people refer to as the "hoot owl." The Ojibwe name for owl is *gookooko'oo* and the white man's hooting rendition for this owl is "who cooks for you—who cooks for you all." This owl with the booming voice is perhaps the most vocal of all owls that inhabit the Northwoods. Besides its common "who cooks for you" call, it has a wide repertoire of wails, screams, screeches, cackles and hoots. When people hear the mysterious wailing or cries of the banshee or other unknown entity, it is in high probability they are hearing the barred owl.

Besides being a talkative owl, the barred owl is also abnormally inquisitive. Based on my experience with this owl, it is easy to call one in with a simple imitation of their hooting. Whether we have been in the wilderness regions of the Boundary Waters Canoe Area, Quetico Provincial Park of

Ontario, Woodland Caribou Provincial Park of Ontario, or in our backyard, this owl remains the same in characteristics and habits which include readily responding to imitations of its hooting. There have been many occasions at our cabin, or in wilderness areas, around a campfire, that my wife and I have had up to four different barred owls respond to our hooting by flying into trees above us, with our campfire light reflecting off their front sides, while the wild hooting session may go on for a half hour with a cacophony of hooting and wailing of owl talk. It is at such occasions when we humans can owl-talk with an owl that we may sense a feeling of equality, but I know that we are not equals. At night, the owl's abilities are far above ours in its world. As Thoreau said, owls are a different race that "awakes to express the meaning of Nature there."

The barred owl is the only non-horned owl with black eyes in large ringed facial disks. Of course, the horns are not horns but feather tuffs. Owls have ears that are offset, one ear being lower than the other ear, which aids them in triangulating prey. The ears are usually located in the large eye disks in which the disks act like a TV dish, aiding in gathering sound. Their hearing is so acute that an owl can hear a rodent under the snow or concealed in grasses. Though owls have excellent night vision, nothing can see in total darkness, so the true gift of the owl is its hearing, and that is what it depends on for survival.

The largest owl in appearance is the great gray owl, but this is deceiving, as plucked of its feathers, the great gray is smaller than the great horned and snowy owl. It is the dense feathered covering that makes the great gray appear larger, though he is in reality smaller and lighter. Though they are not found in abundance, great gray owls are isolated and occasionally seen. If they are present, they are likely seen as they tend to perch high in a prominent black spruce or tamarack in some lowland conifer swamp during the light of day. Being more an owl species of the far north, they have adapted to daytime hunting, which makes them more visible to the birder.

In the winter of 2005, an unusually large and significant owl eruption occurred in northern Minnesota and northern Wisconsin. This owl influx was an extremely eventful year for birders as it brought people to this region from as far away as Europe to see the concentration of northern owl species, but it was not a good thing for owls. The reason for their journey was to find food as the vole and lemming populations that they preyed upon in the far north had precipitously dropped. I recall making the half-hour drive to Bemidji with my wife and counting five great gray owls. Prior to that year it was rare to see any.

Besides the great gray owls during this influx, there were also hawk owls and boreal owls making these extraordinary migrations out of their homelands. Normally we do have breeding pairs of either boreal or hawk owls in the country around where I live, and I once had a miniature boreal owl, less than eight inches in height, visit a campsite on a remote border lake in the BWCA. I was relaxing at my campfire in the evening after a long and grueling day. I heard him first, a series of rapid, short, high-pitched whistles. Then I saw him in a small spruce near my fire. He was rather tame and continued his song for ten or fifteen minutes. The rapid tempo of whistles sounded like water dripping. I clearly recall hearing a story from an Ojibwe or Cree legend that told of a great owl who had the hubris to try to drown out a great waterfall with its booming hoots, but instead offended the water spirit who shrunk this great and powerful owl down in size to what's now the petite boreal owl and reduced its booming hoot, in which he tried to make more noise than the great waterfalls, to the sound of dripping water.

The saw-whet owl, who is slightly smaller than his cousin the boreal owl, is our smallest owl in the northland, and, even though common, is rarely seen as it is strictly nocturnal. The only time I have seen this little owl in daylight is when he is flushed while grouse hunting in woods of thick cover, and when hunters do flush him, he is often mistaken for a woodcock by his zigzag flight pattern. He gets his name from his raspy whistle that is slower in tempo and raspier than the boreal owl and sounds like a lumberjack filing his saw, hence the name saw-whet. When in his breeding season of March and April, his saw-filing whistle can go on for hours without a pause. This persistent calling can be his undoing as bigger owls like the barred owl will zero in on him as prey.

One warm evening I was sitting outside in the total darkness with a flashlight at my side. As I sat there in the quiet and darkness, I heard something scurrying on a limb of a large red pine within ten yards or less. I was perplexed at what would be running back and forth on this limb, so I slowly raised my flashlight and pointed at where I thought the scurrying was emanating from and turned it on, and to my surprise I saw a saw-whet. It sat on the horizontal pine limb and started these wild and bizarre gyrations with its head. It was like a scene out of *The Exorcist* as its head was placed in such unbelievable positions that it didn't seem physically possible. At one point it had its head nearly upside down and between its feet. It let out an alarmingly loud, high-pitched, and piercing whistle that could be compared to a siren, and then it flew in a wide circle in a fluttering manner and landed on the same spot of the red pine limb and started the wild body gyrations over again, only to repeat the flight again on precisely the same route as before, as though it was attached to a wire. It just goes to show us humans that the plants and animals we share the earth with have physical abilities and talents that go unrealized and unnoticed by us. Over the eons, life on our planet has taken so many twists and turns and given out so many remarkable gifts and talents. We think in terms of our small and sheltered worlds, little realizing the miraculous around us. Appreciating the gifts and abilities of so small an animal as the saw-whet owl is a lesson in humility and respect.

Swans

Those who contemplate the beauty of the earth find reserves of strength that will endure as long as life lasts.

— Rachel Carson

It was about twenty years ago when I started to regularly see trumpeter swans in the region of northern Minnesota where I live. A friend and I had notified a local radio station of our trumpeter swan sightings and they announced this, but cast doubt on our identification and stated that what we saw were undoubtedly tundra swans. We knew they were wrong as we had seen breeding pairs, and upon hearing a trumpeter, even if it's the first time, there is no mistaking what species of swan you are hearing. Their horn-like blast is something unmistakable.

As an avid canoeist, I spend much of my free time paddling in the backwaters and off the beaten path. At first our swan meetings were rather uncommon, but they have become more common as time goes on. All the swans we have seen were in remote locations and that appears to be a common rule among breeding swans; they need privacy from humans and to obtain that they breed and nest in relatively remote areas.

The other native species of swan found in North America is the tundra, formerly known as the whistling swan, which breeds in the far north above timberline. Both species are very large but the trumpeter is larger, though this is difficult to distinguish in the wild unless the two happen to be seen together. The trumpeter swan, when resting in the water, often holds its neck so there is a slight kink where the neck meets the chest and at the base of the upper mandible is a faint streak of red or yellow. Aside from this, the best way to distinguish these two swans is by their calls, the trumpeter being a loud horn blast and the tundra sounding like a wheezy whistle. Tundra swans migrate through in spring and late autumn in large flocks and in impressive numbers, and sometimes they can be seen and heard all morning in their great journey. When the tundra swans are moving through, they signal the last of the autumn bird migrations. Trumpeters move about in smaller numbers and some of the birds winter over where there is open water. It is not that unusual to see a small group of trumpeters in winter.

Trumpeters gravitate to small and shallow lakes, for it is in such watery habitats that grow the various pondweeds, smaller water lilies like water shield, algae, sedges, and other similar vegetation that swans are fond of. They have much longer necks than other dabbling and water surface feeding ducks, so they can reach down further and get food that a mallard or other dabbler cannot reach. They even use their huge webbed feet to stir up the bottom and loosen plants and roots in order to access more forage. Cygnets (newborn swans), like the young of other plant-eating birds, will eat much insect food before becoming vegetarians.

Trumpeter swans are the largest waterfowl in North America with wingspans stretching to seven feet or more in length, and weights up to thirty pounds, almost twice the size of tundra swans. It takes at least one hundred meters of open water for them to run along and flap their wings in order to get airborne. When inside my cabin with the windows open or out in the yard, I can easily hear these big birds take off as their powerful flapping of wings and big webbed feet slap the water as they run across the surface, and they sound like a small herd of horses stampeding as they struggle to get their bodies airborne. When I see a flock of twelve to fifteen trumpeters flying, usually just above treetop level, I know it is safe to assume that this is an extended family. Swans, like most waterfowl, are family orientated and form close bonds. They mate for life and mated pairs, a cob and pen (male and female), may pair off and select where they want to nest when less than two years of age, but they generally wait several more years before actually breeding. If a cob should lose his mate, he might never mate again.

Prior to settlement of North America by Europeans, the trumpeter swan covered most of the continent in great numbers. In the National Geographic book *Water, Prey, and Game Birds of North America,* I found an interesting account of an apparent road to extinction of this magnificent bird:

"Clearly, the largest of our waterfowl was abundant and widespread in the wildlife paradise that once was America. Trumpeters bred across northern Alaska and Canada east to Hudson Bay and as far south as Iowa and Missouri. They wintered along the Atlantic seaboard to the Carolinas, in the Mississippi valley, along the Gulf coast, and westward to the Pacific."

The book continues to state that "Between 1853 and 1877 the Hudson's Bay Company handled some 17,000 swanskins, many of them from trumpeters. The beautiful plumage was sold on the London Market for adornment and to make powder puffs and down coverings. ... By 1900 the trumpeter was nearly extinct. In 1918 the Migratory Bird Treaty Act outlawed the hunting of trumpeters. But it was almost too late. In 1933 only 66 of these great swans were reported in the United States."

These big birds are one of the great success stories in our country. Nearly fifty years ago, little would I have realized that these wonderful birds would be making my small lake their home. Most of the success of the trumpeter here in Minnesota is due to the efforts of Carroll Henderson of the Minnesota DNR. He brought back a suitcase full of swan eggs in 1986 from Alaska and transplanted them here. I now see them daily flying over from April to December, but the great thrill for me is to have had them frequenting my small lake. Often I count as many as a dozen in the autumn, but the real thrill was in 2014 when a pair chose to nest on my small lake.

The nest site was a small, grounded chunk of peat. The swans built it up with material composed of mud and vegetation. Each wad of mud and grasses resembled croissants. The nest was approximately five feet in diameter and two to three feet above water level. On this mound was a depression that contained five beige eggs that were between four or five inches in length. We were jubilant that these trumpeters had chosen our humble little lake to reproduce. Almost daily I would hike down to the lake to check on the progress of the swan family, and each trip I would find the pen (female) on the nest with her neck stretched out and flattened to the nest structure in an attempt to make herself as inconspicuous as possible, which was rather absurd for such a highly conspicuous bird to do, and the cob would swim away from the nest, doing his job to attract my attention away from his family.

The earliest date that I observed a swan sitting on eggs was May 21, and from that date forward the pen would only slide off her nest and eggs due to a disturbance on the lake. After almost daily checks on swans and nest, it was late in the evening, within an hour before sunset, on June 24 when approaching the lake that I saw both adults standing on the nest with four tiny, pure white cygnets between them. I was surprised at the whiteness of the cygnets as I have observed subadults during the ricing season of early September and they were more gray than white.

The successful hatching of these eggs was a red-letter day for me. To think that slightly over seventy years ago these great birds were on the brink of extinction with fewer than seventy existing in the lower forty-eight states. By 2005 a survey done in North America had found that the trumpeter swan had increased to 35,000 and was steadily increasing.

Within a week after hatching, all the swans — both adults and newborns — had disappeared. I was greatly disappointed and could not fathom what happened. Did a predator, like an eagle, pick off all four cygnets? If so, where had the adults gone? I mulled their disappearance over in my mind but could not come up with a plausible explanation for this complete disappearance, and then I did some research and found that often swans and cygnets, less than a week old, could walk more than a mile. It was then that my thoughts were on a small and undeveloped neighboring lake within a straight-line distance of less than one mile from my lake. I foolishly wondered how they could find their way through the woods to this neighboring lake, but then I thought of the many times these birds had flown between these two lakes and the excellent aerial view they had. I became cognizant of how much better they knew their way around than I, who mostly stuck to game trails and old logging roads, knew my way around. Shortly thereafter, my wife, granddaughter, and I loaded up our canoe and made the short drive to a small creek crossing a nearby road. This creek flowed out of the wilderness lake that I suspected the swans had hiked cross-country to and afforded us the opportunity to access the lake. As soon as we had paddled down the creek about a quarter mile and opened into the lake, I immediately saw in the distance two adult trumpeters, and at least two cygnets as they scurried into the dense cover of emergent plant growth. I was satisfied that these were the same swans, and by late September I had three swans back on my lake, one of which was clearly a subadult. They stayed here until the lake froze over in mid-November, and prior to ice cover the lake had groups of swans numbering up to fourteen, all busy foraging on the lush growth of pondweed and the nut-like seeds just below the surface.

As soon as the ice went off the lake the following spring, the cob and pen returned and refurbished their nest. I was now convinced that Amik Lake was, in their minds, a home with everything they needed to survive: solitude, good food sources, and nesting grounds.

Early in the swan residency on my lake, both cob and pen would swim to the farthest side of the lake at my approach. As my wife and I began to check on them daily, they came to know we were not dangerous and intended them no harm, and they would swim to within ten yards of us and show interest. I almost always bring my dogs with me, and the swans approached them even closer than they would us. As they swam along the shoreline, they would continue to follow us as we walked the lakeside trail, and they would make soft utterances and cooing sounds. People say animals can't talk or communicate with humans, but I do not concur; you just have to be open and recognize when and how they communicate. As my late friend Larry Stillday said, "When people are balanced and in harmony with our Earth Mother the animals know that, that's what the old people used to say, the animals are talking to us, sometimes they use sound, but most of the time they use their behavior, it's therefore up to us to be able to read what they're acting out."

Then a sad event occurred during the swans' second breeding season on Amik Lake. Sometime in early June, and after several weeks of the swans incubating their eggs, I had a bear visitor late one night. We woke up to shine a light on the bear and it went about its business in my cabin yard and then left. Shortly thereafter, we heard the swans making a commotion on the lake. The next morning I walked down to the lake to see both cob and pen together on the far side of the pond, and the nest was littered with broken eggshell fragments. It was obvious what happened. The bear left the yard and followed the well-beaten game trail and path alongside the lake and he saw the white swan on the nest, fully exposed, and swam out and ate the eggs. Though I was saddened by this event, I knew it was something that was repeated uncountable times in the natural world. To the bear, it was a stroke of luck to come upon the nest, but to the swans and I, it was a sorrowful event. If I were a bear, I do not know if I could pass up such a delectable meal of four or five jumbo eggs. The swans did not attempt to start over again as they likely knew better than I that it was too late in the season to lay eggs, incubate, and see their progeny reach maturity before the autumn set in, but they remained on my lake until it froze over.

The autumn following the tragedy had the entire extended family of my two swans coming and going every day. Some days there would be as many as fifteen swans on Amik Lake. They would be in physical contact with one another with lots of swan talk going on among them. It would be the same as a family reunion for me but they had this reunion on a daily basis. Plus, they all became fattened up on the prolific pondweed that does so well here.

This same autumn one beautiful evening in October while in my bow-hunting stand near the lake, I suddenly heard what sounded like a number of large animals running through the woods and coming my direction. It was not particularly loud but had the sound of a number of animals running fast in unison. My first thought was a pack of wolves chasing a deer, and for a moment I froze in the tree, then I turned to the direction the sound was coming from and my attention was immediately drawn skyward to see a dozen swans no more than a few yards above the treetops, banking in complete unison as they turned over my head. It is at such times I become mentally and emotionally inspired. It is at these moments when I realize that we are all related and these relatives of mine are more than just birds, they make up one of many miracles that I experience on a daily basis. I owe them much gratitude for enriching my life.

When I bought this land in 1970, if someone would have told me someday I would have trumpeter swans residing here, I would have thought they were crazy, but here they are and what a success story it has been to witness.

I feel a great sense of satisfaction that these big birds have made a remarkable comeback from the brink of extinction and have chosen my small lake as home. They have also taught me several valuable lessons in life, and they have communicated to me by their actions the importance of family. Their work and effort in building their nest mound, their dedication to incubating and raising their young, their connection and bonds to their extended family or ancestors, all have shown me the respect for family and the love that is the basis of family. Trumpeter swans, like wolves, have felt the havoc of mankind. We owe them a great debt that can only be compensated by leaving them in peace to fill the role that the creator set for them. They have far more value than powder puffs or other adornments; they are an achievement of evolution and a means to inspire and create wonder.

The Tribe of Cranes

The quality of cranes lies, I think, in the higher gamut, as yet beyond the reach of words.

— Aldo Leopold

When I bought this land in 1970, there were no sandhill cranes here. Occasionally I would see them soaring high in the sky on their way to the big bog country northwest of me. I had no cranes to interact with until twenty years ago. I can vividly remember the morning in spring when I heard a strange loud rattling noise in the sky, and I was surprised to see two cranes fly low overhead and land on the bog bordering my lake. Since then, cranes have become more numerous each year.

I have read that cranes can live thirty-six years or longer.

This age was ascertained by banding a crane in Wyoming in 1973 that was found again in 2010 in New Mexico. But the age of cranes as a species is what really blows my mind. Fossils of cranes from ten million years ago have been found that are identical to our sandhill cranes of today. It is no exaggeration to say, as Leopold so articulately put it, that when one hears the crane he is hearing "no mere bird. He is the symbol of our untamable past, of that incredible sweep of millennia which underlies and conditions the daily affairs of birds and men."

This past July I was standing in my garden when I heard cranes, and I stopped to watch ten cranes fly over me at treetop level. I have my resident cranes that nest and spend the bulk of daytime in an open wooded cow pasture of a neighbor about a mile away. Late in the evening, these resident cranes fly to my pond where they hunt for frogs, rodents, large insects, and snakes on the bog. I am confident that it is the same pair I have seen every year for the past decade or more. It is in early summer when driving by the cow pasture that we always see one or two crane babies, which are called "colts." Whether the parent cranes are standing still or moving, both adults are close on the flanks of the colt or colts and never more than two or three feet away from their young. When I walk down to my lake to see them, they are extremely wary of me and generally disappear as soon as they see me. I know they remain on the lake all night as they often wake me, on and off, with their calls, and I can always rely on them to wake me well before sunrise with their vocalizations which sound prehistoric with the loud volume and horn-like notes and rattles.

Leopold loved cranes and I am beginning to feel the same. They are symbolic of our inner struggles and exterior struggles with the land and wild places. They, like other plant and animal communities, are links to our distant past. We are just a moment in the span of existence of cranes; they witnessed our arrival and the demolition of so much of earth's ecosystems, and hopefully we will learn to see the value in them and the rest of the life on earth, and we will live with them in respect. As Thoreau said, "In wildness is the salvation of the world," and so it is in the world of the crane, and so it should be in ours too. The more diversity of life there is in this world, the more stability there is. Diversity and stability equate to strength and health. Maybe this is the lesson of the crane. I think the answer lies in change within all our institutions. We must stop seeing the natural world as a commodity and start seeing it as we would see a family member — something to love, protect, care for, and cherish.

Fierce Hawks of the Northwoods

For many, the thrill of seeing a live goshawk is greater than seeing ruffed grouse.

— Gordon Gullion

I love to walk the woods with my old twenty-gauge side-by-side hunting grouse with my old dog. Up here where I live you never know what sort of critter you are going to run into while grouse hunting. It is as unpredictable as the weather. You could come face-to-face with a wolf or bobcat. Grouse hunting is difficult. They are called feathered rockets for good reason.

From the time their wings explode, you have less than a second to get off a good shot. The best of hunters only succeed a third of the time, and at my age, it isn't getting any easier. I would estimate that for every ten birds that my dog gets up, I will get shots at three or four due to being either out of range, or an obstruction like a spruce tree or some other object that I can't shoot through. Of the third that I get shots at, it'd be mighty good to get half of them, or in other words, considering my aging reflexes, it is an exceedingly good year if I put eight to ten birds in the freezer. With a good bird dog, I am at an advantage over those who do not have a good dog. Further complicating my success is all the distractions in the woods. The forest is a diverse community and there is always something to get your attention besides the hunt, and even when you are not distracted, a flushed grouse makes an explosion of thundering wings that one never gets acclimated to.

The relationship a hunter has with his bird dog is special. If my dog couldn't go with me, I would not go. It is indeed a joy to watch the dog work, nose to the ground, sifting through a thousand scents for that one which unites our combined efforts together and gives our relationship meaning above her just being my pet. We are a team; she knows exactly what her job is, better than I do. I never grow accustomed to the ability of a dog. Every year, as we walk down an old trail, she will pick up a grouse scent, and with nose to the ground go off into the woods on my right, and then suddenly put the brakes on, do a 180-degree turn, and then go back the same way she came, cross the trail to my left, and with nose still on the ground continue on and flush a grouse. This all translates into her being able to tell what direction the bird is walking by the strength of the scent; the scent was getting weaker, and she could smell this, so she turned and went in the direction in which the scent was getting stronger. I have learned to never, ever doubt the wisdom of my dog. She and all the dogs I have had before her are far better hunters than myself. They are better equipped. She is the wolf that lives in my living room. She has the ability to run all day, has astonishing olfactory glands, and I believe has senses that I cannot understand.

No matter how accomplished a grouse hunter may be, there is one that reigns head and shoulders above the rest as the supreme hunter of ruffed grouse: the goshawk. This hawk, the largest member of the accipiter family, may be the fiercest hawk in the forest.

There are three species of accipiters in North America; the smallest member is the sharp-shinned, the next larger member is the Cooper's, and biggest is the goshawk. All three are principally bird hunters and all three have the same aerodynamic flight design: short powerful wings and a long broad tail. The long tail enables them to maneuver through the thickest of brush and the powerful wings enable them to do so with astonishing speed. The sharp-shinned and Cooper's are called "blue darters" in parts of the country, and another name they have been called is "bullet hawk." All three have a reputation for fierceness and persistence.

I recall reading in an old bird book an anecdotal account of a goshawk chasing a hen into a farm house where the hen sought shelter from the fearsome hawk under the ankle-length skirt of the farm wife, and the goshawk followed in pursuit. The deadly hawk was killed by the frightened woman's stomping. I have witnessed the sharp-shinned pursuing a white-throated sparrow into a thorny blackberry, and to my amazement the hawk maneuvered through this thick and thorny briar with unbelievable speed and agility and exited with the sparrow in its talons. The sharp-shinned hawks make their appearance in great numbers during the spring and autumn sparrow migrations. When these sparrow migrations occur, it is in staggering numbers. This great migration goes unnoticed by most, but it is epic in size. During the peak, I may have hundreds in my yard, and in many locations the forest floor appears as if it had been thatched as thousands of sparrows scratched up the duff on the forest floor for food. It is this mass movement of sparrows that brings the sharp-shinned hawks. I have compared this sparrow and sharp-shin relationship to migrations of wildebeest in Africa with the lions following them, or the great migrations of caribou on the Canadian tundra and the wolves that move with them. When the sparrows pass through the Northwoods, so goes the sharp-shins, as the two are intrinsically linked.

The Cooper's hawk—larger cousin of the sharp-shinned—resides a step higher on the food chain. They are far less common than either the sharp-shinned or goshawk, and like the sharp-shin they migrate further south during the winter months. The Cooper's can take small squirrels, mice, and larger birds. A friend of mine watched a Cooper's stalk and kill a brood of three pileated woodpeckers that had recently fledged. When these big woodpeckers first leave their cavity nest, they cling to the trunk of the tree for a day or two. It was at this unfortunate time that the Cooper's hawk dispatched all three because they would not fly off from their nest tree.

The real evolutionary achievement of the accipiter group is the goshawk. This bird of prey can chase and catch a ruffed grouse on the wing in the thickest of forest cover. There is some question as to how it got its name. Many North American upland bird hunters say the "gos" in "goshawk" comes from grouse, but I have also heard the "gos" comes from goose as the European goshawk that is somewhat larger than his North American counterpart was used by falconers to bring down geese. Whatever the case, this fearsome hawk is the master predator of grouse. Many times I have observed this large hawk suddenly and silently appear with its wings set as he glides smoothly and effortlessly under the canopy in the forest. He is impressive as he sails with only sporadic wing beats to maintain speed as he disappears almost as suddenly as he made his appearance. I see and hear many bird hunters shake their head in disdain when the goshawk is mentioned as they perceive this raptor as only bad news. We humans that only have an incomplete connection and understanding of predator/prey relationships dislike this hawk who can be perceived as diminishing the quality of our hunt. Some may even take a shot at a hawk or owl in ignorance, but such behavior only demonstrates how our culture has failed us all by not instilling in us an understanding of the complexities of all the interconnections in the natural world.

Goshawks have lived in conjunction with grouse and other game birds for millions of years without either one diminishing the survival of the other. In fact, the goshawk has strengthened the grouse rather than jeopardized its existence through the tests of the chase. The grouse that survive are the ones that have some edge in speed, maneuverability, alertness or camouflage. The grouse that do not have a survival edge or ability end up as a tasty meal for a goshawk. Those that eluded the hawk through having the edge survive to pass on their survival traits. The feathery rocket that hunters seek is the product of the goshawk.

Native game birds like the ruffed grouse do not need management in the terms we see game management today. If the habitat is there, grouse will prosper. Intensive logging will only increase grouse numbers to a degree. Much of our present state forest lands resemble aspen monocultures which may appear as a good omen to grouse hunters, but the ruffed grouse in its year-round lifestyle requires more than aspen lands. A healthy forest for all its occupants is a diverse forest and a diverse forest is a "mighty fortress."

I have been hunting ruffed grouse in the forests of the north for over fifty years, and at one time considered myself an accomplished shot of this bird, but lately it is the goshawk that teaches me a lesson in humility. The most recent lesson came this October when I was in a slump concerning my ability to put a grouse in the frying pan. One morning, as my dog and I were taking a break and relaxing on a stump and I was smoking my pipe, a goshawk came cruising through the woods. We finished our break and continued our hunt in which we thus far had missed a couple of grouse. Nearing home, we were walking a game trail through a thick second-growth forest with a dense understory of hazel, and we found a pile of grouse feathers adjacent to the trail, and a little further down the trail found a grouse carcass with its succulent breast meat gone. This scene in the woods brought home to me the reality that no matter how good I think I am as a grouse hunter, I am only an amateur to the goshawk, the greatest upland bird hunter in the entire northern hemisphere.

Tweety Birds

Yes it's true; we can and do learn a lot from Nature. She's always teaching us, even when we think there is nothing but empty space. In truth, when it comes to Nature there is never an empty space. The only empty space that exists is in the human mind that thinks it knows a lot.

— Chi Ma'iingan

As a small boy of perhaps eight or nine years old, I was captivated by foldout artwork of a dozen or more song birds in the Minneapolis Sunday paper. I was fascinated by the colorful and intricate patterns, and I removed this foldout from the magazine and tacked it on my bedroom wall. For years these birds remained the only artwork on my wall, until I grew into my mid-teens and got a car and a set of binoculars. I remember visiting the T. S. Roberts Bird Sanctuary in south Minneapolis in spring during the peak of migration and seeing the birds on the foldout tacked to my bedroom wall come to life. It was as if a miracle had happened; those little birds with brilliant colors and exquisite markings were now living, breathing, and moving in the branches of shrubs and treetops. I may not have grasped the change that these little tweety birds were having on me at that moment, but I do now. I was seeing for perhaps the first time one of the miracles of life on earth: hundreds, if not thousands, of species on great migrations whose ultimate goal was creating new life and perpetuating their existence. This spectacular event every spring is nature's celebration of life and renewal.

Since my interest in birds developed into something more than watching their migration patterns, I have begun to keep a chart of when individual species return. I have found that the exact date different species return is so predictable I can almost set a clock to their arrival. I know that on May 10 when I get up in the morning, I will see my first rose-breasted grosbeak, as this is the date I see the first arrival year after year. March nineteenth marks the return of the first red-winged blackbird, and so forth, with almost every migrating species. Only weather can alter these arrival dates, such as a late ice-out for waterfowl, but the overall regularity is astonishingly punctual. Such timeliness must be a law within the bird world, for if tardiness be the case, the great cycle of life behind this migration will be disrupted and mating, nest building, birth, and maturing will all be set back and jeopardize the continued existence of birds.

This timeliness in the circle of life reminds me of Larry Stillday and the Teachings of the Seven Grandfathers, and especially the teaching of "Truth." The Grandfather of truth is *Mikinaak*, the snapping turtle. This truth is forever represented by the turtle with the markings on the back of his shell; there are twenty-eight markings around the outside edges of the shell. These markings, or configurations, denote the twenty-eight-day cycle of the moon (from full moon to full moon). Within these twenty-eight outside markings on the shell are thirteen contained markings or configurations which represent the thirteen moons, which represent the truth of one cycle for the earth's rotation around the sun and the four seasons that make up this cycle.

As Chi Ma'iingan taught:

- The turtle represents: self-containment, creative resource, Mother Earth, adaptability, love, healing, and knowledge.

- When the Great Spirit gave us these laws the turtle was present to ensure that the laws would never be lost or forgotten.

- Our bird relatives are more intimately in tune to these laws of natural truth than we are, for they represent Mother Earth's clock upon which all life depends for consistency and well-being.

For over fifty years, I have cherished the great arrival of birds in the spring. It is as important to me as making rice, making sugar, and deer hunting. Every year since that first spring at T.S. Roberts Bird Sanctuary, I looked forward to this event, and rarely does a day go by that I am not out in the woods with my birding binoculars scouring the trees and bushes for the newest migrant to arrive in the Northwoods. Besides the enjoyment and satisfaction I get from seeing these birds, I have learned much from this endeavor. I have learned what patience is all about and that when birding you must use all your senses. You have to stand still for lengthy periods of time looking and listening. Full concentration of one's senses is mandatory, and the acknowledgement that birds live in other dimensions of time and space than we do, and that we must adapt ourselves to their world. Everything about the world of these small birds is in fast-forward. From their heartbeats and breathing to their motion and habits, everything goes forward faster than the realm of time we live in. And when I am bird watching, they do not give themselves up easily. It may take much time to finally have the sought-after bird reveal itself to me.

Aldo Leopold wrote about 65290, the band number that he placed on a particular chickadee and his subsequent live-trapping of 65290 for five consecutive winters, the longest-living chickadee in Leopold's trapping and banding career. Leopold gained two lessons from chickadee 65290; the first was that chickadees can live up to five years (I learned from a naturalist at a park reserve that they had a chickadee who lived eight years), and the second was that 65290 had an "extraordinary capacity for living." What exactly is that capacity is less clear to us humans. As Leopold noted, chickadees have two weaknesses: staying out of windy places, and do not get wet before a blizzard. I would add that we need to think time is relative, not only in bent space, but right here, on earth, before our eyes. I would argue that a year in the life of a chickadee would equate to several decades for us. The reference of time to a chickadee would be easier for us to understand if it were compared to watching a DVD movie. What would be a two-hour movie for us would be months for a chickadee. If we were to play the movie in fast forward, it may appear in real-life speed to the chickadee. It is possible that the electric signals or messages in the brain of a chickadee or any other small bird are faster than ours. Birds live in a different realm than we do. Whether 65290 had a higher degree of smarts than his fellows, or was just luckier, who can say? But I do believe that all birds have that extraordinary capacity for living and in this capacity is the greatest lesson to be learned from birds.

Having looked at the little chickadee, it is time to note that the chickadee is a sedentary bird; he is a year-round resident. The wood warblers, vireos, tanagers, and flycatchers are all migratory. Some may migrate no further than from Louisiana to the Northwoods of Minnesota, while others like the blackpoll warbler migrate epic distances, wintering from Venezuela to central Chile and summering in the northernmost forests of Canada and Alaska at timberline. I have read accounts from ornithologists that, when birding in Central America or the Amazon rainforests in December or January, mention a great bulk of the birds they saw were our summer residents. Contemplating that many of these same small birds we see here in summer make epic journeys twice a year covering thousands of miles makes our journeys seem small in comparison. When I ponder my own roaming and wanderings with these little tweety birds, it truly is miraculous and creates a great deal of respect and awe in my mind for these small creatures. When I consider the preparations that these birds make, putting on reserves of fuel in the form of body fat to provide the energy to travel thousands of miles, and their ability to know when their time has come and navigate from summer to winter homes, it is truly amazing.

One early September, some bear hunters who were hunting over a bait site that had some meat and animal fat came to me and asked if I would know what all the scores of birds were they had around the bait site. I asked them to describe the birds to me and the response was "Little brown birds." My first response was that there are hundreds of pages of "little brown birds" in every bird field guide. So I went to the bait site and saw numerous ovenbirds all around eating the maggots that were crawling on the putrid meat. I informed the bear hunters as to what the bird was, but I am certain that by now they have long forgotten about ovenbirds. It is a rather unfortunate state of affairs that so many hunters and outdoorsmen would not be more familiar with "tweety birds." These small birds go unnoticed as do so many life forms, both plant and animal. Many hunters see them as beneath their dignity, but herein lies the error of their ways.

As a hunter myself, I understand the key to success in hunting, whether it be big game or small game, is to know what is going on in the plant community and what the birds are up to, and to understand the interconnection of it all. On a different occasion I was asked the same question as to what birds were hanging around a bait site, and this time there was no meat, only oats and molasses. I was confident that it was not ovenbirds, since they are insect eaters, so I investigated and found it was a flock of white-throated sparrows feasting on the grains of oats. Perhaps if these bear hunters would spend a little more time becoming familiar with the lives of small birds, they may have a better appreciation for the beauty and mystery of the woods and see it as more than the chance to shoot a bear and begin to appreciate it as a place of enrichment of the mind and body.

There are surely better places for spring birding than where I live, but here I can walk out my door and be rewarded with scores of new arrivals every day from mid-April to the first of June. When I do go, which is often, I slowly make my way to Amik Lake, as small woodland pond edges make ideal birding locations, with the warming shallow waters of spring, which are the breeding sites of a myriad of insects, from mosquitoes to dragonflies. This is a buffet that any insectivorous bird cannot avoid. It is here that I not only add to my bird list, but feast with eye and ear on the beauty of colors and song, something that over the years I never tire of doing.

Every year the first wood warbler to arrive is the myrtle warbler, now called the yellow-rumped warbler with his yellow cap, tell-tale yellow rump, bluish back and white breast with yellow flanks. Often the myrtle is accompanied by the palm warbler with his constant pumping of his tail up and down. Also seen early is the black-and-white warbler who acts like a nuthatch, going up and down the trunks of trees with her intricate black-on-white designs. And so the springs go every year with a parade and proper sequence of birds. By mid-May I am rewarded with some of the most brilliantly colored birds of the Northwoods such as the Blackburnian warbler whose orange head makes an orange fruit appear dull in comparison. I recall the first time I laid eyes on this bird; I could not believe or understand that nature could create such stunning color. The famous ornithologist, Elliott Coues, wrote of the Blackburnian, "There is nothing to compare with the exquisite hue of this Promethean torch." No living thing but plants exhibit the spectacular color of birds.

The scarlet tanager, known as the "firebird," may even outdo the Blackburnian warbler. Elliott Coues said of the scarlet tanager and the impact this bird had on him, "I hold this bird in particular, almost superstitious, recollection, as the very first of all the feathered tribe to stir within me those emotions that have never ceased to stimulate and gratify my love for birds." This bright red-and-black tanager winters in the Amazon rainforest, and that is where he gets his name as the Tupi Indians of the Amazon call him *Tanagra*. As for many of the birds that do not have the brilliant colors, like the vireos, they outshine others with their pleasing songs and the persistence of their singing. The red-eyed vireo starts his territorial and mate-attracting song as soon as he arrives. He sings, "Here I am, up here, up here, see me, hear me, up here," and the song goes all day long, without a let up. Some call the red-eye the "preacher" due to his sermon going on at great lengths of time.

The kingbird gets his name from the habit of, when seeing a hawk or crow, leaving his perch and flying after the hawk or crow and harassing it by diving down and pecking at it, even plucking feathers. Of the flycatcher family, the kingbirds do not have the brilliancy or vocal attributes of the showier birds, but they do have courage.

Nature abhors a vacuum. No life form demonstrates this

more than birds. They inhabit every niche in the forest, from the ground to the tops of the trees and every strata in between, even in the water and in the soil, from water birds like loons and kingfishers to ground nesters like the ovenbird to Blackburnians who nest in the treetops. Even within each niche there are specialists who hunt different and varied insects. The warblers, who are fast-paced and hard to see due to their quick movements, hunt faster moving insects, while the much slower vireos and tanagers hunt sluggish caterpillars and worms, which means they linger longer. Flycatchers hunt from the wing, perching on a limb to spring into flight with mouth gaping wide open and then snapping shut on a moth, fly, or other insect in flight.

The songs of warblers, vireos, flycatchers, and tanagers are all unique. If one pays attention and has good ears, the songs of each bird are so distinctive that one who knows the bird songs can walk through the woods and identify each bird species by their song. Knowing these songs will also help one to know where in the lush treetops to scrutinize for a quick look at these elusive birds.

By mid-June the singing of the warblers and almost every other bird species has gone mostly silent due to the end of claiming territory, attracting a mate and nest building. Now birds are consumed with feeding and raising their young and the woods are mostly devoid of the singing of birds with the exception of a few species like red-eyed vireos and catbirds. By autumn, most have molted and some groups like the warblers have lost the colorful plumage of spring and are indeed drab in appearance. Even the best of birders have difficulty in identifying wood warblers. The young have matured and are fattened up with the prolific insect explosions, and they now know their time has ended in the Northwoods, and they prepare to make another epic journey to other regions.

The explosion of pesky and biting insects — mosquitoes,

deer flies, black flies, midges, and thousands of others that we humans like to complain about—have provided sustenance and life for millions of winged creatures, and the sum total of this has been bountiful forests of beauty and song and diversity unequaled in North America.

Every spring I give thanks that I have lived to see another season and return of these little birds. They have been teachers about the capacity for living, about perpetuation of life, about using your gifts, and about great journeys.

A Curious Transfusion of Courage

Out of the wilderness, has come the substance of our culture, and with a living wilderness ... we shall have also a vibrant, vital culture, an enduring civilization of healthful, happy people who ... perpetually renew themselves in contact with the earth.

—Howard Zahniser (Father of the Wilderness Act 1964)

Chi Ma'iingan told me that to accept and understand the Teachings of the Seven Grandfathers, a person needs to first embrace and understand "love" and "respect." He went on to tell me that to respect the Earth Mother we must understand the importance of the interconnectedness of all life. This is the teaching of *Mashkode-Bizhiki* (bison).

Several winters ago, I had a young male turkey, which are known as a jakes, hang around our yard the entire winter until the sap started running in the sugar maples that spring. In an email exchange with Larry about my turkey visitor, I told him in a less than serious manner that as things get tough in the winter I may have to find out what wild turkey tastes like. Larry wrote me: "I was going to say if you are in need of food then the turkey is there to fulfill the promise made by the Creator to take care of his relative, the human. On the other hand, if you are not in need than he's there as a guest and what do you do for guests? Feed them. Well sounds like the turkey will live to see its grandchildren run around in Nature, thanks to you."

The teachings of respect are deeper than they first appear. This notion of respect applies to cutting down a tree, picking wild greens, or killing a deer. It also applies to the water and air. None of these things need us, but we need them. When harvesting wood or killing a deer, disrespect will lessen us as human beings. Respecting all life, whether it is food or just enjoyment in observing, will make us better people spiritually, emotionally, mentally, and physically.

Larry's teaching of Respect:

- Respect is represented by the *Mashkode-Bizhiki*, the Bison.

- The bison provided food, shelter, clothing, and utensils for daily living.

- The bison, through giving its life and sharing every part of its being, showed the deep respect it had for the peoples

- The attributes of the bison are: life, sacredness, healing powers, abundance, stamina, provider, and sacrifice.

- The spirit of respect is to be given toward all life, we must live and understand our interconnectedness to all life.

• Once we realize our connectedness, we will get a clear understanding of our dependence on the land, therefore give the land and its resources absolute respect.

Larry's teachings arrive at respect and spirituality. Aldo Leopold arrives at the same conclusions but he gets there academically and through science. Leopold, in *The Land Ethic*, wrote essentially what Larry arrived at in spiritual terms: "In short, a land ethic changes the role of *Homo sapiens* from conqueror of the land-community to plain member and citizen of it. It implies respect for the community as such."

The need to make respect and love for the land part of our national consciousness is a long-term struggle, and in order for change to come about, we need a radical shift in the philosophical point of view in all our institutions: politics, economics, religion, and education.

I came away from my years in the public education system with no notion of respect toward the land and I received no education about Native American culture. These were learned when I came upon the writings of Thoreau and Leopold and was fortunate to become friends with Larry Stillday. These values and teachings I learned are far more than interesting ideas; they are of paramount importance for continued life on earth.

We have been provided with a road map created by a long line of environmentalists, and this map can guide us in the direction to arrive at truth and success by living in harmony with Mother Earth. They lifted us to within a few steps from the peak, but we seem to be sliding back down. I believe it is time for environmentalism to reach for the Native American spiritual beliefs and understanding of harmony and peace with the natural world. Too often in our civilization, governed by economics, science has been for sale to the highest bidder. This is not a fallacy; it is a fact. Take for example Rachel Carson, the scientist who revealed the dangers of pesticides in her pivotal book *Silent Spring*, and the attacks on her credibility by chemists representing big chemical corporations.

I believe in good science, and I have embraced it, but I am now more inclined to also embrace spirituality, for to me spirituality will better serve us in arriving at the correct ethical perspective in regard to the land and everything in, on, and above it. This is why the Teachings of the Seven Grandfathers are so important.

This is a long-term struggle, and the best way to approach it, as Larry Stillday advised me concerning the fight to save wolves, is to "be the wolf." In other words, exercise humility.

I truly believe in all that I have said, but we must also remain focused on protecting what we have. Saving these tag end pieces of wilderness will allow them to inspire others, as that is how I arrived at where I am today; being in contact with wild America was a renewal and exciting experience that became an integral part of my life. If I had not seen the northern lights while crossing a northern Minnesota lake, heard wild owls hooting at dawn, and had a flock of ducks fly low over cane grass in a wild wetland, I would not be doing what I am today. And I must always remember and be grateful for those who came before me and sacrificed themselves to save our wild lands, people like Howard Zahniser, Bob Marshall, Aldo Leopold, and David Brower, to name a few. But for me, here in headwaters country of northern Minnesota, I have a special place in my heart for a man by the name of Jacob Vradenberg Brower, the Father of Itasca State Park and the headwaters of the Mississippi. I tell this story to show how the beauty and sacredness of America's special places can and does change the way we view the natural world. The struggle to save these special places is a long-term struggle against great odds in which the individual who pursues the struggle is slandered, misportrayed, vilified, and often the work they started isn't finished until after their death. The men and women who speak for earth, though they may not realize it, have seen the bison and do what they do because they understand respect. Jacob V. Brower is one of these saintly men.

Jacob V. Brower:
Father of Itasca State Park

We must understand that the living world cannot be replicated.

—William Kittredge

Jacob Brower was born in Michigan in 1844 and moved to Minnesota where he served with the Union Army, Company D, in the famous and heroic Minnesota First Regiment in the Civil War. After the war he was a banker, seaman, attorney, railroad president, legislator, explorer, land agent, editor, archaeologist, and surveyor. The town of Browerville in Minnesota was named after Brower due to his designing the layout for the town.

The earliest I have come across his name in context with

history was in William Folwell's *A History of Minnesota Vol. I*, where Brower is mentioned as an archaeologist working at Kathio, the former great capital of the Dakota on Mille Lacs Lake.

The archeological survey by Brower about Mille Lacs warrants the conclusion that these settlements were of great antiquity. From such a center it is not difficult for this tribe to dominate the hunting grounds reaching to the headwaters of the Chippewa, the St. Croix, the St. Louis, the Mississippi, and the tributaries of the Red River of the North.

Brower would likely not have entered into the story and history of the headwaters of the Mississippi or Itasca State Park if it were not for a fraudulent exploratory trip and plagiarized report by Willard Glazier about the source of the great river in 1881.

With a controversy swirling about Glazier's fraudulent report, Brower was enlisted by the Minnesota Historical Society on February 12, 1889, to clear the air concerning Glazier and verify the true source of the Mississippi, as first determined by Joseph Nicollet in 1836 and a plethora of explorers who followed Nicollet and Schoolcraft. The purpose of Brower's work was purely scientific and nothing more. The findings of Brower are detailed in his book of 1893, *The Mississippi River and Its Source: A Narrative and Critical History of the Discovery of The River and its Headwaters*.

Something seminal happened in Brower's life while working at the headwaters. Something caused an epiphany in the man who up to this time in his life had been a captain of commerce, growth, and taming the wilderness. Brower began his work as a man of his times but was transformed by the beauty of the land. Surely the beauty of the region had an impact on him, and surely this impact included hard science, and yet Brower was affected spiritually in a major way.

The following information comes from an article in the

May/June 1967 issue of the *Minnesota Conservation Volunteer* by Samuel H. Morgan, chairman of the Minnesota Council of State Parks:

"It was not until March of 1889 that an assistant to Brower and his surveying duties, Alfred J. Hill wrote a letter to the editor of the St. Paul Dispatch, raising the idea of a 'real wild' state park be established around the source of the Mississippi River. Eight months later the editor of the St. Paul Pioneer Press followed up on the idea of a state park and urged the Minnesota legislature act on this in its next session. The next documented step was done by a well-known citizen of St. Paul, Emil Geist, who urged the Minnesota Historical Society to 'make history' and turn its attention to protecting the headwaters of the river. The MHS formed a committee that included Brower, who was already well acquainted with the headwaters and surrounding country. Brower prepared a map and cost estimate but by then, the MHS decided it would be better for the state legislature to handle a future park so they asked Brower to author a legislative bill, which he did."

Upon enactment of the bill which would allow for creation of Itasca State Park, Brower stated that "no one will ever fully realize how necessarily strenuous were the exertions which finally resulted in establishing Itasca State Park."

Now that the park had been established, the real heavy lifting would begin. There were four entities owning land within the park boundaries: the federal government, railroads, private ownership, and Weyerhaeuser Timber Company. On August 2, 1892, a bill was passed and signed giving these federal lands to the state with the right of forfeiture "if at any time it shall cease to be exclusively used for a state park, or if the state shall not pass a law or laws to protect the timber thereon."

During all this, Brower was serving as park commissioner with no salary and all costs coming out of his own pocket.

With the federal land acquired, Brower went to work on securing the railroad lands belonging to Northern Pacific in which he succeeded by getting Northern Pacific to agree to fifty cents an acre for 2,450 acres. Grudgingly, the state accepted the offer as it was really more a gift from the railroad than a sale.

Brower's term as commissioner ended in 1895, but he continued to work hard at his vision of a park though his efforts to gain the timber holdings through condemnation "were largely of battles lost." Brower wrote to Governor Knute Nelson that he felt "entitled to different and better consideration and treatment, even at the hands of demagogues, temporarily placed where they can do the greatest harm to the greatest number."

On May 7, 1901, Brower submitted his survey and appraisal with Attorney General Wallace B. Douglas intending that Douglas, as written in the bill, acquire the private timber holdings "expressly for the purpose of rescuing Lake Itasca and its beautiful shores from the devastating grasp of advancing lumberman, not a single pine tree had been lumbered off the area of the state park."

The fight to save the old-growth pines in the park had become a race for time. The clear-cutting was rapidly advancing up the headwaters of the Mississippi and closing in on the park. Unfortunately, after January 9, 1901, with the retirement of Governor John Lind, a friend of the park, the condemnation of the remaining timber holdings became one of inaction and depredation. Attorney General Douglas left the remaining timber lands in timber company ownership and stated that "the purchase [by the state] of all standing pine situated in the park would be an idle waste of money." The State of Minnesota continued to allow logging in the park and the construction of a dam at the outlet of the Mississippi which inundated much of the shoreline of Lake Itasca.

Jacob Brower died on June 1, 1905. A great lodge was built later that month but was not named in honor of the man who gave his life to save the beautiful trees of the park and protect the headwaters of the great river, but instead it was named for W. B. Douglas who, according to Samuel Morgan, "had neglected to carry out the legislative mandate for land acquisition, but had been one of the parties executing, on behalf of the state, some of the very contracts which enabled lumbermen to do substantial damage to Itasca's lands, lakes and timber."

After Brower's death, his close ally, Portius Deming, continued the work in Minnesota's legislature. In 1913, over twenty years after the establishment of the park, and almost a decade after Brower's death, Deming secured $250,000 to pay off the timber companies and other private holdings in the park. These same lands could have been bought in 1899 for $40,000. The park was now whole and protected but not until after nearly two decades of heroic efforts and Brower's death. Deming said in a letter to Brower's daughter, "I did this work largely in remembrance of him [Brower], and of what he would have done had he been living."

Every time I have visited the park, I have had to stop in awe of the majestic three-hundred-year-old red pines, for they are not a few scattered stands here and there, but extend for great distances throughout the park. They dominate the park and impress hundreds of thousands of people annually. They are arguably the greatest remaining stands of red pine in the upper Midwest. A survey by the DNR of visitors many decades ago found that the majority of people visit Itasca State Park to see the source of the Mississippi River, but return to see the majestic trees.

When my wife, granddaughter and I visit the park, we too draw a curious transfusion of courage, the kind of courage that Jacob Brower was made of. Having these special places on earth not only enriches us, they make us better people.

Jacob Brower's spirit lingers over Itasca and the Headwaters; it will be there for a long time to come.

The Last Remaining Wilderness on the Infant Mississippi River

In the United States there is more space where nobody is than where anybody is. That is what makes America what it is.

—Gertrude Stein

We who live in Minnesota and love wild river trails that are interspersed with lakes and in a Northwoods setting are blessed as there are more opportunities here than anywhere else in the lower forty-eight. If one wants to get out in this watery backcountry, the first place that comes to most minds is the Boundary Waters Canoe Area Wilderness (BWCA) of over one million acres in size, which gets over 250,000 visitors annually. This vast region containing arguably the epitome of Northwoods character and canoeing is a national treasure that has influenced and afforded ordinary people a chance to experience wilderness in an ordinary way without costly trips into the far north or elsewhere.

I love these waters of the Canadian Shield and have traveled thousands of miles in the BWCA and neighboring Quetico Provincial Park in Ontario. Many of my most precious experiences of wilderness were of my trips into this area. But Minnesota also has many designated canoe routes throughout the state that offer a wilderness experience that rivals the Boundary Waters. Some of these are well known and some that are right under our noses are not so well known, but there is one that has special meaning to me in north-central Minnesota and that is the last remaining wilderness on the infant Mississippi River, or as it's known to the Ojibwe, *Misi-ziibi*, the great river of life.

Minnesota's Itasca State Park is where the *Misi-ziibi* begins. On the north end of Lake Itasca the great river begins as barely a trickle that one could walk across without getting one's knees wet. As the infant river flows north, it feels its Canadian urge as many of Minnesota's northern rivers are drawn to Hudson Bay, but when it passes through Bemidji, it begins to turn east as if Lake Superior, the largest surface area of fresh water on earth, is exerting its influence and pull, but by the time it has stretched to over 150 miles, it begins to arch around to the south where the continental draw to the Gulf of Mexico over two thousand miles away has captured its heading.

If you look at a map of the upper Mississippi, the river from its source at Lake Itasca to the Twin Cities five hundred miles south, it resembles a shepherd's staff, and within the crook of that staff is what we call "headwaters country." It is within headwaters country that one finds a diversity and richness not to be found anywhere else in the Northwoods.

Within this region are not only found the headwaters of the Mississippi, but many other well-known rivers that originate here in headwaters country.

The name "Itasca" was suggested by Reverend W.T. Boutwell, a member of Schoolcraft's 1832 expedition to the headwaters, by taking the last syllable of *veritas* and the first syllable of *caput* to create the word "Itasca." *Veritas caput* is Latin for true head. I prefer the name that Ojibwe people used, *Omashkooz*, which translates to Elk or Elk Lake. The French called it *Lac la Biche*. Looking at an aerial photograph the shape of the lake may suggest an elk head, or perhaps the region had elk present which surely would attract Native hunters. This site was favored by Ojibwe communities as made evident by the presence of mounds, prehistoric hunting sites, and its draw for hunting opportunities up to present times which are well documented.

The early French fur traders that were the first white men to enter headwaters country called the rugged moraines that extend through the region, west to east, the *Hauteur des Terres,* or height of land. What attracted these men to this region was the prolific amount of fur bearers. The land features in the *Hauteur des Terres* were shaped by the glaciers of the last ice age. The land here is still young, as it was less than ten thousand years ago that the last movement of glaciers retreated and formed the landscape.

People from the North West Company, American Fur Company, and unlicensed fur traders who ventured here to exploit the abundance of fur, referred to this specific trading zone of northern Minnesota and a portion of northwestern Wisconsin as the Fond du Lac Department, and this department proved to be one of the most profitable districts in all of North America. Minnesota historian Larry Luukkonen, in his book *Between the Waters,* notes that the Fond du Lac Department within the North West Company had, in 1805, "one hundred and nine men employed at a wage of sixty-three thousand and nine hundred thirteen livres. Returns for 1807 indicate that the production of furs in the Fond du Lac Department was second only to Athabasca."

Local history cites Schoolcraft as the first white man at the headwaters in 1832, but the truth is there were many whites before Schoolcraft. The fur trader of the North West Company, and later the American Fur Company, William Morrison, was likely the first white man there. It was in 1803 on a trading visit to Rice Lake in White Earth that Morrison ventured by Elk Lake. It is documented that Morrison was at the headwaters again in 1804, 1811, and 1812. Men like Morrison were not interested in being discoverers; they were only interested in making money and furthering the company's business. Schoolcraft was a great self-promoter and was notorious for an inflated ego.

Henry Rowe Schoolcraft wrote in his journal about his expedition to the headwaters of the Mississippi in 1832 that the fur post on "Leech Lake has been one of the principal posts of the fur trade in the northwest since the region was first laid open to the enterprise of the fur trade, and it has probably yielded more wealth in furs and skins, than one of the richest mines of silver would have produced."

Lieutenant James Allen, who accompanied Schoolcraft and commanded an escort of ten soldiers of the United States Army, was selected by Schoolcraft due to his map-making abilities, and he kept a journal noting the strength of the Indians and their attitudes towards the United States and fur traders. Allen makes some observations about the geographic aspects of Leech Lake, the bountiful game and other sustenance of this great lake, and the independence and deport of the Leech Lakers: "Their country abounds in furred animals and game, and the lake affords abundance of fish … Deer and bears are the principal animals of the forest which are hunted for their meat; and beavers, otters, martens, and muskrats are the chief furred animals, which are taken in such great numbers as to make this one of the most valuable posts of the north for the American trade."

The historian William Whipple Warren wrote in his *History of the Ojibway People* about the diversity of headwaters country: "The region of country from which the Mississippi derives its source, is covered with innumerable fresh and clear water lakes, connected with one another, and flowing into the 'Father of Rivers' through rapid and meandering streams. ... In former times this region of country abounded in buffalo, moose, deer, and bear, and till within thirty years past, in every one of its many water courses, the lodges of valuable and industrious beaver were to be found."

Ojibwe people must have thought people like Schoolcraft were a bit crazy coming into their country and proclaiming themselves as discoverers when Anishinaabeg people had been living and thriving in headwaters country for thousands of years and thought of this great river as sacred. Native peoples preceded whites by 12,000 years in headwaters country. We are relatively newcomers as evident at the Itasca Bison Kill Site, which is 7,000 to 8,000 years old and located at the south end of the west arm of Lake Itasca.

It is with some trepidation that I speak of this relatively unknown stretch of river, lest it become too well known, but pondering this question, I think the best way to protect it is for people to experience it, as I believe anyone who spends time on this river will love it. It truly is a treasure to have this section of river where we and our children can experience what headwaters country was like a hundred years ago. In a way, it has become a museum piece of wilderness on the mighty Mississippi.

Nearly all of this first forty miles of river lies within Mississippi Headwaters State Forest. The state forest is fragmented with county administered land and some private land. Inside the state forest boundaries, 60% of land base is within one thousand feet of a river or stream. Where there's clean water there will be life abounding.

This infant Mississippi is not an easy river to traverse. There are some lengthy stretches of rocky riffles that can challenge any paddler in high water and create obstacles when in low water, plus three large wetlands where even the most experienced wilderness travelers can find themselves lost. The river alternates between fast segments of river within boreal forests with pine and fir, high sandy banks, and places where the channel can completely disappear, such as vast open marshlands of bog, fen, cane grass, cattails, and wild rice.

One of these segments of fast water is Kakabikans rapids which is three and a half miles in length and commences below Kakabikans Falls, or as it's known today "Vekin's Dam." There is a portage around this picturesque waterfall which is bordered with bloodroot, and when in bloom during springtime this flower causes one to pause and admire its beauty. Another set of rapids is sixteen miles further downstream, known as Stumphges Rapids, which I personally feel is one of the most beautiful stretches of river anywhere in the state. The immense and infamous Rice Lake Bog is further downstream, between Pine Point campsite and the Iron Bridge campsite. The straight-line distance in this immense bog is slightly more than three miles, but by paddle this meandering maze is at least three times that distance. From Pine Point downstream near Rice Lake are great beds of wild rice. As the emergent vegetation develops in summer in this large wetland, any semblance of a channel disappears. Normally the rule of thumb is to follow the current, but in this big bog, there is current everywhere. It's best to tackle this tricky wetland early in the year before the vegetation gets too high. Many experienced paddlers have found themselves unable to navigate this puzzle and have had to turn back. It is unwise to try crossing this bog late in the day, as you may find yourself sleeping in your canoe in mosquito heaven.

Many specific sites and camps along this stretch of river have names that resonant with the human history of the river; Wannigan, Coffee Pot, Bear Den, Fox Trap, and Pine Point.

The infant river abounds with diverse and unique wildlife and plant communities.

I have been canoeing the headwaters for most of my life, and it has, in many ways, defined my life. It is the great river of life. The immense influence the river has had on my life is due to its wilderness qualities. Though the expansive wilderness doesn't compare to the one-million-acre Boundary Waters Canoe Area, the region still has enough wild and semi-wild lands remaining to give one the feeling of being in a remote and wild place. What it has that the BWCA does not is a more diverse community of both plants and animals. The region here has seen the deciduous and coniferous forests advance and retreat. With the retreats and advances in the timber line the prairie has come and gone. Three biomes come together here: prairie, hardwoods, and conifers — which gives the added scope of diversity. The sandy and loamy soils also provide richer nutrients for the base layer on the pyramid of life. Other soils here have been acidified by jack pines for thousands of years, which has hampered diversity, but in turn these soils have become habitat for endangered species such as the ram's head orchid and other species that favor these acidic soils.

On many trips to the Boundary Waters, I have been disappointed by the large numbers of people; after all, it is the most heavily visited wilderness area in America east of the Rocky Mountains. When I put my canoe into the headwaters of the Mississippi, I rarely see another human. A good friend, Rob, and I took a trip five years ago on a Memorial

Day weekend and never saw another canoe or boat for a stretch of sixty-two miles until we arrived at Lake Bemidji. Rob has spent a considerable amount of time in the BWCA and I had encouraged him to join me on this trip as I believed he would be impressed with the diversity of life here. It was May and the river and forest were bursting with life. I can see the river in my mind today as clearly as if it happened an hour ago.

We were in the canoe and moving fast through Stumphges Rapids where the stream narrows in the quick water and where high focus is required as the rocks and boulders must be negotiated or you will dump. Hardwoods and conifers populate the steep slope down to the shoreline, and we could see warbler species like Blackburnian, magnolias, redstarts, and many more perching on these overhanging limbs and darting out from them. This caused us a minor dilemma as we had to decide if we should do some birding, or navigate the canoe around the rocks.

We made camp that night at a place called Fox Trap which afforded us a high vantage point of up and down the river corridor. As we were enjoying the campfire and the thousands of wood frogs and spring peepers clicking and peeping in an almost deafening orchestra, we were interrupted by a bear visitor to our camp and no harm was done. Later that night we were awoken by a pack of wolves howling at perhaps a quarter mile away. The next morning after breaking camp and continuing downstream, we passed a small pond adjacent to the south side of Rice Lake, and we counted seventy trumpeter swans in one large group. The abundant and diverse wildlife here was itself worth the experience.

It was while we were gazing upon the swans that I told my friend Rob of a couple of small streams just north of where we were that emptied into the north side of Rice Lake. These two streams are now named the Little Mississippi and Grant Creek. Long ago, the Little Mississippi, according to what

Schoolcraft said he was told by his Ojibwe companions, was called *Piniddiwin*. It was on this creek that a band of Dakota warriors entered Manoomin Lake and proceeded down to the shoreline, not far from where we were in our canoe, where there was an Ojibwe lodge and all present were killed.

Throughout the two days we spent in the state forest on the river, we identified just about every species of waterfowl native to the state, including cranes, herons, shorebirds, and rails, plus all the wood warblers, vireos, and other inhabitants of these forests. Rob agreed that there was a bonanza of life here.

I have described the river through Mississippi Headwaters State Forest, which is forty pristine river miles. As one leaves the state forest, the river for the next twenty-two miles is a mix of Northwoods, some homes, and a few farms until Lake Bemidji, which is called *Bemidjigamaag* in *Ojibwe Mowin* (Ojibwe language), which means where one leaves the river and traverses across the lake. When entering the river at its exit from the lake, the next stretch of river was called by the Ojibwe *Midaaswi*, which means ten, for there were ten rapids between Lake Bemidji and Big Wolf Lake which is a distance of thirteen miles. Today there is a small hydro-electric dam about seven miles downstream from Lake Bemidji which has inundated all the rapids between the dam and Bemidji, but below the dam the Class 1 rapids will still catch your canoe and carry you into the past when the Ojibwe, and Dakota before them, ruled the land and the great fur traders from Montreal, Sault Ste. Marie and Mackinac plied these waters for furs. This stretch of river has seen much shoreline development since I first paddled these waters, but the river here, with its beautiful mix of hardwoods and pines and its stiff current and crystal-clear water running over a bottom of rocks and clam shells, makes it one of the finest stretches of river in the region.

In this same stretch, between Bemidji and Wolf Lake, thousands of suckers make their spawning run every spring. The river bottom here, washed clean of silt and mud by the stiff current, provides a pebbly bottom ideal for fish eggs. When this fish-run is taking place, a sight to behold occurs every year—the feast of *Migiziwag* (bald eagles). My wife and I paddle this stretch when the sucker run is in progress, and one spring we saw over one hundred eagles in the *Midaaswi*. On some large white pines along the shore there were as many as ten eagles perched on the limbs, tearing apart the meat from suckers they had snatched out of the water. The suckers were so plentiful that the river smelled of decaying fish. Seeing all these eagles together feasting on this run of fish and vocalizing that high-pitched chirping trill of theirs and soaring high and low, some only a couple feet above the water, with their great wingspan, was reassuring to us that, at this time and place, the world was in alignment and all was right.

After crossing Big Wolf Lake, a short stretch of river to Lake Andrusia, and a short paddle across Andrusia, you enter a segment of river that is only a couple hundred yards long and you are in Cass Lake, known to the Ojibwe as Upper Red Cedar Lake or *Gaa-miskwaawaakokaag* (place of many red cedars). Cass Lake has a surface area of nearly 16,000 acres and is ten miles long and seven miles wide. There are three islands on the lake: Potato, Cedar, and Star islands. Star Island is the most interesting and famous island as it was formerly known as Grand Island or Kitchi Miniss. The island itself is one thousand acres in size and on the island is Windigo Lake which is 199 acres in size: a lake on an island on a lake. The island now is mostly United States Forest Service land within Chippewa National Forest with the exception of some scattered private parcels on the eastern half. The island is forested with magnificent old-growth red and white pine and has some fine campsites for the canoe traveler on the Mississippi. For untold centuries, Kitchi Miniss was home to a large Ojibwe community.

I have walked about in the area on O'Neil's Point where the old village was located and have found a number of old rice pits used by the Ojibwe in the process of chafing off the hulls from the parched rice. While I lingered about the old village and the lake, with the water lapping on the shore and the wind whispering in the big pines, I felt for a moment to be back in time among the Ojibwe families going about their business. For myself, having spent much time in the backcountry, I often feel the spirits of those many people who preceded me, who lived here, walked the forest, paddled the waters, and loved the land as I do. Through a common love and respect for the land, I can sense their spirits.

From Cass Lake, there are a number of watery travel routes one can take. I think of northern Minnesota as a complex network of highways and roads, but they are not land-based, rather an interconnected system of streams, rivers, lakes, and ponds with portages linking them. You can go anywhere you wish by water, and in fact, many of the old roads we drive today are improvements of Ojibwe trails. From Cass Lake, I could go up the Turtle River to Red Lake, or I could go south through Pike Bay, called the Pike Bay Connection, which has been used for thousands of years and follows a series of small lakes and portages to Leech Lake, the third largest lake in Minnesota. Or I could continue down the Mississippi for eleven miles to Big Winnibigoshish Lake, the fourth largest lake in Minnesota. Besides the three I mentioned, there are innumerable smaller routes emanating out from all these larger lakes. For the Native people who preceded us and still live here, traveling great distances by canoe was normal and they did it without the aid of maps. For them, travel as far away as Sault Ste. Marie (approximately six hundred miles) was a reasonable thing to do.

For many Minnesotans, or many other Americans, this pristine segment of the Upper Mississippi River is unknown.

This poses a dilemma for conservationists: protecting a wilderness means introducing people to it. For many of us who live in headwaters country, protecting this last remaining wilderness on the infant Mississippi seems like the obvious or logical thing to do, but the actions by our state government and county governments suggest the opposite. In the 1970s, the federal government proposed listing the Upper Mississippi, through the eight counties from its source in Clearwater County to Morrison County in central Minnesota, as one of its protected rivers under the Wild and Scenic Rivers Act. The federal Wild and Scenic Rivers Act would have created a one-thousand-foot buffer zone along each side of the river. This was shot down by pro-development and property-rights-leaning elected officials and county governments. Their efforts to keep the federal government out resulted in the creation of the Mississippi Headwaters Board (MHB), which was essentially to assure the feds that equal or similar protections would be provided, yet keep the river corridor in local control. It is my opinion those equal or similar controls have not been implemented or have not been enforced, and in the meantime the river and lakes through which it flows are being overdeveloped, leading to the drastic altering of shoreline habitat, the grubbing out of emergent and submergent plant species that provide wildlife habitat, more faulty septic systems, and the construction of starter-castles on these lakes. All this is having a monumental and catastrophic impact on the esthetics and ethics of the headwaters corridor. In 2014 a process began in which two oil pipelines, a thirty inch and a thirty-six inch, were to be laid side by side, and would ultimately cross the headwaters and run adjacent to Itasca Park. The threat posed by these pipelines jeopardizes the quality of this Minnesota treasure.

A primary focus to preserve and protect the wild qualities in the last remaining wilderness of the Mississippi River should be keeping off-road vehicles out of this portion of state forest. This is not asking for too much to preserve the historical, ecological, and wild characteristics of one of the great rivers in North America. With the rest of the river converted into a series of pools, locks and dams, jetties, sewage receptacles, and intensive development, it is imperative that this small segment be preserved as a museum-piece of history, for both its natural beauty and human history.

The Minnesota DNR had the opportunity to implement some important protections for the Mississippi Headwaters State Forest when it began to review the area for possible placement of ATV trails. The forest had been victimized by ATV damage, and even the river itself was used for riding in and crossing. A public process was initiated whereby the DNR assembled a work team made up of DNR staff members from the divisions of wildlife, eco-services, enforcement, forestry, and trails and waterways. The work team voted three to two to close the forest to ATV use. The citizen involvement during the written comment period was overwhelmingly in favor of closing the forest to ATV use. Yet, DNR administrators overturned their own work team and negated the citizen input and implemented one hundred miles of ATV trails. This raised the question, who does the DNR actually listen to in their public process?

While I was attending a Mississippi Headwaters Board meeting, there was a mention that the Minnesota DNR was in violation of their own policies, on account that their own signage at campsites or access points prohibited ATV, dirt bike, and ORV use within a quarter mile of the river. The response from the board members was that since the trails would be on existing roads or trails it was allowable. We were also told that their job was to approve variances of which over 90% are approved.

It should be pointed out that board members of the MHB are made up of one county commissioner from each of the eight counties through which the upper river flows. Traditionally, county commissioners are more concerned about development and increasing the tax base and less concerned about the health of ecosystems and wilderness as these values get in the way of development.

But special interests prevailed over the wishes of its citizens and now approximately one hundred ATV trails lace this area around the infant river, some of which go directly to the water's edge.

In twenty years of advocating for special places on earth, I have too often seen the outcome of these issues as being counterproductive to protection of the land and inclined to development or exploitation of the land. I have seen too many treasured places here and in other states being used and viewed as marketplaces or resources to make a profit. It is unlikely that our relationship with the land will change until there is a diametric change in all our institutions; political, economic, educational, religious, and social. Until we see the land in a different ethical context, and see use of its resources in a far more sustainable way, and approach them with care and respect, I do not see anything but shrinking returns for those of us who love and respect the complex, interconnected, and interrelated plant and animal communities that we as people, and the institutions that make up our society, rely on for our very existence.

As Americans, we have two choices: we can sit by and watch the loss of wild places to greed and profit, or we can fight to save them. After all, what's best about America and what's best about being an American? It is our public lands, national parks, state parks, national forests, and protected wilderness areas that strengthen us and make us who we are. When defining America, what comes to mind but the land, the grizzly, the wolf, the moose, even our national symbol *Migizi*, the eagle. Ponder for a minute a nation without a few free-flowing rivers and without its original animal and plant communities intact. This is a place of wilderness where we can recharge our inner batteries and find God himself as did Jesus, Buddha, and Muhammad. Without these things and places, we would cease to be the people we want to be.

In the words of Chi Ma'iingan: "The Creator so graciously put in place an interconnected system so we can thrive in this world. Along with this interconnected system he gave us seven laws, one of those laws being that of respect, this respect means we honor our relatives including the four-legged, the winged creatures, those that live in the water, and our plant relatives for taking care of us by giving of themselves and all they ask is that we honor their spirit for giving us their flesh to sustain us. This law is still as relevant as it was in the beginning, this respect includes us as human beings, and in fact this lesson applies especially both ways."

Approaching the Fork in the Road

There is magic in the forest, magic to heal the wounds made by men.

— Helen Hoover

Three years ago a deer hunter who hunts near where I live and whom I casually know and see only during the firearms deer season, told me that his name was drawn through the DNR wolf hunt lottery to receive a wolf-hunting license. This deer hunter had previously explained to me that he would like wolves to continue to roam the Northwoods of Minnesota, but would like to kill one wolf so he could have a trophy on his wall and that would be enough for him.

As he proceeded with his story and his quest for a wolf pelt, he told me of a recent day when he was in a tree stand

and heard something coming through the woods and readied himself for what he assumed was a deer, when to his surprise a large black wolf appeared. As soon as I heard this my heart sank as I thought of the black male wolf that is the alpha of my local pack, but I kept silent as he continued his story. The wolf was unaware of his presence and he put the cross hairs of his scope behind the wolf's front shoulder, knowing that he was about to get his wolf, but he said he lowered the gun and couldn't shoot. I asked him why. His reply was simply five words: "It didn't seem right then."

Three years ago I was visiting with an independent logger who has done some prescribed logging for me. Our conversation was mostly about critters of the woods and eventually drifted to the many bear visitors I have at my cabin. After a few of my bear stories, he told me of a bear that had denned for the winter behind his home. He said some acquaintances had wanted to shoot the bear but the logger told them no and said, "It would simply be murder." The bear left the den that spring and for all I know is still roaming these woods.

I was reading an article in the *Minnesota DNR Volunteer* (NOV-DEC 2015) about a bear known as Number 56. She had XXL yellow tags on her as identification so hunters would pass up on her. Number 56 was 39½ years old, the oldest living wild bear "of any species in the world." The author, DNR bear researcher Dave Garshelis, noted that the bear lived in an area in Northern Minnesota that is popular to bear hunters and was seen at baits by numerous hunters who all let her live. He wrote, "Bear 56 lived so long because for most of her life she was skilled at staying away from people. But she also needed some luck and some compassionate people to allow her to live the full life that she did." She died naturally in her sleep that summer.

Last night, I stepped outside after midnight on the first day of March, knowing that a new year and new life were about to commence. The cold sub-zero air was hushed in utter silence and the night sky was crystal clear as the Milky Way cast its illuminating band across the heavens. Orion, the hunter, was in the south and Ojiig, the fisher, was in the north. As I stood in the cold, my thoughts were of the dismal forecast for the health of everything wild and free on this planet. Besides the ominous course we are taking, I pondered the turtle, the beaver, and the other teachings they represent and the great mysteries that surround me, and then I heard it, first a low chesty howl that penetrated the night sky, then a second howl joining the first, then one or two more joining in. The wolf vocalization told me that they were about to commence the hunt. The howling lasted no more than a minute, and then silence again, but I knew they were near, gracefully stalking through the dark forests in hunting mode; there is no free lunch for a hungry wolf. Then in the quiet of the night, I heard a heart beating. A slow steady beat: ba-bump ba-bump, ba-bump. Was this my heart? It was the heartbeat of the natural world like an Ojibwe ceremonial drum, the heartbeat of millions of interconnected living organisms, uncountable micro-organisms in the soils, ancient white cedars that have been listening to this same beat for hundreds of years in their coniferous swamps, the waterways that have nourished this land for ten thousand years, the plant communities that form the basis of life itself, and complex animal communities of which I am a part. It was the heartbeat of the land organism.

I see the fork in the road ahead for mankind, wondering which road we will take: the scorched road or the green road. At least during that moment, the world seemed in balance. I walked back inside with a feeling that maybe there was hope.

For further reading about Chi Ma'iingan and his teachings of reconnecting to the natural world, check out our other title, *Road to Ponemah*, by Michael Meuers.

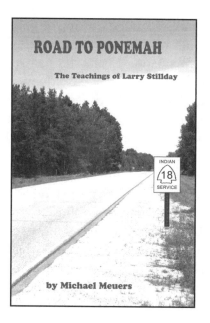

www.riverfeetpress.com

Acknowledgments

It would be remiss of me not to mention the following for their support and help in the making of this book, for without them, it would not have happened. The most important person is my wife, Linda Mae, who has supported me in my passion and advocacy for the outdoors all my life. Secondly I need to thank my Father-in-law, Kenneth Liljeberg in his support, and my close friend, Michael Meuers, who has continually voiced words of enthusiasm. Thanks to Mrs. Larry Stillday (Violet Stillday) — her assistance in Larry's teachings and her friendship played an important role in this book. Also thanks to Larry's extended family, including Rose Cloud, Vickey Fineday, Wesley and James Cloud. Larry's sons, Larry Jr., Leigh, and Randy, and many more from Ponemah. Thank you to all. Special thanks to Maureen Hackett (Founder of Howling for Wolves) for her friendship and her monumental effort in standing up for the wolf. Special appreciation goes to Daniel Rice of Riverfeet Press for accepting my work and giving me a chance and allowing this book to go forward. Without his advice and work it would never have happened.

photo by Daniel J. Rice

Barry Babcock lives off the grid in the Mississippi headwaters country of northern Minnesota. His lifestyle is one of simple and self-sustaining existence. He gathers what he needs from the land by gardening, hunting, harvesting, and his only electricity is harnessed from the sun, his water from a well which is pumped daily by hand. He lives an intimate balance with the natural world.

He has pursued a way of life distanced from the economic and consumptive norms which he believes can hinder a persons connection to the natural world. He truly lives on the perimeter of society.

With a deep love and respect for the land, he has been active in curbing the transformation of northern Minnesota which has been enacted by extractive industry, motorized recreation, and development. For over two decades, he has been active with the Tri-County Leech Lake Watershed Project, and is the founder of the grassroots organization Jack Pine Coalition. Since the delisting of wolves from the Endangered Species Act, Babcock has been pro-actively fighting to protect this animal. This has included speaking to legislature in conjunction with the non-profit group Howling for Wolves, and starring in the documentary films *Medicine of the Wolf* and *Wolf Spirit*.

www.riverfeetpress.com
printed in the USA